Ourselves and Others

The New History of Scotland
Series Editor: Jenny Wormald

Original titles in the New History of Scotland series were published in the 1980s and re-issued in the 1990s. This popular and enduring series is now being updated with the following published and forthcoming titles:

Vol. 1 *Warlords and Holy Men: Scotland AD 80–1000* by Gilbert Markus (new edition to replace original by Alfred Smyth)

Vol. 2 *Kingship and Unity: Scotland 1000–1306* by G. W. S. Barrow (reissued edition)

Vol. 3 *Power and Propaganda: Scotland 1306–1488* by Katie Stevenson (new edition to replace *Independence and Nationhood* by Alexander Grant)

Vol. 4 *Court, Kirk and Community: Scotland 1470–1625* by Jenny Wormald (second revised and updated edition)

Vol. 5 *Crown, Covenant and Union: Scotland 1625–1763* by Alexander Murdoch (new edition to replace *Lordship to Patronage* by Rosalind Mitchison)

Vol. 6 *Enlightenment and Change: Scotland 1746–1832* by Bruce P. Lenman (second revised and updated edition of *Integration and Enlightenment*)

Vol. 7 *Ourselves and Others: Scotland 1832–1914* by Graeme Morton (new edition to replace *Industry and Ethos* by Olive and Sydney Checkland)

Vol. 8 *No Gods and Precious Few Heroes: Twentieth-Century Scotland* by Christopher Harvie (second revised and updated edition)

www.euppublishing.com/series/nhs

Ourselves and Others
Scotland 1832–1914

Graeme Morton

EDINBURGH
University Press

For Angela, Sam and Evie; themselves living out of Scotland

© Graeme Morton, 2012

Edinburgh University Press Ltd
22 George Square, Edinburgh EH8 9LF
www.euppublishing.com

Typeset in 10.5/13 Sabon by
Servis Filmsetting Ltd, Stockport, Cheshire, and
printed and bound in Great Britain by
CPI Group (UK) Ltd, Croydon CR0 4YY

A CIP record for this book is available from the British Library

ISBN 978 0 7486 2048 7 (hardback)
ISBN 978 0 7486 2049 4 (paperback)
ISBN 978 0 7486 2919 0 (webready PDF)
ISBN 978 0 7486 5518 2 (epub)
ISBN 978 0 7486 5517 5 (Amazon ebook)

The right of Graeme Morton to be identified as author of this work has been
asserted in accordance with the Copyright, Designs and Patents Act 1988.

Published with the support of the Edinburgh University Scholarly Publishing
Initiatives Fund.

Contents

Tables and Figures

TABLES

FIGURES

Acknowledgements

The patience of a publisher should, I think, go along with that of Job. This book was commissioned when its author was on one side of the Atlantic and completed, a little later than intended, on the other side of that ocean. I am, without reservation, indebted to Edinburgh University Press for persisting with me. As, too, did Jenny Wormald, the academic who waited. Thank you for being the most generous editor one could wish for. To Trevor Griffiths my profound appreciation for reading an earlier draft of this book and for the hospitality that makes my visits home the transatlantic equivalent of comfort eating. And to my family, including the furry and pedantic members, my thanks for reading as well as 'being' major parts of this book.

Introduction

If there is an overused descriptor bestowed upon contemporary experiences, it was the 'singularity' of that society. As a metaphor for the age, it smacks of amazement, incredulity and historical inimitability. Historians are wont to impress the uniqueness of their period upon their readers, and to avoid disappointment such claims are made here. The span 1832 to 1914 is when the technology of modernity came firmly into view: the electric telegraph, the motorised omnibus and the sailing ship that no longer depended on nature to propel its passengers and cargo. Above all, the steam railway shrank the temporal distances criss-crossing the Scottish mainland as it did the connection to England and, through the country's ports, passage to the wider world. Not that the Scottish people had ever been hermitic, but this was an age marked by the movement of people and the flow of information – both in and out of the nation.

The steam-powered rotary press brought down the cost of printing, increased the speed of publishers' output and better helped the Scots to read about themselves and learn about others from any number of standpoints. Prior to 1830, 131 newspapers had been registered in Scotland. Over the next two decades, 169 new newspapers were established and more than 100 more were added each decade throughout the century. The unstamped press flourished around the time of franchise reform in 1832, with fifty-four of these publications in Glasgow alone. With a partial reduction in the cost of the stamp tax in 1840 and removal of that tax in 1855 the advent of daily news had come. Periodicals were strongest in the first half of the century, regional newspapers in the second half. *The Orcadian* began publishing in 1854, *The Shetland Times* rolled out its first edition in 1872 and the Dundee publisher D. C. Thomson dominated the reading matter of Tayside and Fife after 1905 with its mixture of provincial newspapers and weeklies for women. The *Celtic Magazine* and other nineteenth-century periodicals – such as Tait's and Blackwood's (both Edinburgh), Fraser's (London) and Harper's (New York) – fed the minds of Scotland's learned civil society. When *Chambers's Edinburgh Journal* started in 1832 it quickly gained a readership of 80,000 before shifting focus to London under new editorship in the 1850s. But with a range of publishing houses on their doorstep, few others were compelled to follow the path south.

The evidence suggests Scotland was a more literate society than England, a consequence of its many schools (religious and secular), its universities and a civil society bulked and developed by early urbanisation. Publishing brothers William and Robert Chambers informed readers of their *Information for the People* (1856) that Scotland had long benefited from the advantage of a 'universally diffused means of elementary education'. In their view it established the Scots as steadfast people, examples of fidelity and perseverance, each possessing 'some tincture of literature'. While imagined from afar as preserving an essentially oral society – from which the much-translated ancient poetry of Ossian had sprung – the Scots would be more likely found reading their political economy, their tracts and their mechanical descriptions, nurtured under the guise of 'improvement'. Begun in the 1840s, mechanics' institutes drew members for the newspapers, periodicals and manuals stocked in their libraries and reading rooms, and for guidance to the manufacturing processes taught in their classrooms. Practical and prosaic, reading was not just for pleasure or debate.

Such pathways to learning enabled a wide array of contrasting ideas to penetrate, any choice of which will seem diverse: exiled from both Switzerland and France, the Italian nationalist Giuseppe Mazzini established himself in England as a literary commentator in 1837; Karl Marx published *Das Kapital* in 1867 written from his favourite seat in the British Library; Sherlock Holmes first pitted his intellect against London's criminal fraternity in *A Study in Scarlet* in 1887; Peter Rabbit bounced quietly into print with a limited private edition of his *Tales* by author Beatrix Potter in 1901. Lauded by John Stuart Mill for giving a fresh perspective to Britain's tendency toward cultural insularity, Mazzini was read in Scotland not least through his contributions to *Tait's Magazine*. His one-time collaborator Giuseppe Garibaldi – who was likened to William Wallace – found that Oban Town Council had placed a steamer at his disposal so he might complete the 'experience' of touring Scotland in the 1850s by journeying to Staffa and Iona. Once *Das Kapital* had been translated into English in 1887, radicals and later socialists could read for themselves the ideas of the man they had learned about in the monthly journals *Modern Thought* and *Contemporary Review*, both London-based periodicals that circulated north of the border. Scottish-born Arthur Conan Doyle's connections with the nation were impeccable; he lived at various addresses in Edinburgh before moving south, and based his detective on the forensic science of Dr Joseph Bell from Edinburgh University's medical faculty. In contrast, but just as perceptive on human relations, Peter Rabbit was welcomed to Scotland from the Lake District. His *Tales*, a potential Christmas gift in 1902, left *The Scotsman*'s critic delighted with Peter's childlike actions that were so appealing yet without ceasing to be those of a rabbit.

These stories and much more arrived to shape the culture of the Scots. Connection through the electric telegraph and the transatlantic cable mid-century meant this small north-western European nation was imbued increasingly deeply with values from other nations as well as those from its own people. When Paul Reuter moved to London in 1851 and made use of the new communication technology, he endeavoured to send news around the world, counting the Scottish newspapers amongst his clients. News from the agency that took his name was printed regularly in *The Scotsman*, in one instance reporting from Paris that the French royal family 'mingled their regret and grief with the Royal Family and the English nation' for the death of the Prince Consort in 1861. The column also contained snippets from Prussia, Herzegovina, the Brazils and America, and reports on the *Bombay Mail* and the eruption of Vesuvius. Like nations on both sides of the Atlantic, the Scots were intrigued by the new communications. A lecture the next year on the technology of telegraphy by Major J. H. A. Macdonald, of the Edinburgh Rifle Volunteers, and in support of that regiment, explained the different approaches and exhibited part of the failed transatlantic cable which had a tendency to unravel because of the direction of the join – one twisted to the right, the other to the left – a problem confirmed by two independent assessors.

This singular age in Scotland's history can be pitched as opening the nation to the movement of people, ideas and information more intensely than before. There was nothing static or moribund here, even for the most immobile handloom weaver, stable lad or domestic servant. Strangers, travellers, tramps, tourists and economic migrants were commonplace, as Chapter 6 and Chapter 11 will show. News was circulating, and it was more recent news than their grandparents' generation would have known. News, indeed, had become an industry. Information was packaged and manufactured just as any piece of wrought iron or woollen hose added value to the raw materials they comprised. These Scots had the means to know more about themselves than their forebears knew about themselves. They especially had greater opportunity to learn about others, whether they resided inside the nation or outside its boundaries. Being Scottish was not simply being other than English or being other than Catholic. Being Scottish was not a rejection of the unknown, but a reflection of the known. In this age of deepening information flows, the nation's history was in dialogue with the nation's identities.

THE SOCIOLOGY OF OBJECTIFICATION

Very lightly, this book will make use of objectification theory to frame its analysis. Borrowed from gender studies, the theory is formed to show how society objectifies women to separate their sexuality from their personality. In turn it leads to self-objectification, where the observer's perspective is internalised and taken to be one's own. The French philosopher Michel Foucault explains how objectification is achieved by dividing sections of society into distinct groups, by the application of (claimed) scientific classification and then by the subjectification of self. By believing in how others have objectified our history, by the self-objectification of that view because it is presented to us rationally, we internalise ourselves as subjects and deny our own agency. For good reason the late Victorian theorist Ernest Renan explained that getting history wrong is essential to how nations are formed.

To better explore Scotland's history and identity during the rise of modernity, self-objectification will be used to analyse the inter-relationship of ourselves and others. The evidence comes from what contemporaries thought was happening, and what it meant for them as a people, and what they thought of 'others' both inside and outside the nation. By the same token, it is a reflection of what contemporaries external to the nation thought was going on in Scotland, and thought they knew about the Scots, and what they told the Scots about themselves.

Such echoes may be artifice; these observations may be distortions; the contemporary conclusion may be misplaced. So this intellectual interchange will be presented alongside the socio-economic history of a near century of transformation. As much as *Ourselves and Others* is a narrative history book, it is story formed in the interplay of personal identity (*myself*), the framework of the nation (*ourselves*) and the knowledge of others.

A YEAR OF BEGINNINGS

In both Scotland's and Britain's capital cities, the discussion of 1832 was all about politics, and in particular the 'Nation's Bill'. *The Times* caught the mood:

Everything now announces that this great restorative of a decayed constitution will be realized. The Sovereign is, as he ever was, staunch to his conviction, and to his Royal word once given: in the Cabinet there is not a shadow of difference upon the course to be pursued. The people of Great Britain are alike unanimous; what, then, can an expiring party do?

The Parliamentary Reform of 1832 – expanding the franchise to allow those owning property to the value of £10 to vote in general elections – was enacted by separate English and Scottish legislation. It pulled proportionately more Scots into the voting booths and produced a system for both countries that was more reflective of recent population settlement. The Reform also invigorated the link between politics, a progressively dominant industrial economy and the new media nurtured by civil society.

In the interpretation of *The North American Review* in January 1832, reform of Westminster was 'an American question', not one simply for the people of Scotland or England. This was not for the principles of democracy, but for the commercial relations that crossed the Atlantic. Those whose income and wealth came from trade and industrial endeavour had pushed for political power to be opened and while the British electoral system had led the world with this initial expansion, ground was steadily lost. America, Australia, New Zealand, Russia and Germany all widened their electorate later but then more extensively than Britain. Indeed, most adult Scots had no entitlement to vote for or against their government. In 1911, only 54 per cent of men in Glasgow (and 60 per cent of men for the whole of Scotland) were entitled to vote. Women lacked even that, despite the increasingly vociferous campaigning of the suffrage movement from 1867. Women ratepayers could vote in Scottish burgh elections in 1884, in county elections in 1894 and in parish council elections in 1894 (the only instance of the three where they could stand for office). The position of town councillor was a privilege open only to men until 1907 as was that of county councillor until 1914. Scottish women in some parts of the diaspora were granted the legislative vote earlier than their sisters, mothers and daughters back home: in New Zealand (1893), in Australia (standardised under the Commonwealth Franchise Act 1902, while indigenous women remained excluded) and in Canada (1917). In 1918 women over the age of thirty who owned property could cast their vote at a British general election, but not until 1928 were women and men enfranchised equally.

CHOLERA: MORIBUS AND SPASMODIC

Concurrent with the agitation around electoral reform, throughout 1832 the people had a new threat to deal with. It came from cholera, and it caused fear for the ease with which it had spread since its first appearance the previous December. To some, the consequences of the disease were being overstated, more mirage than reality, a political tool used to stifle free discussion amongst the working classes and to further impose external morality on their behaviour. When *The Loyal Reformers' Gazette* told its Glasgow-dominated readership that this new health scare was but a distraction from the Reform debate, they argued it gave the Tories reason to delay action in Westminster. With an average monthly death rate of twenty to thirty in Edinburgh, cholera did not seem especially virulent. In Glasgow, 106 cases resulted in forty-six deaths. For England and Scotland combined in the year, there were 5,064 cases reported and 1,496 deaths confirmed from the disease. The *Gazette*, in spiteful jest, even offered a cure:

> Take a full and fair representation of the people, the whole people, and nothing but the people; let the House of Commons, this chosen, immediately reduce the taxes; let the poor obtain cheap bread, wholesome food, and warm clothing, in exchange for their labour, and thus they will defy the Cholera.

It was a debate about social class, with consumption and typhus associated with the undernourished poor, whereas until understanding developed in the 1860s of how cholera was transmitted through contaminated water, that disease induced panic across the social orders. Despite the *Gazette*'s accusation that they were mere operatives of the state for their intervention into the cleanliness, intemperance and eating habits of the poor, the Scottish medical profession took a line that marked a difference from the sanitary strategies introduced in the English towns and cities. They encouraged ventilation in housing and discouraged people from going out at night when the disease was present. The Boards of Health of Dundee and Edinburgh asked the populace to eat before leaving the house, to dress more warmly than usual and to avoid large gatherings of other working-class people, even at church.

Spasmodic cholera had been long known in India and contemporaries traced the current problem to a particularly virulent attack that moved to Calcutta in September 1817. The disease then spread throughout the regions and into the army, causing watery purging, first without pain, then sickness, then pain rising up from the toes, through the legs and inducing a burning in the stomach, with death coming within four to six hours of onset. It moved to Persia in 1821, the Mediterranean in 1823, Tehran in 1828, Georgia in 1830, then ravaged the Russian and Polish armies in the spring of that year. Paris was badly affected, and by October the disease had made its way to Sunderland and into an emigrant ship spotted at New Ross in Ireland. London at this point was only mildly affected, and various reasons were posited: their meat diet, perhaps, or the sulphur from their coal? Was it the narrow and thickly populated areas that experienced its effects more widely than the wider-built areas? In Scotland, East Lothian saw some of the earliest cases of the disease, in Musselburgh, Tranent and Prestonpans. It seemed to miss some regions completely, to travel great distances without losing its virulence, to backtrack on itself and to spread against the prevailing winds. It was made worse in Musselburgh because of the presence of typhus before and during the epidemic, while in Prestonpans, the beggars, colliers and 'dissipated persons' were most afflicted.

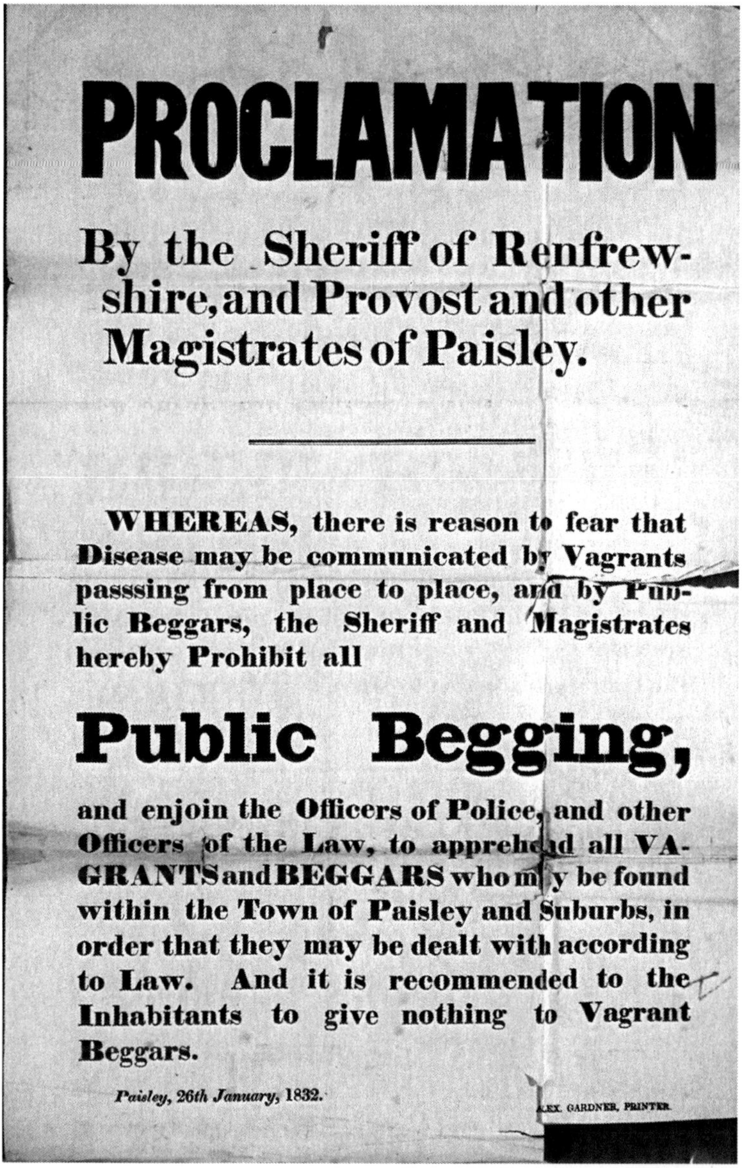

PROCLAMATION

By the Sheriff of Renfrewshire, and Provost and other Magistrates of Paisley.

WHEREAS, there is reason to fear that Disease may be communicated by Vagrants passsing from place to place, and by Public Beggars, the Sheriff and Magistrates hereby Prohibit all

Public Begging,

and enjoin the Officers of Police, and other Officers of the Law, to apprehend all VAGRANTS and BEGGARS who may be found within the Town of Paisley and Suburbs, in order that they may be dealt with according to Law. And it is recommended to the Inhabitants to give nothing to Vagrant Beggars.

Paisley, 26th January, 1832.

ALEX. GARDNER, PRINTER.

Figure I.1 *Cholera! No public begging permitted in Paisley, 1832.*
© Renfrewshire Council, Local Studies Library.
Licensor www.scran.ac.uk

SPINNING THE INDUSTRIAL THREAD

While franchise reform was a positive reinforcement of the growing influence of capitalists and industrialists, the movement of Scotland's trade around the world carried the threat of previously unseen diseases landing along with passengers and cargo. The Scottish economy of the 1830s was filled with latent transformative power. This came with the partial replacement of industry around textiles with processes powered by coal and steam.

Mechanisation and the factory were to become the new mark of Scotland's economy; iron, steel, chemicals and shipbuilding fired a small nation to increase its GDP by 10 per cent, close enough to England's lead and well in front of Germany, the Netherlands, France, Italy and Austria. It was an uneven story, as Chapter 6 shows, and small industrialists continued apace. Indeed, even the largest concerns were dependent on human capital rather than physical plant. Around one million more jobs were created during the period in focus here, but wages remained some 10–20 per cent lower than for similar work in England. The near constant movement in search of work was the norm for most, and for many that journey took them overseas.

SCOTT IS DEAD. LONG LIVE SCOTT-LAND

One who opposed the Reform legislation but welcomed the economic benefits of political union with England was the celebrated novelist Sir Walter Scott. His narrative and poetic writings were to define the age with their mixture of romance, Jacobitism and historical reflection. The year 1832, however, marked his death. The first stroke came in February 1831, a second shortly after and a third more serious one in April, as his daughter Anne recounted:

> Papa is recovering slowly, but mere acquaintance would think him quite well. In mind he has always been the same. In this last attack he has never lost it, but I think his speech is not quite right yet.

Indeed, till it comes round the disease is still, I fear, hanging about him. He is very irritable, and will not believe but it has been my insisting on him being bled that has made him ill.

Scott's failing health was headline news around the world and of concern to monarchs and compatriots alike. In October Scott travelled to the Mediterranean, given passage on a man-o'-war at the insistence of King William. *The Scotsman* thought it necessary to report on letters that had arrived from Malta on 24 November 1831 announcing that Scott had survived the journey and the general improvement in his health. In January, he was presented to the King of Naples who offered to order any excavation of Pompeii that he may desire. Instead Sir Walter chose a trip to Athens, with Sir Frederick Adam offering passage on a government steamer for his convenience. On hearing of the presentation, the satirist within the *Pittsburgh Gazette* suggested the 'King of Naples has the honor of being presented to Sir Walter Scott'. The novelist began his return in May of that year, but suffered a fourth stroke in Nijmegen, delaying his return to Scotland. In June, under 'English news', his state of health was reported in *Courrier de la Louisiane*, a daily published in New Orleans. The fulfilment of his wish that he return to Abbotsford was reported in the *American & Commercial Daily Advertiser*, and under 'European News' the likelihood that Scott's life would soon end was reported in the *Geneva Gazette*. Scott died at his Abbotsford home on 21 September 1832 at around 1.30 p.m. This was the passing of a celebrity. The obituary for the 'wizard of the north' was reproduced worldwide. The *Pittsburgh Gazette* heard 'a universal echo this side of the Atlantic' for his mourning. The *Connecticut Courant* copied its account of Scott's celebrated life from *The Times* and *Fraser's Magazine*, explaining that the major events in his life were so known to the world that they did not need repeating.

Despite Sir Walter's passing, Scott-land continued apace. Boosted by the quixotic descriptions in *Marmion* and *Lady of the Lake* especially, foreign visitors and others had long been attracted to Scott's romanticisation of the west coast to gaze upon a coastline and a people that were 'unchanged', appeared unworldly and offered a looking glass into an earlier time. This the outsider contrasted with their own life: of towns, fashion, of being fashionable and an intellectual exchange so different from the people one nodded recognition to at the church hall, the coffee house or the dinner club.

The ever-quotable English critic Dr Samuel Johnson, encouraged by his Scottish-born companion and biographer James Boswell, was an earlier tourist in search of authenticity. The tales of the Hebridean poet Ossian were a sensation from 1760 via the antiquarianism and writings of James Macpherson (1736–96). It created Europe-wide shorthand of what Scotland and its people were to those looking in from afar. Johnson made this judgement despite *A Journey to the Western Isles of Scotland* (1775) being published at the zenith of the Scottish Enlightenment. Ossian was at the centre of 'sublime existence', offering a guide to travellers in search of a 'physical' or a 'metaphysical' experience. Another who came was the composer Felix Mendelssohn. The year was 1829 and he was twenty years of age. Mendelssohn had followed the path of romantics before him, braving seasickness to take the small rowing boat to the island of Staffa, located in the Hebrides off Scotland's western coastline. The cave became his inspiration to write *The Hebrides Overture (Fingal's Cave)* the next year and then *The Scottish Symphony*, although it would be another dozen years before it was finished. Mendelssohn, like the others, came looking for Scotland and for the Scots. His music would be his discovery, objectifying Scotland's pre-modern past into aural shorthand for the pleasure of a modern society. Like Scott-land, *The Hebrides Overture* summarised its subject.

SEEING OURSELVES AS OTHERS SEE US

These visitors were in search of landscape and emotion, of essential Scotland more than the everyday Scot. But what did the people look like in this period? Their clothing and fashion are examined in Chapter 7, most of it remarkably uniform.

Their physical features are not so easily catalogued. One English art critic's description of the Scots comes from Lady Eastlake, who gave some thought to this question in her diary entries for 1844:

> On first returning to Scotland you are struck with two prominent national physiognomies. The one, the accepted type of the Scottish face – long in the chin and high in the cheeks; the features large, all but the eyes, and as ill put together as the limbs of the body; the upper lip turning out, and as large as the lower one; the hair reddish-grey, straggling, and coarse; the skin tight and freckled, and the working of every bone in the face seen under it. But occasionally good teeth and good humour enliven the face: honesty you expect from it, and vulgarity you are not surprised at; much sense and no vice are to be found in it. The other is very different; but, I fancy, equally Scotch. A small, well-set head, going up straight from the back, with clean-cut, sharp, hard features; small, light, and very red-lipped mouth, the long slender nose rather drawing it upwards; complexion clear, with a set colour; hair black and plentiful, and deepest eyes of a peculiarly dark slate colour, with a fine, tight-skinned, slightly wrinkled brow, which looks as if it worked hard for its owner. A face of no softness and no openness, but intensely shrewd and intellectual, and one which you are long in trusting and never tire of examining. The women have, many of them, wide open faces, with their features, the moment they speak, flopping back like the borders of their caps.

Other descriptions flowed from cultural stereotypes. *Punch*, for example, tended to eschew the simian features it assigned for the Catholic Irish and instead used highland garb in its satire to distinguish all Scots from ourselves. Scientists also offered some descriptions. John Beddoe's presidential address to the Anthropological Society in 1872 reflected on Scottish ethnicity and its association with national identity:

> Blood may rule the physique, but climate and other media, and linguistic, religious and other history all act, of course, upon the character and sympathies of a people; and as personal identity has been affirmed to consist in the consciousness of personal identity, so it might be argued, not without some appearance of plausibility, that

national identity consisted merely in the consciousness of national identity.

Beddoe's earlier work had seemingly identified a distinctive distribution of eye and hair colours, with light hair and eyes in the east, especially the south-east, light eyes and dark hair in the west, and an increase in darker shades in the towns and cities. Much of this research was impressionistic, and in 1908 Beddoe unsuccessfully employed colour cards to measure and debate J. F. Tocher's observations the previous year on the connection between physical characteristics and insanity. Tocher had studied over 50,000 school children to discover the preponderance of red hair in the north-east of Scotland, precisely the area where most asylums were to be found.

This research in turn built on John Cleghorn's 1868 inquiry into whether Scottish character could be deduced from the attributes of the soil. Cleghorn attempted to compare Scots in the east with those in the west, and to compare the Scots with the English. Findings from Board of Trade returns showed him there was little difference between the amount of corn and the number of cattle and sheep under cultivation throughout Scotland, but their value was greater in the east than in the west: 'The want of soil, the want of food, on the west, is further seen in the Gaelic, for it and heather go together'. Confidently he stated that the 'east man is taller and his head bigger' than his western counterpart. In the east there have been religious revolutions, but in the west they 'move in masses' – where 'Papacy is the religion of poverty'. His answer for progress was to mix up the soil and mix up the species, because the 'character of the Scotch is the expression of the soil of Scotland'. Respondents to the paper were not wholly convinced with his classifications, however, conjuring up examples throughout Continental Europe where the soil was similar but the character different.

In these examples of seeing ourselves as others see us, Scott, Mendelssohn, Eastlake, Beddoe, Tocher and Cleghorn all sought to objectify Scotland by dividing the nation into distinct groups: a Jacobite heart and sublime landscape by Scott; an aural Ossian

by Mendelssohn; the nation's physiognomies by Eastlake, Beddoe
and Tocher; the character of the nation formed from its soil by
Cleghorn. Through the rationalisation of these classifications –
and the historical, cultural, aural and scientific objectification
of Scotland – the national self was subjugated, historical agency
was downplayed and Scottish identity was formed.

WE MOVE ON

Ourselves and Others is a social history based on a question
so simple yet so difficult to answer: who were the Scots? When
we look at the great changes that took place in Scotland, and
explore the factors affecting how many Scots were being born,
the rate at which they died, the numbers who left for a life
elsewhere, those who returned and those who came from other
countries, we are moved to try to understand the lives of the
Scottish people and those who lived in Scotland. Consciously,
this is a history of Scots within the nation, within Britain, and
also distant of Scotland.

The chapters are set out to investigate Scotland as a society
structured by its institutions, its economy and its political and
constitutional framework, along with multifarious customs,
beliefs and accepted ways of doing things. The denominational
differences within Protestantism, and Presbyterianism most
especially, and the growth in the number of Irish Catholics mid-
century were reflected in marriage, childbirth, illegitimacy and
social mores, as well as cultural control and legal and social
punishment. Religious beliefs and practices structured many
different aspects of lives that were ordinary as well as the experiences of extraordinary people in this period. And the churches,
too, structured the lives of Scots overseas. The number of
Presbyterian churches to be found throughout the 'new world'
is testament to that, with by comparison nary an Anglican
church to be found in the Maritime Provinces of Prince Edward
Island or Nova Scotia, for example. But this is also evidenced
by a debate that strained the Free Church of Scotland immediately after its creation in 1843: should it take much-needed

financial help from Scottish slave owners in the southern states
of America, or was that help tainted beyond its monetary value?

Ourselves and Others is a blended history of the Scots in a
period of major transformation. It is not about 'the other', for
that is only part of how life was envisaged and identities were
formed. 'Being Scotland' is about the blend itself. We do not
simply reflect ourselves in England's economic and constitutional development or in Ireland's Roman Catholicism; we are
part of that development, as it is part of us, of being Scottish
within the united kingdom of Britain. The wearing of multiple
hats – one or another, but never more than one at a time – or
imagining identities as if they were a Russian doll – each self-
contained but subsumed beneath a larger identity – was not
being Scotland in the 1832–1914 period. There was no zero-
sum or sliding scale here. Rather, it was a relentless eddy of
historical developments from home and away, some engaged
with completely, most only elliptically; in other words a blend
of our history with a chaser of others.

1

Being Scotland

LAND OF BROWN HEATH AND SHAGGY WOOD

Where 'being Scotland' first formed was upon the land. Not by itself an island, Scotland nevertheless meets the sea with 6,100 miles of coastline. The nation's single land border is to the south, shared with England, and little changed over centuries. The North Channel and the Irish Sea take the Scot to Ireland and the Atlantic Ocean to the west; the Pentland Firth joins the Atlantic Ocean and the North Sea to the north; the North Sea ferries the Scot east to Scandinavia and the Low Countries and, once the journey around England has been made, the English Channel to the European Continent completes the circuit. Scotland is a narrow country. From Berwick upon Tweed in the east to the Solway Firth in the west the distance is around sixty-eight miles. Scotland is no easy shape to measure, but estimates made to the Board of Agriculture mid-century came to the conclusion that its landmass comprised 18,944,000 acres, with 5,043,450 acres that were cultivated and 13,900,550 acres that were not. Of this number, Scotland's islands comprise around 4,000 square miles, and its lakes and rivers around 638 square miles. Measured in 1870, there was 3.5 million acres of arable land, with the remainder being grassland, used primarily for hay. The biggest of Scotland's islands are nestled in the Outer Hebrides to the west and Shetland to the north (covering 352,337 acres) with around twenty-five of its ninety islands inhabited in the 1830s. In total, the Scottish nation comprises

upwards of 790 islands with many of these little more than out-
crops while others were populated seasonally or when moving
cattle or sheep from grazing grounds to market.

Great Britain is the largest island in Europe and Scotland
takes up around 30 per cent of its landmass. There are twenty-
six square miles of land in Britain to every one mile of coastline,
a remarkably low figure, with vaguely comparable estimates
for the continents showing Europe at around 229 square miles
per mile of coastline, America 437, Asia 500 and Africa 741.
Divided by the Highland Boundary Fault, which travels from
the north-east to the south-west of the nation, separating highland from lowland, there are three great regions of the nation:
the southern uplands and central belt around the Firth of Forth
and Firth of Clyde; the central area of Tayside and Perthshire
going north to Inverness-shire and the north-east; and the highland area to the west of the Great Glen. So variable is Scotland's
topography that there is much difference in how land was put
to use, its mountainousness being the origin of rivers as well
as of the absence of plentiful rich soil. Scotland is a small land
mass, and only around a quarter of its acreage was cultivable
in this period. Nor was agricultural work helped greatly by the
weather. Scotland has a temperate climate, a wet and windy
one, not conducive to the cultivation of the wheat and corn
that was found in greater abundance in England. Wheat generally struggles to grow above 500 feet (700 feet maximum), and
while oats are not fond of elevations above 1,200 feet, along
with barley and the potato these were mainstays of Scotland's
cash crop production and the nation's diet. The figures in Table
1.1 refer to Scotland after the potato blight had all but passed
and the highland region was slowly regaining its output. The
potato crop yielded 529,915 tons in 1854 and 732,141 tons in
1855. When all produce is totalled, 'man and beast' of Scotland
produced 1,532,004 tons of food in 1854 and 1,592,604 tons
in 1855.

It was the nation's western and highland lands that were
'the mighty impulse' that inspired both Scott and Wordsworth
into poetic excitement, such was its polar contrast to lowland

Table 1.1   Major crop yields, 1854, 1855

	1854	1855
Wheat	608,063	632,817
Barley	954,950	761,613
Oats	4,231,789	3,758,893
Beans and peas	135,115	147,956
Total (in quarters)	5,927,917	5,301,279

Source: Ministry of Agriculture, *Agricultural Statistics. Great Britain Historical GIS Project 2004.*

Scotland and urban England. Yet 'being Scotland' included some less obvious juxtaposition, too. It is in Dumfries (Wanlockhead at 1,295 feet) and in South Lanarkshire (Leadhills at 1,280 feet) that Scotland's two highest villages are found, not in the Highlands. And in contrast to the romantic appeal of the nation's glens and lochs, diverse local enterprise developed as much from below the ground as above. Professor James Nicol's survey of 1861 divided up the 31,000 square miles of Scotland into 15,500 square miles of gneiss, granite, mica slate and quartz rock; 2,700 square miles of trap; 4,900 of old red sandstone; 4,750 of slate; and 1,750 of coal – the latter in the south of the nation.

BEING SCOTLAND

On top of this geological matrix, Scotland's rural life, its fishing industry and animal husbandry and, as we shall see more fully in Chapter 6, its mining industry all underpinned so much of the nation's economy and society. How the identity of the nation as a landmass and as a people of the land flowed into cultural constructions of ourselves and others can be distilled from two inter-related sets of historical developments. The first was a continuation of mid-eighteenth-century attempts to advance the productivity of agricultural work and the living standards of the rural population, the philosophy of 'improvement'. The mid-nineteenth-century arrival of *Phytophthora infestans*, potato

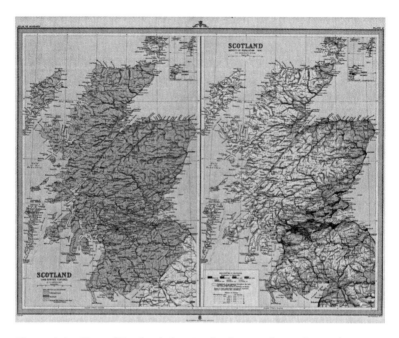

Figure 1.1   *Map of Scotland showing land-use and population density,*
1895. © National Library of Scotland. Licensor www.scran.ac.uk

blight, challenged this philosophy and added an edge to how
the highland Gael (and the Irish immigrant) was objectified.
The second, also based on older debates, is the consequence of
Improvement for ownership of the land, from the great highland
estates to the small crofts. If outsiders, absentee Scots and elites
predominated in owning Scotland, what did it mean for ourselves as a community if we had limited or no legal entitlement
to the land of our fathers and mothers? The crofters' war of the
1880s was an important part of the answer.

ON AN ISLAND, WITH THE ANIMALS

Because they lived on an island, guaranteed water was important
to the Scots. Food and fuel were caught from the sea and rivers

or scavenged from the beach: the harvesting of kale created its own industry. The herring industry added around £1 million to the British economy each year in the 1860s, employing 91,139 people directly, including 39,266 as fishermen. The Shetland Islanders described themselves as fishermen with farms while the Orcadians to their south were farmers with boats. When cash-rich lowland capitalists partnered with locals in Caithness and Sutherland to invest in larger boats to fish the northern and western waters in the 1840s, it led to an expansion in related jobs in gutting, curing and drying fish for wider markets. From mid-century the crofting people, cottagers and tenant farmers went in significant numbers to temporary employment in fishing fleets operating out of these two counties and around the Clyde coast. These examples are reminders that in this age of steam, the sailing boat continued to have a relevant economic role.

Animals, too, were central to changes in local economic activity. The Marquis of Breadalbane converted 240 square miles of land around Glencoe into a deer farm in the 1820s for hunting, catering for outsider engagement with the highland estates. Mid-century the Mar estate employed fifteen gamekeepers to attend its hunting visitors and added construction jobs to build fencing and rounds (towers) to meet the new leisure requirements of the land. With an estimated 2 million acres given over to farming deer for hunting in the 1860s, the waste of cultivable land was loudly questioned. The sport proved lucrative for the landowners who could attract hunters to their straths and glens, but it was a recurrent complaint amongst locals that sportsmen, gamekeepers and their dogs would trample over the fields of corn 'for such a paltry thing as a dead grouse'. Primarily amongst the more moneyed English, deer stalking increased in popularity in the final quarter of the century as royal and ennobled patronage – backed up by society magazines and retail promotions – injected the masculine blood hunt with a feminine romance divorced from the reality of rural transformation.

Deer were not the only animals whose cultivation had a major cultural impact on 'being Scotland' even if of less emotive appeal. Horses were expensive to own and were used intensively throughout the year. The 1857 agricultural census returned 185,409 horses at work on Scotland's farms – 126,471 under three years of age, 34,947 over three years of age and another 23,991 owned for leisure and transportation.

Their value was reflected in the bothy ballads of Scotland's north-east. This was not simply an indication of the animals' cultural appeal and the affection in which they were held, but society's measure of a master, recalling how well he treated them as an economic resource. Far from universal, the bothy system has come to represent some of the hardship of all rural life. The large single room that housed a group of male farmworkers was popular only in areas where there was little work for women.

Cows were kept for beef in the north-east and for milk in the south-west. In the east of Scotland in the 1840s pork and bacon were eaten if pigs were kept locally. By 1901 sows kept for breeding represented only 12 per cent of the total number of pigs; the rest were for sale. Of all Scotland's animals, sheep had the greatest economic, social and cultural impact. Their numbers at the end of the century were well above the human population (of 4.5 million in 1901).

The price of cattle had halved between 1810 and 1830, while sheep prices remained more or less unchanged. It was an encouragement for farmers to invest further in the animal, and the land-hungry Blackface and the Cheviot sheep had already been introduced from the middle of the previous century. In 1800 there were an estimated 35,000 sheep in Inverness-shire; by 1880 this had increased to 700,000. Sutherland had seen an earlier and quicker increase, from 15,000 in 1811 to 130,700 in 1820, and the numbers in Argyll increased at a similar rate, reaching one million by 1880. Karl Marx had denounced the Countess of Sutherland as 'a female Mehemt Ali, who had digested her Malthus' for her attempt to increase financial returns with the introduction of sheep on her land. By 1835 her scheme had removed 15,000 people and replaced them with sheep farms run by a single family, comprising 131,000 animals. Reflecting on those tenants who objected to their forced removal, the Countess's estate factor Patrick Seller pleaded in

Table 1.2 Censuses of animals in Scotland, 1870–1901

Year	Horses	Cattle	Sheep	Pigs	Poultry
1870	172,871	1,041,434	6,750,854	158,690	
1871	174,434	1,070,107	6,882,747	195,642	
1877	188,736	1,102,074	6,968,774	153,257	
1884	187,803	1,136,604	6,983,293	159,560	2,307,092
1885	188,292	1,176,004	6,957,198	150,984	2,325,354
1901	194,893	1,229,281	7,401,409	124,821	

Source: Ministry of Agriculture, *Agricultural Statistics. Great Britain Historical GIS Project 2004.*

1845 that '[t]he Sutherland Question does not I think need one word more to be written or said on the subject in Scotland'. He felt himself a 'Dwarf in the fable' and that 'our cause has been just, but, then, every battle cost me a leg or an arm . . . I defy the world to say, with truth, that in any part of my conduct, there has been injustice, harshness or unmanliness'. Seller argued that it was the Poor Law that needed attention for the treatment of the cottars, yet the narratives of forcible eviction and the stories of emigration have played an important part in objectifying the landless Scot. Indeed, research suggests that the headlines have masked a more sober judgement that economically the move to sheep farming was a response to rather than a cause of highland poverty. Masked also, argues historian Eric Richards, is the management structure of the sheep farms, which could have been run differently without so drastic a loss of population.

In the 1840s agricultural work was still paid predominantly in kind, shielding the communities from downturns in the market, but also hindering the accumulation of even small amounts of capital. The agricultural labourer's contract detailed how much barley, oats and other grains were to be exchanged, with employment contracted for six or twelve months. This relationship and the ownership of only small amounts of land on the croft or tenant farm made it inherently difficult for rural Scots to escape a life of subsistence. For the years 1856 and 1865, the average value created by a croft in the highland counties was £33, yet it was estimated that land to the value of £40 or £50 was needed to support a family who had no other source of income. The contemporary calculations indicate that highland agriculture returned little more than £7 per annum on average, meaning that without a good crop and a ready supply of potatoes and fish, then the wellbeing of the family would be quickly undermined.

Before 1832 the majority of Scots were employed in agricultural work, but this declined over the period until 1914. In the census return of 1891, over half of Scotland's population was returned in the towns rather than the countryside. Between 1851 and 1891 the numbers employed in agricultural fell by 41 per cent, with the biggest loss coming during the agricultural depression of 1873 to 1896. The debates surrounding the over-population of the countryside were well rehearsed in Archibald Alison's *Principles of Population* (1840), William Thomas Thornton's *Over-Population and its Remedy* (1846) and John Stuart Mill's *Principles of Political Economy* (1848). Yet throughout this period, neither these trends nor the Malthusian fear diminished the economic and cultural importance of rural and agricultural work to 'being Scotland', with most Scots still of the land, or only one generation removed from it.

Despite the undoubted mundanity and fragility of agricultural work, and – from the outside – its associations with drudgery, poverty, the highland Gael and then the Irish immigrant, estate work was varied. The harvesting of kelp, the digging of canals, the building of roads and fencing, and cattle and sheep rearing were all part of the early-nineteenth-century improvement of the countryside. Enclosure marked out the landscape in the first half of the century; erecting dykes and planting hedges had the benefit of providing work during the off season. Peat was important as fuel in the early decades but lost out to coal and the development of the fireplace to burn the 'smokeless' versions later in the century. Horse-drawn ploughs, the rotation of seeding to gain greater productivity and the use of alternative crops like turnips were part of the intensification of lowland farm life. Before the 1840s, and increasingly so afterwards, highland workers would tramp to lowland farms for seasonal employment, which brought much-needed cash back to the highland economy. Importantly, it better enabled the northern parishes to hang on to their population over the longer term, allowing stomachs to be filled that would otherwise go hungry.

Along with the intensification of sheep farming and seasonal and temporary migration, the harvesting of seaweed and the creation of kelp from burning it was a third source of cash income in the highland counties. Kelp was used in the production of soap, glass and iodine, and its trade provided a boost to the west highland economy in the years from around 1760 until the 1830s. It was not an industry that developed any infrastructure, however. The collapse in price that followed the reopening of trade routes at the end of the Napoleonic Wars caused a major loss of cash income. In response to the continued decline up to 1845, the Highland and Agricultural Society of Scotland put out a call to establish the most economic and straightforward means by which iodine could be extracted in situ from seaweed. The extraction of salt from kelp was chemically difficult and of no commercial gain, even if undertaken in specialist facilities in Glasgow. Iodine, however, was a better bet. Kelp could yield three to four and a half pounds of iodine per ton, and drift-weed could produce six to ten pounds per ton. It was work that could be carried out in the croft, keeping Highlanders in their homes. But the cost of iodine was on a downward trend, collapsing from 30–40s per pound in 1845 to 16s per lb the next year. The discovery in France of the means to convert iodine into a range of permanent dyes, through combining it with metals, had driven the price upwards in 1849, but still the returns did not recover sufficiently.

The loss of profit from kelp undermined landowner attempts to establish long-term industrial activity on the coastal fringes while intensifying crop and animal husbandry in the hills and glens. Improvement was variable in its impact and take-up by those instructed in new techniques. Agriculture was only slowly progressing in Orkney in the 1830s with the move away from the single stilted plough to its replacement with the 'common kind', with iron-toothed harrows and rollers to ease progress. The use of guano as fertiliser was popularised after 1840, with experiments showing that foreign guano produced 530 stones per Scots acre of turnips more than farmyard dung alone for little more than half the cost. When overseas supplies of guano dried up, ammonia was used, supplied by William 'Paraffin' Young's Oakbank Oil Company. Agricultural improvement was thought not only to aid living standards but also to keep people on the land. In the contemporary analysis of the Rev. David Esdaile, minister of Rescobie in Angus, the acquisition of landed property was the most natural and efficacious remedy to poverty and degradation in the rural areas. This was a desire, he thought, especially strong amongst Scots. His solution was not the forced subdivision of land from the wealthy, but to push the landowner or the cultivator of land to appreciate the happiness engendered if many could enjoy it. They would be wise, he chided, to heed the Wisdom of Solomon: 'the profit of the earth is for all: the king himself is served by the field'. This ministerial contribution to the *Journal of Agriculture* countered Lord Brougham's suggestion that small amounts of land, peopled by a few in constant toil, was no solution to either finding work for the masses or lifting their moral spirits.

FIXING THE ROOF

The philosophy of agricultural improvement and its application mixed internal and external objectifications of highland society. From local lairds at home to external landowners in Edinburgh or London, the ideas combined intimate knowledge of Gaelic and rural society with rational science framed by advanced theorising on civil society. An example of how Improvement was applied in the first Victorian decade is the reconstruction of simple cottages at Abbeymains in the Lennoxlove Estate of Lord Blantyre, redeveloped in the 1840s under the watchful eye of the Highland and Agricultural Society of Scotland. The old cottages consisted of one room of 20 feet by 15 feet; the beds were used as the divide from the kitchen and the pantry. The walls were clay, the floor unplastered and there was no ceiling below the rafter board. The cottages had gardens behind, with dunghills and ruinous pigsties in front. The conversion turned the eight cottages into six larger ones with two new additions built. Outhouses were constructed for each cottage, and the windows were replaced with cast-iron frames. The rooms were provided with a mixture of wooden flooring and Caithness pavement. Ceilings were installed, the walls plastered and a fixed bed, shelving in the pantry, grates and sweys (to swing the kettle out from above the heat) added in the kitchen. The cost for improving the cottages was £233 12s 6d, with a further £84 12s spent on improving the associated offices. On average it cost £38 18s 9d to improve each cottage and £13 2s to provide an office for each (with each dwelling allowed a privy, coal-house, pigsty and ash-pit).

The Society's impetus for this investment came from criticism voiced in England about the condition of the Scottish peasantry. Stung by this rebuke from afar, the Highland Society offered premiums to reward the best-kept cottages and gardens, with their gold medal offered to the proprietor who erected on his estate the greatest number of approved cottages. Of particular concern were further reports received about the poor condition of workers' accommodation in the bothies. So, in 1847 the Society offered for the first time its gold medal to whoever constructed the most approved farm steading on his estate for farm-servants. The aim was to encourage the habits of cleanliness and order, but also to better the health and comfort of the rural population through the improvement in the warmth, ventilation and drainage of the accommodation. The Earl of Rosebery, who had more than once addressed the Society on the importance of representing those who were unable to argue their own case, displayed special attention for these workers. Building new cottages would be the best answer, but Rosebery did not want the pace of change to be slowed, accepting that the cheaper option of renovation should be followed 'to ensure this national problem is addressed'. While there was no profit to be made, it was 'one of the most important duties to which a public society could direct its attention'. The philosophy of agricultural improvement was also one of morals. The idealism and spirit of discovery, which had been present in its Enlightenment roots, were now transformed into characterisations of the industriousness and self-worth of the individual, a personification of race in the face of the imperatives of capitalism within peripheral and undercapitalised agriculture. This moral indignation focused with greatest hostility on the Gaels, and on the highland Celt more widely.

BLIGHT AND FLIGHT

If there was to be one solution to the Malthusian darkness of a rural society increasingly unable to feed itself, then the introduction of the potato seemed to be the answer. Known for two centuries or more, the potato began to overtake oats as Scotland's food staple from the late eighteenth century. The great advantage of the potato was that nutritionally it could sustain a denser population. Sir John Sinclair estimated that four times as many people could be supported by an acre of potatoes as by an acre of oats, and it was a crop more resilient to the mild and damp Scottish climate. The use of the potato also meant non-arable areas were now being inhabited where once they were empty, creating population spread but also dependence on the crop.

Shocked by the unfolding disaster in Ireland, the Highland and Agricultural Society of Scotland sent out surveys to establish the extent of the potato blight in various parts of the country, both highland and lowland. In the autumn of 1846 the blight's appearance was logged. It had first appeared ten years earlier in Argyll, but the spread and extent was now much greater, destroying nearly all of Scotland's potato crop in only a few short weeks. It had been a long year of waiting to see if the catastrophe would be transferred from Ireland, and correspondents increasingly documented the unwelcome evidence. On 19 December 1846 John Hutchison of Monyruy, near Peterhead, recorded that unlike the previous year, 'I cannot now hear of a single instance within many miles, where the potatoes have escaped'. Conscious efforts were made to defeat the disease, such as that of Thomas Aird, a weaver in the parish of Darvel, who sowed the seeds first in his garden hotbed before trans-planting then into open ground; while the tubers grew to be as large as plums the blight came and the stems decayed. Some tried leaving their potatoes in the ground over the winter and ready for the spring, others dug their potatoes daily until the frost came, but no one in this part of Aberdeenshire escaped unscathed. The respondents were asked to comment on the weather, concluding that dry or sometimes very wet weather accompanied by humid conditions brought on the blight. The parish of Lanfine in Ayrshire found the blight to be particularly bad despite different varieties of potatoes and manures being tried; even with only slight evidence of disease these crops failed.

Government officials led by Sir Edward Pine Coffin, church representatives and newspaper reporters commented back from the Highlands to the rest of Britain, and to the world, of the despair. In 1847 lowland aid was newly coordinated by the formation of the Central Board of Management for Highland Relief, coming together from the Edinburgh and Glasgow relief committees and that established by the Free Church of Scotland. Before the year was out, an unprecedented £210,000 was raised. Relief came in the form of seed and meal, with work given in exchange. In some parishes as much as three-quarters of the population was dependent on hand-outs to avoid starvation. Yet these were distributed unevenly and there was fear that the help either was too generous or was turning the Highlander into an indolent pauper, dependent (forever) on charity.

Estimates of the number left hungry or starving by the potato blight suggest that around 200,000 Highlanders were affected. Contemporary claims of 300,000 going without food and half-starving were explosive, but exaggerated. Proportionately few died from the consequences of the blight in Scotland compared to the devastation in Ireland. Outside of the six years of potato blight, Scotland was spared the kind of agricultural shortages that affected earlier periods, but price fluctuation was significant to livelihoods and the choice of food upon the kitchen table.

The costs of the relief on the landowner were also noticeable, with some selling off land to raise capital and others using what funds they had left to assist in the emigration of their tenants. In the estimate of population historian Michael Flinn and his colleagues, 9,000 more emigrants left Scottish ports in 1847–9 compared to the departures recorded in the three years before famine struck. Yet there was no immediate abandonment of the Highlands, with preference first for internal movement. In most cases of western and island depopulation – ranging from 12 per cent in South Uist to 21 per cent in Barra and 23 per cent in Coll – much was already in progress before the blight took hold. The parishes of Inverness-shire and Sutherland in the east, and the towns of Dingwall, Tain and Stornoway, increased in population between 1841 and 1851. It is suggestive that emigrant flight during blight was not coterminous when accounting for the 60,000 highland Scots who were displaced in the period 1841–61. Only after the Emigration Act 1851 was there government finance to help with the cost of passage for those otherwise held in place by the debt of rent arrears.

Newspaper coverage of the potato famine would frequently summon up the spectre of race rather than God's will to explain the destitution. Seeing idleness all around, Highlanders were reported to be refusing to work for what seemed a fair wage. To those outsiders who travelled to see the effects of the blight at first hand, it was the Highlanders' living conditions that appalled most: 'it is a fact that morally and intellectually they are an inferior race to the Lowland Saxon,' reported *The Scotsman* in January 1847.

OWNING SCOTLAND

One fall-out of the potato blight, exacerbated by the famine in Ireland, was that it confirmed to some observers that the Celtic races no longer had a place in society, at least not a productive one. Once economically 'of the land', the Celt was objictified into an older Scotland, one confined to the nation's past. No longer modern, the Celt and the Highlands were objictified through cultural consumption: as landscape to visit, to hunt, to improve and to contrast in painted image, song and social investigation.

For all these changes to society, and the propensity of highland Scots to temporarily relocate in lowland Scotland or to emigrate, big landowners remained dominant in the late nineteenth century. In 1872, 93 per cent of Scotland was held in estates of more than 1,000 acres, in contrast to 78 per cent in Ireland, 61 per cent in Wales and 56 per cent in England. At this time, four out of the top ten great British landowners were Scottish – the Dukes of Buccleuch, Bute, Sutherland and Hamilton – and nine of the top twenty-nine had Scottish estates. The 1,500 largest landowners controlled 90 per cent of Scotland; it was a dominance that had dropped only marginally thirty years later. Land reform against the landed classes was a feature of late-nineteenth-century Ireland and Scotland, most acutely in the crofting areas of the north-west, whereas rural England was not similarly challenged. This economic domination was reflected in political control at the local level. In 1892 two-thirds of the thirty-three conveners of Scottish county councils were landowners, of whom seven were peers and five were also lord lieutenants. We owned Scotland's land, and others owned Scotland's land too, but most of us owned nothing or very little.

There is interest in examining any of Scotland's counties in some detail, but for its royal connections focus here falls on Aberdeenshire, including what became known as Royal Deeside, where there were 4,489 landowners recorded in the return. There were 869 people named as owning one acre or more, totalling 1,252,100 acres at a combined value of £768,791 4s. Ten estates were over 20,000 acres in size and these landowners controlled 561,498 acres, or just under 45 per cent of Aberdeenshire (see Table 1.3).

Opposition between the 'have much' and the 'have little' manifests itself in religious divisions and class antagonism alongside more everyday concerns of underwork, poverty and migration. The one major legislative attempt to redress some of the iniquities for the very poorest came with the Crofter's Holding

Table 1.3 Distribution of land ownership over 20,000 acres, Aberdeenshire, 1872–3

		Acres	Value
1	Trustees of the Earl of Fife, Duff House, Banffshire	139,829	£17,740 5s
2	Colonel J. Ross Farquharson of Invercauld, Invercauld, Braemar	87,745	£9,567 3s
3	Marquis of Huntly, Aboyne Castle	80,000	£11,215 5s
4	Duke of Richmond, Huntly Castle	69,600	£24,747 15s
5	Earl of Aberdeen, Haddo House	63,442	£40,765 11s
6	Her Majesty The Queen, Balmoral House	25,350	£2,392 16s
7	James T. McKenzie of Kintail and Glenmuik, Glenmuik House	25,000	£1,116
8	Sir Charles Forbes of Newe, Bart, Castle Newe	29,238	£5,992 7s
9	W. Dingwall Fordyce of Brucklay, MP	20,899	£12,743 19s
10	John Gordon of Cluny, Cluny Castle	20,395	£13,713 10s

Source: *Land Ownership Commission 1872–3.*

Act 1886. The crofter's plight drew contemporary comment of Parliamentarians, too. It was one of the few Scottish issues, along with the Disruption in the Church of Scotland (1843), that garnered significant attention in the Westminster chamber. Both were insular debates, yet because of the nation's inter-relationship with its near neighbours, each was driven by the concerns of the shared Parliament.

Because the newspaper editors of Edinburgh and Glasgow were at times reluctant to provide a sympathetic interpretation of tenant poverty in the Highlands, it left a gap for John Murdoch to fill with the establishment of the *Highlander* in 1873, promoting a strong highland economy and culture from within the region, and informing supporters in the central belt towns and cities of the issues at hand. The influence of the press was behind the land agitation of the 1870s when both the *Highlander* and the writings of Free Church minister John MacMillan criticised the actions of Aberdeen paper mill owner [and later MP] A. C. Pirie in 1879 for forcing his tenants to work on his estate or face eviction. It led to warnings that unless reform was forthcoming, then troubles akin to the situation in Ireland would arise.

Greater concern came along with shock and disbelief at the severity of reaction in what became known as the Land Wars of the 1880s. Memories of the Sutherland Clearances between 1807 and 1821 were the backdrop to highland anger towards any forcible efforts to move people from their homes. The Battle of the Braes in Skye in 1882, when the crofters asserted their 'historic right' to graze their animals on land owned by Lord MacDonald and used for his own sheep, was reported throughout Britain. With the tenants refusing to pay rent if access continued to be denied, and soldiers dispatched from Glasgow to quell the 'troublemakers' – leading to crofters being beaten and prisoners taken to Portree – the right to own land was an issue for both local and national government.

The Royal Commission of Inquiry established to consider this agitation published its report in 1884. The Commission was accused of being landlord dominated, but still much evidence came from factors and crofter leaders. The outcome, the Crofters' Holdings (Scotland) Act, received Parliamentary assent in June 1886. As a philosophical reflection on the moral right to own land, the legislation was a dramatic change in the law, taking from the landowner and giving to the crofter the heritable right to the land. But in reflecting the historical narrative of 'being Scotland', it was less unexpected because it fitted the experience of improvements to crop and animal husbandry, attempts to improve the rural house and home, and a pattern of land ownership that remained the most concentrated in Europe despite the imperatives of the modern age.

THE CELT FROM TEMPORAL AND GEOGRAPHICAL DISTANCE

In the examples of housing improvement, blight and land reform, contemporaries framed the socio-economic and political influence of 'the Celt' within a particular objectification of the Highlands. This came from various directions, for good and ill, and kept the Improvement philosophy at its core. Whether it be to advance living conditions and diet, agriculture and industrial output, or belated land reform at the century's end, the cultural objectification of the Celt and the highland region was built on economic and philosophical changes premised on an interpretation of what a successful highland society would look like.

Throughout all this, respect for the highland soldier and Queen Victoria's affection for Deeside ensured a place in popular and intellectual discourse for the ordinary Highlander that was more sympathetic than might otherwise have been the case. In the towns and the cities the Highlander was still thought of as an interloper and an economic threat when jobs were scarce, but when in the Highlands the Celt was simply exotic and peripheral. The Highlands, as a place, was no longer threatening to lowland constructions of self, and their land was now for leisure and sport, insufficient to sustain a viable society to the level it once did. To others, this history of economic hardship and (en)forced migration is evidence of an older society ending, irrespective of the stability in land ownership.

The history of the land and its people supplied the evidence to feminise the Celt in comparison with masculine progress. Matthew Arnold's *On the Study of Celtic Literature* (1867) describes the Celt as 'sentimental', 'sensual' and 'ineffectual in politics'. Arnold saw truth in the 'extravagance of chivalry' in the Celt, who 'has an affinity to [feminine idiosyncrasy]; he is not far from its secret'. Arnold associated the Celt with 'magic naturalism' and special charms and secret powers, producing a decidedly Ossianic definition, where English was the language of importance with Gaelic confined to antiquarianism. The feminised Celt as noble savage was 'owned' by masculine Britain.

The feminisation of the Celt was reinforced in affinity with 'shared' societies. The encounter of Scottish Highlanders with colonisers paralleled the experience of North American Indians. Both were oral cultures based on myth, kinship and natural resources; each lay in shadow from a core civilisation. Kin-based communities, a distinctive clothing that signalled 'savage' against the refinery and fashions of the urban world, they were peoples subjected to pacification. Scholars make the argument that the masculine core of England/Britain 'oppressed' both the Celt and the Native American, undermining, appropriating and adapting their symbols as and when needed. In each case 'nature' was used to classify the everyday life of ordinary people in ways that made sense to contemporaries at a distance. In this context, and with a widespread cultural resonance that continued throughout the century, the lines of Scott's *The Lay of the Last Minstrel* encompassed the objectification of the nation and its people through 'the land':

O Caledonia! stern and, wild,
Meet nurse for a poetic child!
Land of brown heath and shaggy wood
Land of the mountain and the flood,
Land of my sires! what mortal hand
Can e'er untie the filial band,
That knits me to thy rugged strand!

That the character of the Scot was formed in relation to the nation's soil, and the Celt was believed closer to nature – as Arnold's theories were followed and given currency by the likes of Beddoe and Cleghorn – then 'being Scotland' flowed out of the natural environment. To investigate this further, our eyes gaze upwards to the clouds in the sky and to the nation's weather.

2

Weather Scotland Will

One part of Scotland's identity never constrained by national boundaries is the weather: it always comes second hand. Lying along the northern 55th parallel, Glasgow and Edinburgh are on the same latitude as Moscow and Copenhagen to the east, Quebec and Alaska to the west. The Gulf Stream hits the nation's west coat with warm but moist air from the Gulf of Mexico; in chilly contrast blasts from the north polar continent spread cooler but drying air to the east coast. For most months in the year, Scotland is the wettest and the cloudiest part of Britain, and it can be windy, too: the Hebrides and Shetland experience on average thirty-five and forty-two days respectively of gales each year. Even though it is a narrow country, Scotland's coast is sunnier than its interior, with the highest average sunshine recorded each year in Moray and the Outer Hebrides at around 1,300 hours (although Shetland measures only around 1,100 hours). And while the northernmost parts of Scotland can average four hours more daylight than London during the height of the summer, on average Scotland's crops are warmed less by the sun than in the farms of England, with the southern coast of Britain benefiting from over 1,750 hours of sunshine on average each year.

Throughout the 1832 to 1914 period, the number of hours of daylight affected not just agricultural and other work outdoors, but spinning and craft, leisure and everyday life in the home. Heavy rain, wind, hail and frost impacted the farmer as it did the builder, the fisherman and the groundsman. It meant the working day would be variable even when disciplined by the clock or the machine. Nor did the move from sail to steam power free the trader from the elements. Rough seas and fog remained variables in the delivery times of coastal steamers and for transatlantic cargoes alike.

It was not controversial for the Enlightenment thinkers David Hume and Adam Ferguson to argue that Europe's temperate climate was one reason behind that region's lead in the path of civilisation. Doubt, however, remained for their contemporary John Miller that the national characteristics of the Scots, the English and the Irish could be explained by weather patterns that, to him at least, seemed too similar to be of great influence. And while the seasonal changes in daylight and in wind, rain and sun were associated with Scottish national characteristics ranging from a dour demeanour that matched the clouds above, the development of muscle and sinew from long summer evenings of athletic activity or a heavy use of alcohol once the sun set early in winter, the nation's climate remained embedded in worldwide weather patterns. The weather of others affected our weather, yet contemporary Scots were at first sceptical that outsiders could offer insight into their national climate. For many, still the best guess to the seasonal changes the weather would bring for the farmer or seafarer was to follow rhymes and prognostics passed down through experience and the trained eye, to trust indigenous knowledge. Even after British national weather forecasts came to Scottish newspapers in 1862, the use of science to describe, let alone predict, the weather was not always adjudged an improvement upon local knowledge.

A story recalled by one critic told of a visit to Perthshire by the celebrated naval captain Sir Sidney Smith (1764–1840), who upon being complimented on his abilities as a seaman to predict the weather, replied, 'I can do nothing among your mountains; but set me afloat in a known sea, with a barometer before me, and I will give you a rough guess of what you may expect'. He could do this, he insisted, because whenever he was posted somewhere new, he would make a point of asking the local fishermen for their signs and observations on the weather, never finding them wrong. The Rev. David Esdaile, a Presbyterian minister from Forfar and scientific sceptic whose story this was, insisted that weather prognostics by fishermen, sailors and shepherds, without any pretension of science, should not be mocked: the scientists should instead read Addison's *Barometri Descriptio*, and 'let them not despise the *empirical* knowledge of the unlearned, handed down from the days of old and trusted in because it was founded on experience'. Writing in 1867, the Presbyterian minister Alexander McLeod insisted the purpose of using science to predict the weather was not to discover the secular truth, but rather 'the entire subordination of all these to His control'.

Some prognostics could be readily proven to convince Scots that the observations of their parents and grandparents remained of value in this age of technological modernity: 'If the first day of Januarie happen to be Fridaye, then shall the winter be very cold and dry, the spring boysterous and wette then drye . . .' Tested in 1864, it was found to be true. And similar unattributed prognostics were repeated throughout the century. Spring, for the farmer, was the crucial period for sowing:

> Nae hurray wi' your corns,
> Nae hurray wi' your harrows;
> Snaw lies ahint the dyke,
> Mair may come and fill the furrows.

The farmer and sailor alike were keen to know what kind of winter they would endure:

> If Candlemas-day be dry and fair,
> The half o' winter's to come and mair:
> If Candlemas be wet and foul,
> The half o' winter's gane at Yule

Cirrus clouds, known as mare's tails, were thought to indicate wind to the seafarer:

> Mackerel's scales and mare's tails
> Make lofty ships carry low sales

Animals, too, were predictors of the weather in many parts of Scotland. Swine carry straw in their mouths before a storm; cats scratch a post or wall before wind, wash their face before a thaw and sit with their backs to the a fire before snow. Humans, of course, developed their own weather sense, being more likely to feel pain or rheumatism before a change from dry to wet weather or from mild to cold weather; listlessness or unease were often felt before a storm. When milk suddenly and unexpectedly went sour, then a thunderstorm was said to be at hand.

Some of these predictions had implications for the nation's health: 'a green Yule makes a fat Kirkyard' came from the belief that frosty weather is healthier than damp weather. And there were a large number of popular prognoses regarding all manner of weather characteristics, confirming its importance to those working out of doors or at sea. A cloud on top of Sidlaw Hills is a sign of rain soon to come to the residents of Carmylie; when there is mist covering the summit of Bin Hill, rain is likely in Cullen; and a similar covering of the Paps of Jura indicates to the people of Kilcalmonell and Kilberry that wet weather is due.

This was not so much a national preoccupation with the skies as a test of the value of science and its application in the parishes of Scotland. One correspondent to the *Scottish Farmer* in 1863 explained that although popular prognostics were rarely valid for more than the next twenty-four hours, natural signs of old differed little from those provided by Admiral FitzRoy 'with all the meteorological science of the present day at his command'. FitzRoy, of whom we shall soon learn more, was mocked for offering predictions only one week in advance, whereas 'the weather prophet' Thomas Du Boulay, without state support, was sufficiently confident to predict the weather six months in advance simply by observing the vernal equinox. With both 'exposed', the old farmer was thought to know best, whether the prognostics were scientific or not.

While it was almost uniformly believed that the weather followed God's will, some were still prepared to bring earthly theories into the discussion. In 1867 the Rev. Charles Clouston, Minister of Sandwick near Stromness, President of the Orkney Natural History Society and honourable member of the Kirkwall Literary and Scientific Association, as well as a member of

mutual aid societies in Orkney and Glasgow, published a trea-
tise on predicting Scotland's weather. For this man of God there
was no conflict of conscience in waiting for the Newton of meteorology to one day discover the laws by which the Almighty
regulates the weather: 'In the meantime, it must be pleasing to
God, as well as beneficial to man, to throw light on any of these
laws'.

With his time maximised by the isolation of an Orcadian life,
Clouston was able to combine his scientific training and observations with his ministerial and pastoral obligations. His analysis
mixed scientific and religious reasoning, describing the circulation of warm air around the equator that heated up the ocean
and led to rain falling on the more temperate regions as 'beauti-
fully illustrating the wisdom and beneficence of the Creator'.
His principal instrument was the anemometer, used to record
wind speed; government issued, it came by way of the meteorologist Admiral Robert FitzRoy. FitzRoy first made his reputation
as the commander of the *Beagle* expedition served by a young
scientific officer by the name of Charles Darwin from 1831 to
1836. After a chequered career that took him to an ill-fated
governorship of New Zealand, he became in 1854 Britain's first
state meteorologist within the Board of Trade.

Armed with his barometer and anemometer, Clouston
offered the first published validation of popular prognostics
that built upon the classificatory structure developed in Dr
Arthur Mitchell's 'Popular weather prognostics of Scotland'
(1863). Through systematic observation and the recoding of
air and water temperatures, he tested long-held beliefs such as
river fog being a sign of frost or whether Fife coal miners were
correct to suggest that before a storm a sound like a bagpipe
or the buzz of a bee would come from the rocks and minerals,
and that such sounds were significantly quieter before rain.
Similar techniques, measuring water and gas pressure, were
used to investigate whether an increased flow of water, and the
issue of gases and foul air from underground crevices preceded
approaching changes in the weather, a prognostic held by the
miners of Midlothian.

THE WEATHER WORLD

Whatever confidence there was in common knowledge, nascent international measurements and God's will to predict its path, Scotland's weather was wont to play tricks on any who thought it either indigenous to the nation or homogeneous in its effects. The meteorologist Alexander Buchan pointed out that in comparing Scotland's mean temperature of August 1860 with the same month in 1864 an identical figure was found (54.4 degrees), but in 1860 the highest daily temperature was 60.8 degrees and in 1864 it was 62.5 degrees. The higher day temperature helped produce a bountiful harvest; the lower was the chief cause of a poor harvest. For such a small landmass, but a coastal one in the path of significant wind flows, the weather had a profound effect on staples and luxuries alike. The air temperature, compared to the sea temperature, was three degrees higher around the coast of the Orkney Islands than in the south of Scotland. The Scottish Meteorological Society [SMS] found that the average rainfall in the west of Scotland over a six-year period mid-century was 47.38 inches, whereas it was 29.29 inches in the east. In a further striking example of such disparities, Charles Roberts recorded in his *Naturalist's Diary* that even though the west coast of Skye and the Laigh o' Moray are on the same latitude and only seventy or eighty miles apart, with an average temperature difference of two degrees, in Skye the rainfall can be 100 inches or more per year, but in the Laigh o' Moray it is only twenty-six inches. In the drier parish, with bright sunshine, cereals grow well, but not so in Skye. The sun's radiation at 1,000 feet or more can ripen peaches in Fallon in Aberdeen whereas in the south of Scotland it is insufficient to do likewise.

Scotland's weather knew no national boundary; that much is clear. Similarly the regular movement of goods and people by sea was linked to wide meteorological conditions, beyond Empire to all the world's trade routes. Scotland's seafarers required knowledge of favourable wind and current, and as the growth of global capitalism demanded regular and timely

movement of goods, so science was called upon to benefit the
safety of crew, cargo and profits.

In 1853, the US Navy admiral Matthew Fontaine Maury
visited Britain with a plan to raise public support for an international collaboration to document worldwide meteorological
readings. Although he was cautiously welcomed at first, doors
eventually opened once the generous funding he received from
the US government became known, enough for a staff of ten or
twenty. Maury was the leading international meteorologist, his
personal drive flowing from a desire to understand the nature of
storms and 'establish God's pathways through the sea'. Around
1,000 US vessels had been using a standardised reporting form
since 1851 and the first international maritime conference to
agree a uniform system of meteorological observations taken at
sea was held in Brussels in August 1853. Support for international measurement had come from the governments of Sweden
and Norway and, in anticipation, the British government had
instructed the Royal Navy to record the kinds of meteorological
data already being collated by its US counterpart.

In addition to locational information, delegates agreed to
record the direction and velocity of currents, the form and direction of clouds, the quantity of rain, the direction and force of
wind, and the temperature and density of water at the surface
and at various depths. The use of standardised forms replaced
reliance on ships' logbooks and meteorological atlases and
began the process still in place today of the systematic collection
of meteorological and oceanographic data for better guiding
ship movements.

Upon receiving the report from Brussels, government civil
servants wrote to the Royal Society with a series of requests that
led to the establishment of a meteorological office in London
in 1854 as part of the Board of Trade. Concurrent with these
developments, debate on the merits of scientific over culturally formed measurements continued within Scotland. When
the Marquis of Tweeddale lectured the SMS in 1860 that old
customs remained best, he did so with the hope of being proved
wrong. The Society had formed five years earlier from 200

subscribers each putting in £200, with Tweeddale its first chairman. Simply by watching the sky, the ennobled amateur meteorologist later pointed out, a number of shepherds were able to predict the dramatic snowstorm of 1861: why should this be, he wondered. Tweeddale had offered two essay-writing prizes of £20 to the Society, then meeting in the Museum Hall of the Highland and Agricultural Society. One of those was for the best essay on rainfall (achieving five entries and won by Thomas F. Jamieson of Ellon in Aberdeenshire); the other for the best essay on the optimum crops for Scotland's weather conditions (which had no claim upon it, despite the belief it would appeal to Scotland's tenant farmers).

In the spirit of discovery, the SMS was keen to acquire and test out new measuring equipment. With the increase in the interchange of meteorological information between the European nations, lighthouse engineer Thomas Stevenson reported on the six stations around Great Britain and Ireland feeding information into the Board of Trade and, at the request of the mathematician and astronomer Urbain Leverrier, to Paris also. Believing somewhat optimistically that Scotland's trade and extensive fishing fleet would gain to an extent greater than any other country in the world – 'if only the appearance of storms could be telegraphed a day or even a few hours in advance' – the SMS promoted the international free trade of information as a competitive advantage for the nation. The data collected was sent to Edinburgh's Royal Observatory for analysis before the summaries were passed to the Registrar General for Scotland. Charles Piazzi Smyth was Scotland's Astronomer Royal in these years. Born in Italy in 1819, he was the son of London-born Admiral William Henry Smyth and great-grandson of Captain John Smith (1580?–1631). Through his sister's marriage, he became uncle of the hero of Mafeking and scout leader Robert, Lord Baden-Powell. Admiral Smyth was an amateur astronomer and Charles gained his exotic middle name from his godfather, the Sicilian astronomer Giuseppe Piazzi, later taking it as his forename. Smyth was educated in England and trained at the Royal Observatory at Cape Hope in South Africa. Observing

Halley's Comet in 1835, along with Sir John Herschel he produced watercolours of this 'extraordinary phenomenon'. Smyth took up the position of Astronomer Royal for Scotland and Regius Professor of Astronomy at Edinburgh University in 1846. The work was arduous, the pay low and the office underfunded. He came to rely on his Scottish-born wife Jessie Duncan as his assistant, finding greater success observing the night sky over Tenerife in the Canary Islands than Calton Hill in Edinburgh and publishing the first known book on astronomy containing stereo-photographs in 1858. That expedition had been helped by a grant of £500 from the Admiralty and the use of the 140-ton yacht *Titania* from Robert Stephenson, MP and son of the engineer George Stephenson, for the duration of the expedition.

Piazzi Smyth was a pioneer in the technique of placing telescopes at high altitudes. His photographic experiments had in 1843 produced the oldest known calotypes of indigenous peoples in southern Africa. By his own invention in 1852, he introduced the means to signal the time from the observatory on Calton Hill using a time-ball. Edinburgh's one o'clock gun was added to this service in 1861 and he worked with the local clockmakers James Ritchie & Son to ensure that the citizens of the city would always have a means of telling the time, a system he then spread to Dundee. Smyth's *Astronomical Observations made at the Royal Observatory, Edinburgh* (1863) was widely acclaimed, while his work on spectroscopy, the precursor of astrophysics, was recognised with a moon crater named after him.

Smyth's analysis of Scotland's weather was dependent on the daily information he received from the SMS. By 1857 the Society had established thirty-six measuring stations although some counties were still not covered and the Society found elusive the financial support it needed to fill the gaps. In 1858 J. F. Macfarlan petitioned the Chamber of Commerce in Edinburgh to memorialise the government for a grant on the Society's behalf, receiving the city's unanimous support. It was now, after three years of subscriptions, that these amateur meteorologists pondered closure. If that happened, the Society feared, 'in regard to meteorological observations, Scotland would be behind England'. There was an element of national pride as well as stubbornness in how they valued work that was often painstaking, declaring confidently that if Scotland were to lag behind its southern neighbour in the application of science to weather measurement and prognosticating, then their 'countrymen would come forward to assist'. The stand-off was concluded when the Board of Trade offered to undertake the role of classifying, reducing and publishing the Society's results (done by engaging Smyth in the task). The coverage of Scotland increased, with fifty-four reporting stations operating in the middle of 1860, sixty-five in 1861 and seventy-two the next year. The Society kept up a role as coordinators of the national measurement of the weather as well as exploring the scientific value of their methodology.

By 1865 the SMS was estimated to be the largest and best-organised meteorological society in Europe, tripling in size over the decade to almost 600 members. Beyond recording weather statistics for Scots, the Society was contributing to knowledge of Britain's weather patterns for domestic and international use. Tweeddale gifted the SMS mementos and reports from the Council of India in 1862 and the Society sold over 200 copies of its quarterly reports in 1863, gaining the services of two volunteers in Syria to provide measurements from that region. The rise in membership indicated that meteorology was becoming popular and practical, no longer a mystery to society at large. A new medical department was added to look at the effects of climate on health and disease. One of its members took the practice of reading to the public schools – the Normal School [in Edinburgh], the Dollar Institution, Elgin Academy and Aberdeen Grammar School. To confirm its newly established credibility, His Royal Highness the Prince Alfred became an honorary member – two years before becoming Duke of Edinburgh, the title then revived by Queen Victoria – having had the occasion to visit the Society and examine its measuring instruments in 1864.

Challenges, however, remained. The Society struggled with its plans to establish a meteorological observatory at the summit of Ben Nevis, a point chosen to best record the direction of Scotland's Atlantic storms. After a failed appeal to government, momentum fell upon the endeavours of the Englishman Clement Wragge who not only spent much time clambering around the mountain to take daily measurements, but headed an appeal for funds throughout Britain in 1883 which climaxed sufficiently to open the Thomas 'Lighthouse' Stevenson-designed building in October that year, which remained in operation until 1904. It was Wragge who began the trend of naming cyclones with people's names and in 1886, having returned to Australia upon failing to secure the position of superintendent of the Ben Nevis observatory, he became a founding member of the Royal Meteorological Society of Australia.

'IT'S NO RAINING'

The motivation for Tweeddale's £20 prize in 1860 was his belief that the average rainfall in Scotland – as well as that of Western Europe more widely – was declining. From the evidence of twenty-two recording stations, Thomas Jamieson's winning essay countered that the average was unchanged. But this conclusion was itself challenged by James Glaisher, founder member in 1850 of the Meteorological Society, who suggested the annual rainfall since 1815 was indeed on the decline. That his evidence came only from one recording station in London convinced George James Symons FRS (1838–1900) that the current measure was inadequate. Symons joined the British Meteorological Society in 1856, aged only seventeen, and published the first systematic investigation into British rainfall trends three years later.

His interest was piqued after a succession of dry summers just at the time when the expanding towns were under increasing pressure to bring water supplies in to their residents. Working for FitzRoy in the Meteorological Department, Symons struggled to convince the Admiral of the value of his work. By 1863 with the financial help of the British Association and the Royal Society he was publishing *British Rainfall* each year, which contained 3,500 records from 900 stations. That year Symons had written to Alexander Buchan for advice on the best rainfall measurement gauge, continuing to try different methods throughout his career. Symons was gifted twenty-five years of records from the Board of the Northern Lighthouses in 1866 covering many of Scotland's lighthouses. He used *The Times* as a means of seeking volunteers. In total he benefited from nearly 2,000 amateur observers feeding in data, allowing the creation of tabulations then followed in other countries, although large parts of Scotland in the 1870s were still lacking observers.

In terms of measuring rainfall, developments in Scotland progressed alongside the rest of Britain. It had not been until the beginning of the nineteenth century that a generally accepted method of measuring rainclouds was introduced: Luke Howard's cloud classifications in 1802–3. John Constable pained a number of cloud images in the 1820s to illustrate the classification, but he never painted their appearance in Scotland. In 1838 Sir William Reid authored the first Law of Storms, but measuring instruments were not consistent. At the Great Exhibition of 1851, an animal barometer was exhibited from France where a bell would indicate air pressure according to the movements of a leech. Thermometers had been available since the eighteenth century along with weatherglasses that had been used even earlier. By the 1860s good quality thermometers with porcelain scales might be acquired for a few shillings. Cheaper ones, at one or two shillings, were not thought trustworthy. To test the moisture in the air, two thermometers were needed: one tied to a cup of water with cotton wool or a linen cloth attached to show evaporation, and the other to record the temperature. The budding meteorologist could also purchase a rain gauge in zinc or copper for between one and two pounds. A wind-vane or weathercock could be employed, although the results were often uncertain and weather direction was best observed by following the direction of low-lying clouds or of smoke: the wind will

Figure 2.1 *'We're in for stormy weather': The 'FitzRoy barometer' (1880) popularised after Admiral FitzRoy's death. © Crail Museum Trust. Licensor www.scran.ac.uk*

shift in the direction of upper clouds, so the record made should always note the direction of the lower clouds.

On behalf of the Earl of Aberdeen, Peterhead was one of the few places in Scotland that had a barometer prior to 1850. His aim was to help save lives where no insurance office would offer recompense. Alongside the Lifeboat Institution, the Board of Trade began lending barometers to the most exposed and less affluent fishing villages in 1857, and at the Board's behest *The Scotsman* published in 1860 extensive extracts from Fitzroy's guide to reading a barometer.

As an alternative to the barometer, Smyth advocated the rain-band spectroscope to measure water vapour in the atmosphere as the best and most portable tool for predicting rainfall. Around four inches in length, three-quarters of an inch in diameter and costing £2, it seemed a straightforward scientific means of obser-vation. As the historian Katherine Anderson explains, for con-temporaries the tool appeared to close the gap between science and cultural prognostics. But critics found it vague and 'simply a new sky prognostic' more difficult to use than Smyth claimed.

PHENOLOGY IN SCOTLAND

The tension between scientific measurement, classification and popular prognostics found a middle ground in the popular-ity of phenology. This method of measurement involved the observation of annually recurring events in nature, such as the migration of birds or the flowering of plants. By 1875 there was a network of phenological measuring points throughout Britain, with the most complete survey conducted by the staff at the Royal Botanical Gardens in Edinburgh. James McNab began the survey there in 1850, and with impetus coming from the Rev. Thomas A. Pearson's phenological reports from 1875, McNab was followed by John Sadler (1878–82) and Robert Lindsay (1882–95). An example of this kind of observational evidence comes from A. W. Preston who took time out from his observations around the neighbourhood of Norwich to report on what he found on a trip north in 1888:

In Scotland the crops were as forward by the end of July as in
England, and the root crops much finer owing to occasional refresh-
ing rains. I was told that the spring was much earlier there than here
[Norwich], the laburnums near the Gare Loch (Roseneath) being
in full bloom by May 20th, whereas here my first date for flowering was May 29th, and full flowering June 10th. It was the most
beautiful spring and summer ever remembered in Scotland.

The snowdrop and the hazel were the only two plants to have
flowered all over the kingdom by the end of February 1888,
noted Preston, appearing in Tynron in Dumfries only on
the 27th. For all his use of systematic classification, Admiral
FitzRoy was not averse to observing in his *Weather Book* that
when seagulls fly out early in the morning, then the weather is
likely to be fair, but when they are reluctant to leave the land,
then storm and swell are likely. (The value of such observation,
however, is tempered by the knowledge that there are fourteen
species of gull in Orkney alone and some, like the black-headed
gull, is freshwater-based and rarely goes out to sea.)

It was not just the temperature of Scotland's lochs, rivers and
seas that led to wider attempts at systematic classification, but
what lay beneath the surface, too. Laying telegraph cables on
the seabed required information about potential obstacles, as
well as information on what was in the water and the direction
and pull of currents. Dredging between Scotland and the Faroe
Islands in 1868 pulled up numerous finds for investigation by
Sir Charles Wyville Thomson and Dr William B. Carpenter.
Thomson's groundbreaking *The Depths of the Sea* (1873)
sparked his and the Canadian John Cameron's travels on board
HMS *Challenger* (1872–3) to perform oceanographic research
worldwide, the outcome being fifty volumes published from
1880. On board the *Challenger* was Sir John Murray (1841–
1914): Ontario born, educated in Stirling and at Edinburgh
University, he was Scottish by adoption. Murray established
the Challenger Office in Edinburgh as an international centre of
ocean and marine life research and organised a bathymetrical
survey of saltwater and freshwater lochs in 1897, completing
the Scottish lochs by 1906. He was supported by Frederick

P. Pullar (1875–1901), inventor of the F. P. Pullar Sounding Machine used in the Forth basin, and son of Laurence Pullar of the dry-cleaning business. In more hazardous conditions, the Scottish National Antarctic Expedition, led by William S. Bruce on board the *Scotia* between 1902 and 1904, investigated the waters, environment and wildlife of the polar south.

WEATHER COMMUNICATIONS

The invention that did most to drive real gains for scientific weather prognosting was the electric telegraph. The quick spread of information around the coasts had the potential to save the economy from massive losses of tonnage, cargo and life each year. Six years before the Brussels conference of 1853, the Board of Trade invited international cooperation in providing safety at sea. The first plan was to make the lighthouses at the forefront of this information exchange, and Sir Henry James's experiments in Edinburgh in 1852 using an aneroid barometer – to test the different wind strengths windward and leeward of a house, published in *Transactions of the Royal Edinburgh Society* – was part of the nexus. The application of meteorologic telegraphy established frequent transmissions between widely dispersed recording stations in order that atmospheric pressure be tracked over the whole country. But while the technology existed, investment was needed to build a regularised system and a means of digesting the information into viable communications. FitzRoy championed the value of the new technology and his case gained impetus from the violent storm of October 1857 that started off the Cornish coast before making its way up to the Shetland Islands. This storm caused 343 ships to be lost, close to the British total for the previous twelve months. Two years later, the sinking of the *Royal Charter* off the coast of Anglesey with around 500 lives lost was the greatest single death toll during a storm that claimed nearly 800 fatalities. Included amongst the drowned were four relatives of Charles Dickens, a loss that personalised the tragedy for many. Dickens visited the wreckage and wrote movingly of the events in his periodical *All Year Round*.

Scotland was again hit by a major storm on 3 October 1860 with six steamers wrecked; included amongst them was the *Edinburgh*, a ship Piazzi Smyth had recently sailed in. The momentum for telegraphic meteorology was compelling. The Board of Trade issued its first storm warnings in February 1861 and published weather forecasts based on national information were introduced in August that year and standardised in 1862. They were not prophecies or predictions, but opinions, insisted FitzRoy. It was such candour that fed critics who regarded the collection of meteorological readings, like the collection of coins, as nothing more than a form of antiquarianism. The telegrams sent from the Scottish monitoring stations were received in London at 10 o'clock each morning. Upon receipt they were corrected and standardised then added to prepared forms ready for copying before being distributed one hour later to six chosen outlets: *The Times* (for its second edition of the day), the shipping insurer Lloyd's, the *Shipping Gazette*, the Board of Trade itself, the Admiralty and the Horse Guards. Other newspapers got copies for their afternoon edition before further copies were sent out for the next morning's newspapers. The Board of Trade received around thirty to forty telegrams each day, except Sunday, with the whole of Scotland treated as a distinct district while England was divided into four. Scotland was the first zone worked out by the Board's meteorologists, establishing Britain's weather movement from north to south. It was difficult to get the copied reports to the newspapers any faster, and they were generally too late to advise on the present. If a storm was predicted for Scotland, then warning telegrams would be sent to Nairn; to the Collector of Customs at Aberdeen and Peterhead and to the Montrose Harbourmaster; to the Collector of Customs at Dundee and the Chamber of Commerce in Broughty Ferry; to the Exchange Rooms at Glasgow; to the Collector of Customs at Greenock; to Berwick; to the Collector of Customs at Leith; to the Harbour Master at Granton; to Ardrossan and to the nearest coastguard.

In response to criticism in the pages of *The Scotsman* that the government's attempts at storm warning had failed in

1861, FitzRoy wrote to the newspaper pointing out that such conclusions were hasty since they came before a proper trial of the system. The prediction was a day later than expected, and the storm was also more pronounced, but it came. FitzRoy appended to his letter a copy of the Board of Trade circular identifying the shapes to be displayed upon staffs to indicate the direction and severity of any approaching storm. These physical displays were to be located near a telegraph station. *The Scotsman* carried the wind and weather for the previous day for towns and cities throughout Britain, followed by 'Probable Weather Before Saturday' for North Britain. The Edinburgh newspaper kept using the weather information coming from the Leith Board of Trade Nautical School. As a rule *The Scotsman* did not highlight the London telegrams in its daily reports, but it used the detail collected by the Board in its national information, and used the telegrams directly when storms were likely. On 1 October 1863 the newspaper reported that Admiral Fitzroy had telegraphed that 'Dangerous winds might be expected from nearly opposite quarters successively', and that there was 'the probability of a gale from southwards'. He telegraphed again the next day that 'Dangerous winds might be expected from nearly opposite quarters successively'.

'The Admiral hunts a storm with the vigour of a sportsman, as well as the zeal of a weather philosopher', noted the *Aberdeen Journal* in 1864. But FitzRoy was at times ignored, his warnings accused of interfering in the free movement of trade. On two occasions where it appeared the advice of his office was not heeded then blame came: for the loss of thirty-two vessels and upwards of 100 lives lost in storms in the Liverpool Channel in the winter of 1863, and when the system failed after the telegraph wires were blown down between Northumberland and London.

AN ILL WIND

Never simply ours, the link between the nation's weather and the land, sea and people of Scotland was institutionalised through the SMS, the Royal Observatory, the General Register Office for Scotland (GROS) and the Board of Trade. Smyth's mix of artistic ability, technological inventions and search for the science of prognosticating placed him within the religious values, observations and scientific endeavour of the period. Smyth was a millenarian, and saw clouds as God's work. Fitzroy, however, found science ultimately unable to tame the climatic variations he encountered. His suicide in 1865 was in part explained by the challenge of processing accurate returns while under scientific and (personal and departmental) financial pressure. Uncharitably, *The Edinburgh Review* of 1867 called him 'a gentleman fraud'. By 1866, the Royal Society had condemned the role, and the ability, of the meteorological office to prognosticate, an interpretation seemingly confirmed by the resignation of FitzRoy's long-term assistant Thomas Babbington: the work was too empiricist and too imprecise to advance the processes of science. After this report, the meteorological work was passed over to the Royal Society and the renamed Meteorological Office. Yet at the British Association for the Advancement of Science meeting in Dundee there was much opposition to this 'centralisation' – just as the Scottish nationalists had been opposed to administrative power residing increasingly in London – and instead a demand for the reintroduction of storm warnings was made. Robert Scott, FitzRoy's successor, was forced into reintroducing telegraphed warnings by the end of 1867; but to add to the confusion he determined to present the observations alone, without the prognoses. When in 1871 Smyth wrote up the aftereffects of the 1860 storm in Scotland, he acknowledged that telegraphic warnings would probably not have been sufficient to avoid its worst effects, but still criticised the central state's cancellation of warnings. The need for forecasting 'in the Provinces, so called, though really sitting in the metropolis of the ancient kingdom of Scotland' was, to him, plain.

Scotland's weather did what it always did: the rain fell, the wind blew, the frost came, the snow melted and the sun, on occasion, shone. And while Clouston offered contemporaries

some understanding of why fog appeared, his Orcadian existence would tell him little of the combination of fog and smoke
– smog – that would mark late-Victorian and Edwardian urban-
industrial life. The debilitating effect of various miasmas was a
concern for social reformers from the first half of the century,
shocked by the high death rates in the growing cities, notably
from respiratory diseases. Air currents and air pressure, ozone
gases and the depth of frost and rainfall all had the potential to
worsen any miasma. The arrival and spread of cholera in 1832
and the blight that wiped out the potato crops of the 1840s were
put to this climatic test as scientific understanding was sought.
Both diseases impacted upon Scots' life expectancy. Living and
dying, then, is the theme of the next chapter.

3

We Live, We Die

Fuelled by an increasing number of births over a decline in the death rate, Scotland's population grew from 1,265,380 according to Webster's estimate of 1755 to 1,608,420 people in 1801. The enlargement was sufficient to generate debate within political economy as to how the natural resources of the nation could sustain further pressure on food production. This eighteenth-century concern was prescient of even greater strains to come: over the next fifty years the Scottish population increased three times faster, slowing to a rate still twice as fast during the remainder of the century.

The percentages reveal a stark statistic: that between 1831 and 1911 Scotland's population doubled – from 2.4 million to 4.8 million. This was less than the two and a half times increase in the population of England and Wales, but the number of people living in Scotland went from being less than half the number living in Ireland to numerical equality in 1901 and an excess of 400,000 people in 1911.

A characteristic of Scotland's population was that it was predominantly young and mainly female. In 1851, 36 per cent of Scotland's population was under fifteen years of age and 56 per cent aged below twenty-five. In 1911, the figures had dropped slightly to 32 per cent under fifteen and 52 per cent below twenty-five. Ranging upwards from around seventy-seven to eighty men per 100 females mid-century, only by the end of the century did equivalence near, with around 106 females to 100 men in both 1901 and 1911. Still, some places remained female-

Table 3.1　Annual average percentage increase in population, 1750–1910

	1750–1800	1800–50	1850–1910
Scotland	0.5	1.6	0.9
England and Wales	0.7	1.8	1.6
Ireland	1.1	0.6	0.7

Table 3.2　Comparative population growth (millions), 1831–1911

	Scotland	England and Wales	Ireland
1831	2.4	13.9	7.8
1841	2.6	15.9	8.2
1851	2.9	17.9	6.5
1861	3.1	20.1	5.8
1871	3.4	22.7	5.4
1881	3.7	26.0	5.2
1891	4.0	29.0	4.7
1901	4.5	32.5	4.5
1911	4.8	36.1	4.4

dominated: Edinburgh's gender distribution increased from 119 females for every 100 men in 1901, to 123 for every 100 in 1911. Most consistently of all, Dundee was Scotland's 'women's town' in the nineteenth century through employment offered by the jute industry. Even as those jobs declined at the turn of the century, the city's women outnumbered men by 112 to 100 in 1901 and contributed to a higher than average level of female-headed households. In a survey of 3,000 families in 1905, 23 per cent were financially dependent on one female wage earner, 25 per cent on one male wage earner and 14 per cent on the husband and wife's joint earnings.

　Knowing how many people filled the nation's boundaries was never an easy statistic to uncover. In an address to the Statistical Society of London in 1851, the Scottish epidemiologist James Stark made plain the dangers of continued resistance to the state's questioning of its people: 'There is scarcely a state of Europe relative to whose Vital Statistics we know so little as that portion of the United Kingdom called Scotland'. The burial rate was just one example of bureaucratic failure, oftentimes recorded by an illiterate gravedigger. The Church of Scotland was slow to improve its registration practices and was the chief objector to attempts to create a government department to do the job; secular control of recording births, death and marriages in Scotland was obtained in 1855, whereas the General Register Office in England had been in operation since 1837.

From what we can estimate, the cry of the newborn child was heard more frequently at the start and middle of our period than at the end of the century: the birth rate declined from 35 per thousand in the 1870s to 30 per thousand in 1900 and continued to drop. The death rate started to fall in the 1860s from 22 per thousand to 15 per thousand by 1914. By the first two decades of the twentieth century all of Scotland except some parts of the Highlands and Islands had gone through the demographic transition, the shift from high birth and death rates to low birth and death rates, that was the norm in western countries in the twentieth century. The average number of children born to completed families in 1911 was 5.49, a figure lowered by those with no children in the marriage (the largest category). Then there was a fairly even distribution between two and ten children (with a singleton being less common): the largest reported families of children were three families of twenty-one children, four of twenty-two children, one of twenty-three children and one of twenty-five children. This was a trend accompanied by a decline in the age by which childbearing had ended. In the words of demographer Michael Anderson, 'those [mothers] born in the 1880s had only half as many children to care for, entertain, clothe and feed as their parents had had; their own children had only two-thirds as many as they did'.

Seeing ourselves through the prism of demographic indicators shows the Scottish people in the round: our age and sex distribution, our marriage and reproductive choices, as well as how long we might expect to live. These measurements can also be seen to have distinct regional components when coupled with

internal movements. The western Lowlands was home to just
under 27 per cent of Scotland's population in 1831 but 46 per
cent in 1911. In contrast, the Highlands and north contained 17
per cent of Scotland's population in 1831 but only 7 per cent
by 1911. The rates of birth and death in the decades since 1861
were very similar to those of England and Wales. That Scotland
grew at a lower level was due to the higher rate of emigration,
movement outside the nation's boundaries. It was Scottish men
rather than Scottish women who were the most mobile overseas
and – although less so – also around Britain and Ireland. In
the report of the 1911 census, of the 762,835 Scottish women
returned as married, about 10 per cent had their husbands
absent. Whenever Scotland is described as a masculine culture,
we should keep in mind the preponderance of women in the
nation and female-headed households. And while migrants into
Scotland from other nations can be similarly measured, they
were not the only 'others' in the nation. The Scots overseas were
others, too: not in opposition, but an extension of ourselves.
Both these migrant groups in and out of Scotland will be examined later (in Chapters 11 and 12). For now, moving on from the
headline demographic figures presented so far, the focus turns to
the lifecycle and our lives from birth to death.

COURTSHIP

To get to the stage of sexual intercourse within marriage, young
men and women would learn courtship rituals from friends, relatives and stories, including chapbooks full of references to love,
love lost, love returned and advice from older women on the
vagaries of men's loyalty and conduct. Yet still there is counter-
evidence of brides with little knowledge of sexual intercourse or
the practicalities of birth, with the husband 'expected to know'
(of the former if not the latter). Millwright John Sturrock had a
very sedate courtship of 'his girl' in 1860s Dundee. The couple
enjoyed Sunday afternoon walks in the park, with a friend as
chaperone, or he would pay visits to her family's home. There
was no obvious rush to marriage recorded in his diary entries,

nor any effusive sentiment: there was a clear sense of waiting until economic circumstances favoured conjugal stability.

Less rational, the use of 'trial by ordeal', whereby success in courtship was dependent on the successful completion of some form of challenge, could still be found in this period. In one lowland example a servant's choice of marriage partner to a man of doubtful character was in the balance, the decision dependent on a sign from the 'trial'. First footing was similarly part of the process whereby public approval was sought. In Wigtownshire and Galloway marriage was often celebrated on New Year's Day, and it was common in Edinburgh for servants to induce a sweetheart to visit after midnight on Hogmanay with the expectation of marriage the following day. A number of marriage superstitions persisted. It was thought unlucky to alter the width of the engagement ring; gifts of brooches with pins were thought not to enhance but to end a friendship. On the day of the wedding, if a pig passed in front of the celebrants then it was considered bad luck, but rather than avoid swine altogether, if a pig happened to pass behind the wedding party, then only good fortune would follow. For the couple to have a happy future, then in the south of Scotland they should hope for a dry day or a 'greetin' bride' she would become. A custom of tinkers' weddings was that the couple should hold right hands throughout the ceremony, not unlucky left hands. And if all went well, then when a newly married bride entered her new home, for good fortune an older person would throw cake or shortbread at the door. It remained the custom in Ross-shire into the 1880s to wash the feet of the bride and bridegroom on the evening prior to the wedding and, on the wedding night, to ensure the married couple were 'put to bed'. Salt was a favoured aphrodisiac: 'found o saut, found o the lassies' was a well-used saying, and a chamber pot filled with salt was a marriage gift in the north-east of Scotland. The salt would be sprinkled on the floor to ward off the 'evil eye'. With a little more respect, kirkin' the newly married couple upon their first appearance at an Episcopalian service, marking their transition in status, was another custom in the north-east of the country.

Figure 3.1 *A Shetland wedding march in 1912: led by a fiddler, the wedding party headed for the church.* © *Shetland Museum. Licensor www.scran.ac.uk*

Overseas, Scots men would consider a 'country wife' – a live-in partner while the legal wife was back home, although immigrant Scots' diaries suggest this was more common amongst Irish settlers. An alternative was the 'trapper's marriage' between not only socially but ethnically different people, well illustrated in Alfred Jacob Miller's *The Trapper's Bride* (c. 1837). The American artist was commissioned by the adventurer Captain Drummond Stewart to produce the painting in watercolour for his ancestral home Murthly Castle in Dunkeld. It was then copied in oil along with a further nine versions. Miller travelled with the fur traders and joined the Scots as they exchanged pelts with American Indians. There are a number of reasons for Stewart's preference for this art. Notable among them is the theme of crossing racial and sexual boundaries, and it was said that Stewart's métis manservant on his journeys across America was 'unnaturally' close to him. Research suggests the Victorian belief in female passivity stopped the development of any investigation into lesbianism, and the historical record is equally, but not totally, silent on male homosexuality.

SPINSTERS

Unmarried women were more common in the nineteenth than
the twentieth century. The journalist W. R. Greg's mid-century
scheme to send 750,000 unmarried women overseas to provide
marriage partners for colonial men, for fear they would otherwise fall into prostitution or remain simply unfulfilled, was
not without supporters around Scotland. The cultural place of
the literary spinster was well known to contemporaries who
(uncharitably) preferred them to be unmarried bookish types,
not physically attractive when in possession of a writer's intellect – or, in Miss Mitford's terse judgement, 'all literary ladies
are ugly'. Culturally, this was a middle-class 'problem' of social
place, of the role for a woman without a husband or father to
form the basis of a family network. The position of housekeeper
or governess for a brother or uncle's family was the clearest role
for such women. Living with other women as companions, paid
or otherwise, was also acceptable. But many women did live on
their own unmarried, and for working-class women there were
no such social norms limiting their choice of employment. Both
classes of women were also active as employers, as Chapter 6
shows.

DIVORCE AND SEPARATION

From 1830 all cases of divorce were heard before the Court
of Session. In the Westminster Parliament, in pamphlets and
in speeches, Scottish-born Lord Brougham warned of Scottish
divorces not being recognised in England, resulting in any
remarriage inviting prosecution for bigamy. And while a legal
parting was uncommon, it did occur. Separation and abandonment were the most common means of splitting a married
couple, and death the most straightforward route to remarriage. Divorce was difficult to obtain, and expensive. It seemed
to carry some degree of scandal, inevitably when adultery was
involved. An unremarkable divorce heard before the Court of
Session drew interest because the cited party was the wife, not

the husband, and the pursuer was a Jewish Aberdonian picture-framer, Isaac Barnett. The *Dundee Courier* focused on Barnett's religion, describing the oath of calumny used before giving his witness statement, and the wearing of his hat 'according to the Jewish form'.

Divorce cases could cause also cause mild sensation, as when Scottish military novelist and nationalist James Grant was named in the divorce proceedings of William and Jane Anne Walker in 1870. The viewing area of the courtroom filled over the week in which the evidence was heard, the novelty being that James and Jane secretly communicated to one another through classified advertisements in *The Scotsman*. Having discovered this, William Walker entrapped his wife with a forged note, and plentiful details of the clandestine courtship then emerged: Jane was in the habit of regularly introducing Mr Grant's name into the conversation, suggesting he was the only great novelist since Walter Scott, a claim that was met with laughter from those in the public seats; the servants were out when Grant came calling; Mrs Walker readied herself for a dinner party, yet her dress was of insufficient quality; the side gate was left open; a locket was kept under her dress that piqued the curiosity of the servants; signals were used to indicate that the coast was clear, including a red shawl over the mirror in the bedroom and the blowing of whistles. And then there were the muddy boots after her regular evening walk, not to visit another couple as claimed, but linked with evidence from the Superintendent of St Cuthbert's Burial Ground, where Jane and James were seen together, in the same spot, on regular occasions, kissing and embracing like a courting couple.

In all there were fifty-five witness and 150 pages of evidence conspiring against Jane. What made the association clearly unacceptable to the court, and by extension to the morals of Scottish society, was that the two families were not on social terms. The couple had met in 1868 at a party hosted by Dr Begg. But other than meeting again at a second party, Grant was 'not on any terms' with Jane's husband. Jane's lawyer claimed that if a divorce were granted she would be cast out homeless, without money and with her character so destroyed she would be shunned. Under the Conjugal Rights (Scotland) Act 1861 there was some attempt to protect the property and finances of the deserted wife, but in this case she was the accused. Grant himself was worried about his own reputation, not only failing to appear but hiding behind the veil of Mrs Walker whose defence team asked that Grant's name be removed from the evidence. The case became a point of interesting judicial debate when, after the verdict was passed and the divorce granted, Jane Walker tried in turn to divorce her husband in order that he be liable for the costs, naming four women with whom he broke his marriage vows. This further deliberation did nothing to shorten the attention the case received and the newspaper press overseas picked up the daily coverage.

MAKING BABIES

The 1911 Census of Scotland shows that fertility levels remained high in Scotland, especially for groups where family labour remained important. There was no widespread attempt at birth control within marriage until after the middle of the nineteenth century. Abstinence was the only effective method. Coitus interruptus could be agreed upon, and attempts at washing out the vagina after sexual intercourse, douches and condoms from animal skins were also used. Sexual intercourse while the women was lactating or menstruating was believed a similarly viable method of avoiding pregnancy. Rubber sheaths were not available until the 1920s and abortion clinics were tightly controlled until the 1960s. Backstreet procedures and the use of a knitting needle or similar implement, or a contrived fall down the stairs, were all resorted to that a pregnancy might be forced to abort. The more respectable unmarried woman finding herself pregnant might attempt to elude societal disapproval by leaving town, perhaps to come under the care of a society for fallen women, or to place the newborn child in the care of an orphanage, before returning home.

Babies and infants would be taken into the workplace or left swaddled in blankets nearby when the mother was working in the country or would be looked after by an older child or another woman. Wet nurses, paid to mind and offer their own breast milk to infants not their own, were another option. Yet the wet nurse would often have no milk, being unable to lactate from her own poorly nourished body, and would resort to bluff or the use of substitutes. Sickly cordials were, however, detrimental to the health of the child. In the Edwardian period, the value of a healthy mother for the health of the child was stressed. Advice for new mothers in 1911 was to give the child breast milk until around eight or nine months when other foodstuffs might be introduced, with the child not weaned off the breast until a year had passed. If cow's milk was to be used, the recommendation was to sterilise it by boiling and then cooling rapidly and that it was best if the milk remained undiluted.

Fertility amongst the middle classes was the first to fall, but not until the last decades of the nineteenth century, with little or no decline among the rest of the population until the century's turn. Changes in nuptiality, age at marriage and fecundity, as well as cultural and economic influences, together played a greater role than contraception in explaining this reduction. Infant mortality rates were increasing in Scotland at the end of the century while in England they were falling, but these rates did begin to fall at the start of the twentieth century.

The rate of illegitimacy in Scotland was higher than in England, but there was much regional variation. Historical sociologist Andrew Blaikie shows for Banffshire that rather than a sign of social immorality or of the breakdown in the influence and sanction of the Kirk Session, illegitimacy was a rational response, and at 20 per cent a remarkably normal response, to local economic conditions and the availability of housing. The continued high incidence of marriage to the father of the child after birth was one sign that many were still maintaining the sanctity of the family.

SIGNS OF HEALTH

In evidence running from 1847 to the end of our period, women born in Scotland's cities were a third more likely to deliver babies of low birth weight than mothers born in the Lowlands more generally, the north of Scotland and the Borders. Labouring women in Scotland and those in white-collar but low-paid clerical occupations were 50 per cent and 46 per cent respectively more likely to deliver low-weight babies than women within domestic service and food handling occupations. The nutritional advantage of these latter occupations appeared to lead to healthier children. This analysis by Ward, while necessarily tentative, points to low and declining nutritional standards amongst the ordinary urban Scot. Contemporary John Beddoe's evidence indicated the average Berwickshire farmer in 1870 was 71.3 inches in height and weighed nearly 200lb. His research suggested that taller Scots were to be found in Argyll and in the Borders and that there was not to be found, despite the popular belief, the man mountain Highlander.

Studying the people's height continued to be used as a sign of health and wellness. *The Lancet* produced a series of articles from the 1880s until 1921 on the physical development of children in Britain that indicates the relationship of social class to height and therefore health. Marking off the smaller working class from the upper classes, there was a standardised average difference of four inches for both boys and girls in 1880 (ranging from 53.2 to 57.4 inches for five- to thirteen-year-olds) and two and a half inches in 1921 (ranging from 55.2 to 57.8 inches for five to thirteen-year-olds). In height analysis, these are huge disparities. Evidence from the Glasgow School Board in 1907 found that fourteen-year-olds from the poorer parts of town were on average 4.1 inches shorter than fourteen-year-olds from the better parts of town and 5.4 inches below the national average.

Evidence published in the *Report of the Royal Commission on Physical Training (Scotland)*, published in 1903, estimated that 20 per cent of Scottish children were in bad health and

30 per cent were poorly nourished. Ian Levitt has shown that the investigation into paupers carried out in Glasgow in 1910 found similar differences in stature and height. The introduction of free school dinners was one of the recommendations of the investigation into the high rejection rates returned by the army's recruitment officers during the Anglo-Boer war. Rejection rates of around 33 per cent were the norm, although rates of 48 per cent in 1860 and 34 per cent in 1870 had been known. The report of the Inter-Departmental Committee on Physical Deterioration presented to Parliament in 1904 concluded that overcrowding in the cities had to be regulated. In the House of Lords, Baron Shuttleworth (son of the influential educationalist James Kay-Shuttleworth) feared the lasting effects of the high infant mortality in the Scottish towns, the result of improper feeding or nursing, 'the want, in fact, of intelligent mothering of the children'. He blamed personal ignorance exacerbated by the poor conditions in which the Scottish child lived: 'Slums, back-to-back houses, cellar dwellings, and bad sanitation unfortunately still exist, and the statistics are perfectly appalling.'

Research by economic historians John Cranfield and Kris Inwood on the physical condition of emigrant Scots indicates that it was the nutritionally strongest who left for Australia and Canada in the 1880s and 1890s, and that they arrived into healthier environments, benefiting from a supply of relatively cheaper food. The height of Scots who in 1914 enlisted or attempted to join the Australian Imperial Force and the Canadian Expeditionary Force show no difference compared to English enlistees (whereas across the classes the Scots were smaller than the English at home). Both nationalities were, however, smaller than Irish enlistees which may again suggest the general principle that it was the nutritionally strongest who migrated, although in all cases there was variation between cohorts.

Various reports questioned whether Scottish agricultural workers were consuming sufficient nutrients to keep them at a level of health good enough to foster social stability. What undermined the Scots' diet was the lack of variety in their

Table 3.3 Stature of Australian and Canadian enlistees by place of birth (inches)

Place of birth	Australian enlistee	Canadian enlistee
Scotland	65.8	65.9
England	65.8	65.8
Ireland	66.4	66.4
Wales	65.1	65.7
Native	66.3	65.9

Note: 'Native' means Australian- or Canadian-born

nutritional intake, despite regional variation in what they ate. Research by W. Hamish Fraser shows that the lower death rate in the eastern part of the Scottish Borders, for example, can be ascribed to the peasemeal that, when mixed with barley meal, dominated the daily diet. Fish (fresh or cured), oatmeal, potatoes and milk were common, with fish a regular part of the Orkney diet as in other coastal regions. Herring, white fish and mackerel were the most usual. What wasn't sold at home was exported overseas, especially to North America and Jamaica. Shellfish was prepared in the Scottish kitchen because it was available all year round. The English oyster season ran from 4 August to April each year, the mussel season from 1 September to April, but there was no closed season in Scotland. Two sea lochs, the Gairloch and Loch Ewe, allowed catching the finny tribe (fish): cod, haddock and ling. Some fishermen who took part in the east coast herring industry were in their own boats or in shared vessels, splitting the profits accordingly. Early in the season the salmon would be boiled and packed in vinegar in kegs; in high summer the fish were packed in ice and sent off to London in fast sailing smacks or cutters twice a week to be sold as fresh. John Anderson and Sons in Edinburgh's George Street were 'purveyors of fish to the Queen and the Royal Family' in 1877, including its Royal Emporium that supplied poultry, game, butcher meat and fruit to town and country.

From early in the century butter was consumed by the better off and could be used to preserve meat, with buttermilk consumed by the lower classes. The shift from oatmeal to potato as the staple food in Scotland would have particular problems when blight came in the 1840s. Rurally produced eggs were not eaten but shipped to the Glasgow markets for money. Food was always valued, with little discarded. Throwing bread on the fire was described by a Glaswegian observer as 'feeding the old one' – the devil. Stressing the cultural importance of a filled larder, bothy balladeers sang songs that criticised the quality of the food on their table compared to that of their employer:

> The breid was thick, the brose was thin,
> The broth they were like bree;
> I chased the barley roun' the plate,
> And a' I got was three.
> So unsuccessful was my search,
> My spoon I did throw doon;
> The knife and fork were seldom seen,
> But in the carpet room.

The majority of meals were prepared cold and not cooked in the home because of limited facilities. Based on earlier work by Mrs John Elder teaching 'plain and economical cookery' to women in their home or in the classroom, Mrs Hannah Gordon from the Northern Training Schools of Cookery had identified a continued need for domestic economy for Glasgow girls in 1889. The instruction was to remind the poor of 'the importance of proper food to the human body' and that '[i]t is one of the duties of *women*, and a very important one, to attend to this'. The morality of the message was plain. The advice was to make the most of all scraps of meat, in pies and especially in stews, and to boil bones and vegetables undisturbed in the pot, with the lid on, to keep the nutrients within the water. Gordon's book was part of the movement started by Elder in Govan and included an introduction by Dr James B. Russell, Glasgow Medical Officer of Health: 'it is absurd for a woman to begin the business of housekeeping, without a previous apprenticeship, as it would for a man to start right off as a journeyman, without having been an apprentice'. His message was a crusade of positive

enforcement, that 'A good cook is sure to be cleanly', 'always
thrifty', 'always *religious*' and 'the implements of her craft will
always be scrupulously polished and in their proper places'.
In the most literal sense, he argued, 'The poor man's wife . . .
receives the "daily bread", for which the children pray.'

The children, however, still developed a sweet tooth and the
prevalence of toothache and indigestion was one of the reasons
patent medicines were in such demand. New mothers were
advised against the use of 'soothing syrups', but public education
was slow to progress its message. In the Fourth Annual Report
by Medical Inspectors in 1914, of the 1,282 children examined
in Lewis, eighty had one defective tooth, one hundred and forty
had two defective teeth, thirty-three had four, and sixteen had
five or more. There was negligible difference between defective
teeth in boys and girls (24.9 per cent of boys and 24.7 per cent
of girls upon first examination, and respectively 32.2 per cent
and 28.5 per cent upon second examination), but the children in
the landward schools of Lewis had noticeably better teeth, with
fewer than 15 per cent having one or more defective teeth. It was
also found that fewer than 3 per cent of boys and 9 per cent of
girls had 'nits' in their hair.

ILLNESS

It is difficult to discern just how healthy or not the Scots were
in this period compared to other periods. We know how long
they lived on average, and how tall they grew. Military and
prison data gives us information on their weight, but few could
afford inactivity or to eat themselves overweight. Vegetarianism
was the default when meat was expensive or unobtainable, and
alcohol was readily consumed, mainly in the form of beer with
its low alcohol content rather than spirits, but all forms were
imbibed freely. The environment and what was eaten could be
detrimental to health in other ways: 'Remember that pure air is
food, and that polluted air is *poison*' came the domestic advice
of Gordon. The guidance was to air rooms and bedclothes,
opening windows a little from the top, keeping vents open and

keeping water and waste pipes from the water cistern and the water closet separate.

Most of the large towns had their water supplied as a constant service by mid-century, but smaller areas such as Dumfries, Rutherglen and Barrhead were still waiting on the legislation and the poorer parts of Aberdeen were still dependent on wells in 1862, each being used by up to 400 people and liable to empty in warm summer mornings. It was found that tenants took good care of the water supply when it was brought inside the house, whereas wells supplied by the water companies and situated at the back of the house were often neglected when there was collective responsibility for their care. The provision of a constant service was found to be cheaper than an intermittent supply, with the cost in the Gorbals equating to between 10s and 16s per head from an investment of £110,000 (before additions) servicing a population of around 150,000 people. James Stirrat was the first to suggest for Paisley that the purest and softest water would come from lands lying on primitive rock formations, planning to store water in large and especially deep reservoirs. His observations were based on studies of Glasgow, Edinburgh, Paisley and Liverpool. It was the growth of cities that forced the town councils to look to the counties for the supply of water, often four and sometimes as much as ten or twenty miles distant. Stirling was provided with water from a drainage area of around 150 acres, while for Paisley around 700 acres was needed for the population of 60,000 in 1850.

New options for treating ailments became available as the century unfolded, and not just locally. Eight who were bitten by a dog infected by rabies set out to the Pasteur Institute in Paris on Christmas Day 1894, led by the Assistant Medical Officer of Health, Dr A. K. Chalmers. The use of chemicals offered different solutions to afflictions and infections – formic aldehyde and Cylinn for the disinfection of houses in cases of infectious diseases; if scabies was diagnosed, the linen would be disinfected with high-pressure steam and the body would be varnished with Peru Balsam. Some solutions offered in 1911 were a little bizarre: in addition to adopting a prone position and tightening

one's clothing around the abdomen for the alleviation of seasickness, coffee-mint, beet juice, iced champagne and caffeine
were also suggested as alleviants, along with chloral hydrate and
cocaine hydrochloride.

Folk myths for the causes of ill health and folk remedies to
treat them were propagated alongside the work of the medical
researcher and the epidemiologist. Long-infused tea was identified as a common cause of indigestion; possible treatments
for croup included placing a hot brick into a bucket of cold
water to raise warm vapours for the child to inhale. In hospitals, too, less proven techniques were suggested. James Esdaile
had learned through his brother that the renowned Edinburgh
surgeon James Young Simpson had heard of his experiments
with mesmerism, and offered to help make his work known.
But on sailing from India Esdaile found that Dr Simpson's colleagues did not embrace his account of 161 scrotal tumours
removed while the patients were in a mesmeric trance as 'sufficiently practical'. Hospitals were dependent on private money
and the hospital benefactor gained the cultural, philosophical
and economic position in civil society reserved for the wealthy.
The experimental dangers of medicine made good material for
fiction. Arthur Conan Doyle's short story *His First Operation*
(1894) describes the anxious Edinburgh University student
readying himself to observe the removal of a tumour of the
parotid. A mid-day sherry (or three) at the city's Rutherford bar
was called for first. The patient was brought in and the surgeon
prepared his tools: dressings of carbolic gauze, chloroform and
a small saw in case it was necessary to remove the jaw.

The main cyclical threats to life came from typhus and
cholera. Glasgow's typhus epidemic of 1837 and the epidemic
in Edinburgh ten years later were worse than the outbreaks of
cholera (1848 and 1849 in Edinburgh). The arrival of typhus in
Dundee and Perth in 1847 was similarly worse that the area's
cholera outbreak two years later. Legislation passed in 1832 in
an attempt to control the spread of cholera enabled the Board of
Health in Whitehall to employ a Deputy Inspector of Hospitals
on half-pay (the sum of £31 18s 9d) to make monthly visits

to Glasgow. Where the localities lacked sufficient ratepayer income, the Boards of Health were entrusted with the power to set up temporary hospitals and houses of observation to separate those who may be infected from those who definitely were.

Typhus was endemic, with cycles every five to six years; by contrast, cholera's return followed longer cycles. Both were spread through the coming and going of travellers, merchants, sailors and all that is associated with trade. The *Glasgow Chronicle* blamed the Monkland and Kirkintilloch Railway for the spread of cholera into Coatbridge in 1832. James Stark claimed with regard to Edinburgh 'that ever since the Irish settled here, epidemics of typhus have become more and more frequent, and more and more virulent'. It was a common attribution of blame despite limited evidence, and contemporary newspapers would similarly look for such links. The 'Stranger's Cold', for example, was tied to climatic conditions on St Kilda, because the boat could only land when the wind blew from the north-west.

Other diseases carried their own dangers. In Aberdeen a particularly severe outbreak of measles in 1894 reduced the average age of death in the city from 35.6 in the corresponding month the previous year to 21.8 years, an average driven down by the death rate for children under five nearly twice the average level found over the preceding ten years. Scotland, however, escaped relatively lightly from the influenza epidemic of 1880–90. The epidemic spread in the northern hemisphere contrary to the prevailing winds, spreading from east to west and from north to south. Despite signs of influenza in Scotland in October 1890, its arrival into Leith came only on 17 December that year with a crew from Riga. Other cases were confirmed throughout December in Aberdeen, Inverness and Glasgow, with Caithness and Sutherland the areas worst hit.

The one real success story of medical intervention was a significant reduction in death from smallpox. The Vaccination Act 1863 required the parochial board of any parish or combination of parishes in Scotland to appoint a registered practitioner to ensure all children were vaccinated against smallpox before

Table 3.4 Mean death rates at all ages from all causes per 1,000,000 people living in Scotland, 1855–87

Years	1855–63	1864–75	1876–97	1864–87
All causes	21,051	22,419	19,777	21,016
Smallpox	321	224	6	108
Measles	435	373	330	350
Scarlet fever	841	1,020	405	693
Diphtheria (from 1857)	171	281	221	249
'Fevers'	922	1,012	380	676
Typhus	893	496	53	261
Typhoid (from 1865)	–	403	297	344
Diarrhoea and dysentery	585	608	509	555
Whooping cough	688	619	623	621
Pneumonia	684	777	980	885
Bronchitis	1,368	2,290	2,183	2,234
Phthisis	2,429	2,535	2,146	2,329
Diseases of the circulatory organs	775	1,096	1,418	1,267
Cancer	336	429	529	482

they were six months old. In 1868 only two children died as the direct result of the vaccination. In the years 1883 to 1890 there were twenty-two deaths, a rate of one in every 38,873 vaccinations, compared to one death in every 14,159 vaccinations in England.

Zoonosis, the transfer of disease from animals to humans, was a matter for the town authorities before it was for the hospitals. Post mortems carried out on 300 dairy cows in Edinburgh in 1890 found 40 per cent had tuberculosis and 4.5 per cent had pleuro-pneumonia. The committee formed to analyse the issue heard that the butchers and dealers, the fleshers, felt little compulsion not to sell the infected meat because no compensation was on offer. Dr Littlejohn stated that he had never been able to order an infected animal destroyed because there was no provision for it in legislation. Yet in Glasgow one witness claimed the medical and sanitary authorities in the city had gone beyond 'what is reasonable or proper' in condemning the use of flesh from tuberculosis animals and that butchers should be allowed to sell meat 'very slightly' infected with tuberculosis, a view the committee would not accept. It was an open secret in the 1890s that farmers tried to dump their bad cattle on the Glasgow market because, unlike in Edinburgh, veterinary surgeons were not used as inspectors. In Dundee the process of control involved all dead meat being brought to a clearing-house, where the town expert passed judgement. 'Wholesome' meat was sent on for sale; 'unwholesome' meat was seized and destroyed with the council taking the view that this was sufficient punishment without prosecution. The sanitary inspector in Leith confiscated sixteen tons of meat, valued at £915 17s 6d, and in Perth the owners of infected meat consented to its destruction 'no doubt to prevent exposure', as well as because of the prospect of prosecution.

MENTAL HEALTH

Contemporary investigations into the incidence of insanity in Britain faced the methodological weakness of simply counting the numbers confined in private and public institutions. As a crude measure of mental health in a population, it had obvious downsides in contrasting the (clinical and court) identification and classification of illness, with the final decision dependent on private or state funds for a place. Institutional estimates mid-century appeared to show that England and Wales maintained a higher incidence of insanity within its population compared to Scotland, and that lunacy had the lowest occurrence in Ireland.

One explanation for the difference was that Scotland maintained a system of 'boarding out' to deal with its lunatics in contrast to England where there was greater emphasis on country, borough and district asylums (often with a lower standard of care than smaller exclusive asylums). Scots left their lunatics to live with relatives where they could, and those without such support were boarded out for small sums. If deemed 'fatuous' or 'idiotic' or to possess 'a marked weakness of intellect' again they continued to live and work in the community. Asylums were used for those determined to be criminally insane, with physicians in

Table 3.5   Private and pauper lunatics in public asylums or public madhouses in Scotland in 1847

	Private	Pauper	Total
In public asylums			
Aberdeenshire	45	165	210
Edinburghshire	123	344	467
Elginshire	–	30	30
Forfarshire	84	252	336
Inverness-shire	–	10	10
Lanarkshire	157	388	545
Perthshire	74	90	164
In private licensed madhouses			
Aberdeenshire	15	–	15
Buteshire	2	–	2
Dumfriesshire	64	66	130
Edinburghshire	167	92	259
Forfarshire	2	–	2
Lanarkshire	47	70	117
Linlithgowshire	1	–	1
Renfrewshire	17	112	129
Totals	798	1,619	2,417

residence for institutions of over one hundred beds and only required to make visits to smaller asylums. Contemporaries looked to Empire to explain the levels of insanity at home: the 'most civilized countries' yielded on average one insane person in 1,200 or 1,300 individuals, whereas 'the barbarian countries' yielded one insane person out of every 700 or 800.

Yet the figures for 1847 show no great pattern between the numbers defined as requiring some kind of metal health care and the areas within which they lived in Scotland, be they rural or urban, densely or partially populated. These data stand against one common contemporary belief that the Gaels exhibited a greater level of mental instability.

In Stark's summation, no theory of soil, climate, height or material influences can explain the regional distribution of lunacy within Scotland. The distribution was equal, he argued, between the Saxons and Normans in the Lowlands, the Celts in the Highlands and the Danes, Norwegians or Scandinavians in the far north-east and the Orkney and Shetland Islands. Where he did see difference was in the level of intermarriage: a special dispensation from the church was needed for a cousin marriage in Roman Catholic countries, making them rare, whereas with no such restriction in the Protestant countries, cousin marriages were taking place, and especially so in Scotland.

Legislation in 1862 required mental institutions to be licensed and was the first statutory recognition of the difference between the mentally handicapped and the mentally ill. There was then a gap in legislative intervention until the Education of Defective Children (Scotland) Act 1906. Building on ad hoc schooling for the subnormal in the 1890s, the School Boards were compelled to make provision for such children aged from five to sixteen and the Lunacy and Mental Deficiency Act (Scotland) 1913 required the provision of special schooling.

AND THEN WE DIE

Until civil registration in 1855 there were no accurate statistics on Scotland's death rate. The crude death rate was around 22 per thousand in 1860–2 and 1870–2 before it fell to 19.7 per thousand in 1880–2, 17.9 in 1900–2 and 15.2 in 1910–12. Significantly, the death rate in Scotland's four cities in the 1860s was 57 per cent higher, and the death rate in urban places of over 5,000 inhabitants was 20 per cent higher than in rural areas. By 1910–12, these figures had dropped to 17 per cent and 12 per cent respectively. As the demographers Anderson and Morse explain, social improvements in the four cities meant that by the end of the nineteenth century they no longer had the highest death rates in Scotland, with medium-sized towns such as Dumfries, Coatbridge and Ayr the new deadliest places to live. For this period the death rate was particularly high amongst the very young; the under fives represented the group in which illness and death was rife, skewing the average life expectancy down to 39.8 (males) and 42.1 (females) in 1871; by 1910–12 these rates had improved to 50.1 for males and 53.2 for females.

The General Registration Act 1854, amended in 1860, required a medical person at the death to forward notice to the registrar within seven days, and who was bound to the task by a penalty of 40s. Both embalming and later cremation were stopped if a suspicious death was suspected and in such cases the liver, kidney and stomach were retained for future examination. After a heated debate in the 1870s, and despite opposition from the Burial Reform Society in the 1890s, Scotland's first cremations were possible from 1895. A crematorium and chapel opened at the Glasgow Necropolis in November that year and was first used to cremate sanitary engineer and director of the Scottish Cremation Society, William Buchan, in February 1896.

It is difficult to get figures on infanticide or stillbirth in Scotland. In the years before the GROS, the Burial Register of the town of Perth recorded 42 stillbirths in 1844–5. For the whole of Scotland in 1891, 15,735 stillbirths were interred at Burial Board cemeteries with over 4,500 buried without death certificates. The certificates were not required, however, and anyone could write a note for the undertaker. When stillborn the body was treated as though it had never existed, creating the opportunity for death by violence or neglect to be 'hidden', a practice aided by certain midwives. It was also cheaper to bury a child so certified. In 1892 Scotland's Procurator Fiscal carried out 3,719 investigations into stillbirths – but this was a much smaller figure than the roughly equivalent investigations into suspicious deaths carried out in England. In over 400 cases of 'overlaying' (suffocating the child) in Dundee, there was not one prosecution. The usual explanation was drunkenness. Child murder was difficult to convict even when brought to court. A child found buried in Princes Street Gardens in Edinburgh led to a charge against its parents in 1895, but a verdict of not proven was returned because neither parent could be implicated over the other.

While the symbolism of death blossomed, this was slow to penetrate the Church of Scotland. The Presbyterian minister only gradually became involved in the funeral, which he marked with prayers and the observance of due process at the graveside.

An order of service was produced in 1867 but the Church of Scotland did not officially offer services until 1897. Episcopalian priests did attend funerals and the practice was for a candle to be lit next to the body with a plate of salt placed upon the chest of the diseased. The consumption of whisky, styled as in the tradition of an Irish wake, was followed in Ross-shire for much of the nineteenth century although increasingly frowned upon for its 'evil' and burdensome cost on the family of the deceased. The minister was at times invited to put a brake on the tendency to intoxication. Yet as the funeral party processed whisky would be drunk and a stone thrown to mark each pause taken by the pall-bearers; these breathers would often number the age of the deceased, with the inevitable challenge to sobriety whenever an elder entered the nearer presence of God.

The most renowned Scottish graveyard is the Necropolis in Glasgow. Opened in 1832, it was modelled on Père Lachaise cemetery in Paris. Within twenty years it was the burial place of choice, decorated with increasingly elaborate monuments displayed by friends and family. Charles Tennent, Lord Kelvin and Alexander 'Greek' Thomson are all buried there, as is the Scottish-American industrialist Archibald St Clair Ruthven and George L. Watson, the Glasgow-born ship designer of four America's Cup entrants. One proposal for the National Monument on Edinburgh's Calton Hill was to fund its completion with crypts for purchase, such was the demand for space. Even in the small town of Dumfries, J. W. Dod and Sons could keep 100 memorials in stock at their sculpture works and offered to send skilled workmen anywhere they were needed. The use of black borders around letters to and from relatives of the deceased was a common custom. The child's hand or foot cast in porcelain was another, a practice favoured by Queen Victoria, along with increasingly ornate and inevitably expensive funeral displays. Graverobbing was one contributor to some of the dramatic complexity of grave markers. The barred crypt was not to protect any valuables that might be buried alongside their owner, but to protect the body. Burke and Hare were the most infamous graverobbers, but there were others.

There is a common myth about the placing of a bell in the coffin for fear of being buried alive, with frightening stories relayed in the newspapers. It is possible that this practice was responsible for the phrase 'saved by the bell', although it is more likely that it refers to the struggling boxer.

So much of Scottish life and death was similar but slightly different from the English experience. Included in this are the nation's vital statistics and its customs for courtship, marriage and death. Racial characteristics and degeneration were employed to account for the incidence of lunacy, illegitimacy and infectious disease, but the regional and social class differences within Scotland were more relevant than international or inter-racial comparisons. Scotland had its own heterogeneity of lives lived: they were all ordinary, but they were never uniform or regular.

4

Urban Scots

Despite the Enlightenment classism of Edinburgh's New Town and the commercial grandeur of Glasgow's merchant city, the Scots have sometimes struggled to see 'ourselves' as an urban people. Scots have not thought the urban label applicable, or have thought it an inconvenience. Mostly Scots have regarded living in towns as simply a reality to be endured, thinking – in the heart – 'we are of the land'. With suitable resonance, Kirriemuir became 'Thrums' in the imagination of J. M. Barrie (and the name of a tiny place in British Columbia); it would inspire Ian Maclaren (the Rev. John Watson) to produce one of the best-known kailyard contributions, *Beside the Bonnie Briar Bush* (1894), happily selling more than 750,000 copies. The Gaeltachd, more than most, has been 'where we are from', to others if not ourselves. As ever, there is some truth to this fiction. The Scottish town and city dwellers had every reason to attach themselves in such a way, with so many either temporary or recent urban migrants, or second-generation town dwellers. Few Scots at the start of our period were, *sui generis*, of the towns. The Scots of the 1830s were helped by the generation before them to quickly and aggressively become townsfolk, sustaining a transformation not bettered by any others in the world save the English. Yet the speed was such that the Scots could still perceive the land as their genesis; the rural world was not yet gone.

The proportion of the Scottish population living in towns of over 5,000 people more or less doubled from 31 per cent in 1831 to 59 per cent in 1911. England was the most urbanised

nation at that end date, with 61 per cent of its people in towns
or cities of over 20,000 inhabitants; the Netherlands was third,
with 40 per cent of its population at that level. Scotland bisected
the two with 50 per cent of its people in towns and cities that
were home to 20,000 people or more. What made this shift to
living in towns all the more extreme was its heavy concentration: Scots in towns lived close to other Scots in towns. At least
83 per cent of all Scots breathed their life in the central belt of
the Lowlands from 1801 until 1841, a figure that has not fallen
below 87 per cent since.

An urban place of 5,000 souls mid-century had, in the main,
a cash economy, although still the doctor or the smith would be
partly or wholly paid in kind or with a deferred promise. The
local midwife would be part-time, uncertified and brought in
when needed. The specialisation of function, consumption and
occupation that characterised the urban world from the last
quarter of the nineteenth century was not yet in place. Urban
Scots still largely followed the rhythms of their parents and
grandparents, influenced by their farmer's almanacs and the
astrological information in their trade directories, their timings
governed by natural light. Urban Scotland could still seem a
backward place for all the grandeur and industrial shock that
drove the city's rapid expansion, Glasgow more than most. A
description of the major port of the Shetland Islands in 1860
shows an economy not greatly modernised and a people still
intrigued by outsiders:

> At 9 a.m. Capt. and myself went off to the little town of Lerwick,
> it's very small having only 3,000 inhabitants, the streets are very
> narrow, not room for a cart to pass, and from all I could see I do
> not think they can use anything but thin little ponies. The people
> were all alive with the idea of seeing a few strangers from our ship. I
> bought a pair of gloves and, having posted my letter, I left the shore
> for my ship with the idea that I should never care to see Lerwick
> anymore. I have forgotten to mention that Lerwick, like every town
> in the north of England and Scotland, has its Rifle Corps of 60 men.
> The mail boat came in once a week and goes out once a week; it
> goes to Aberdeen.

Table 4.1 Scotland's urbanised population, 1831–1921

Year	Population in towns >5000 (%)	Increase over previous decade (%)
1831	31.2	28.2
1841	32.7	16.2
1851	35.9	17.3
1861	39.4	16.2
1871	44.4	23.6
1881	48.9	12.8
1891	53.5	17.6
1901	57.6	19.7
1911	58.6	8.1
1921	61.3	7.3

Lerwick seemed otherworldly to this medical student from Glasgow University gaining experience on a whaling expedition, yet still English-born James Taplin (1838–1904) could purchase gloves (perhaps with a choice), he could post a letter in a town with a regular mail service and, like the very best of men in Edinburgh and Glasgow, if he had settled he could join a volunteer force raised in response to the Militia Act 1856.

Time and location saw transformations, of course. One contrast to the island periphery was the north Lanarkshire town of Airdrie in 1896, which boasted a full range of businesses and services within its boundaries: seven banks, seven brokers, nine agents and two accountants were part of the town's economic fabric. Over fifty confectioners and twelve fancy goods merchants kept the town's inhabitants sweet. Food could be purchased from a choice of over seventy grocers plus there were twenty-seven fleshers, seven bakers, thirteen fruiterers, two fishmongers and fourteen provision merchants. Three smiths, eight ironmongers, two slaters, two plasters, one umbrella maker and twenty-four tailors and clothiers offered craft services. Two parts of the country, two periods, and together they mark the growing complexity of the urban experience and its move away from the vestments of rurality. The process, however, would not be linear.

URBANISATION

With urban life not being straightforwardly part of their identity, it is difficult to discern just why the Scots embraced life in the town so wholeheartedly, but the preconditions for this shift have been given some attention. Scottish historian T. M. Devine identifies improvement in agriculture along with an increasing market focus for agricultural output – a change sustained by landowners and facilitated by banks, lawyers and officialdom in the market towns – as key preconditions to the rise of the urban world. Turning these circumstances into what in European terms was a remarkable rural–urban shift was the concurrent economic expansion in the period from 1760 to 1830 – Scotland's industrial revolution.

Perhaps because the central Lowlands became sink traps for population movement, statistically at least urbanisation had some element of uniformity. Scotland, with Glasgow only 2.5 times the size of Edinburgh, was not dominated by a metropolitan city in the way that London dominated England. Whereas Edinburgh had Leith as its port and urban neighbour, Glasgow was surrounded by its substantial satellites: Clydebank, Coatbridge and especially Paisley (with the best claim to being Scotland's fifth 'city'). But just looking at residential numbers, urban historian R. J. Morris explains, masks great variety and an urban experience sorted by economic specialism: Coatbridge, Clydebank, Port Glasgow and Renfrew were the 'metal towns': male- and skill-dominated, they supported the great engineering complexes in Glasgow. There were the textile towns of the Scottish Borders: Hawick, Selkirk and Jedburgh; the linen towns of Brechin and Forfar that used Dundee as their port to both Europe and America; and the leisure and suburban towns of Portobello, St Andrews, Broughty Ferry and Dunoon. Dundee's architecture as well as its economy reflected the importance of its port, where small-scale industries and their workshops filled every available space cheek by jowl with the short streets of working-class housing. There was a concentration of brewing around Edinburgh and Alloa, light iron-founding in and around Falkirk and papermaking in Aberdeen, while Paisley became the world centre for thread and shawls. Edinburgh in 1911 had a well-developed service economy through nationally known hotels, restaurants and distinct retail sectors, with domestic service sustaining the city's largest category of female employment. The capital was home to lawyers, the real estate and finance industries, and large groups of workers engaged in printing and publishing, various manufacturing activities and food production. The demographic profile of each reflected their economic circumstances, adding diversity to the uniformity of the urban experience.

HOUSING STYLES AND THE BUILT ENVIRONMENT

Much has been made of the differences in housing style between Scotland and England. The cost of land and building materials was higher north of the border, although bricklaying and carpenters' wages were generally smaller. Attached to the lease or freehold land purchase, the feu was a legal cost that led to greater density of building in Scotland. The feu system meant that land could never be purchased outright, with an element of rental (the feu duty) payable to the feu superior, the owner of the rights to build on the land. The tenement was the stock response and was found in small towns as well as in the big cities, appearing only sparsely in England, such as in the north-east where rents were high. Indeed it was England, not Scotland, that was the oddity here, since this form of housing was common in much of Europe. The tenement of the 1890s was a regularised structure comprising machine-cut stone on the outside and the parquet flooring of the common stair within. The thick walls insisted on in the police legislation added to the cost, providing high structural quality but at the expense of facilities and space. If the tenement was the visual metaphor for the Scottish home as castle, from which community and social relations formed, then it was matched by heavily constrained personal space. For a population that more than doubled in the 1831–1911 period, Scots lived in very few rooms.

Table 4.2 Percentage distribution of rooms per dwelling in select European cities, 1900–1

City	Year	1 room	2 rooms	3 rooms	4+ rooms
Glasgow	1901	23.8	47.9	17.5	10.8
London	1901	14.7	19.8	17.8	47.8
Berlin	1900	8.0	37.2	30.6	24.2
Paris	1901	26.7	30.1	21.8	21.4

Source: M. J. Daunton, 'Housing', in F. M. L. Thompson (ed.), *The Cambridge Social History of Britain, 1750–1950* (Cambridge, 1990), p. 197.

Glasgow is in many respects the extreme Scottish example because of the particular pressure of low-income migrants from the Highlands and Ireland on its housing stock, but again this pattern was much closer to the European experience than it was to London or England more generally. Whereas nearly half of English dwellers lived in homes of four or more rooms, nearly 90 per cent of Scots did not. Spending so much of one's leisure time outside of the house – in the street, the club or the public house – has a clear context to explain it. A survey of single-room houses in Edinburgh in 1913 found 94 per cent of those who lived in them shared a common water closet and 43 per cent shared a communal sink.

For all that the Scottish skyline was dominated by the stone tenement rather than the brick 'through' terrace (with front and back door) favoured in England, the larger home indicative of suburbanisation was not excluded from the town and city. An English style of housing with an Indian name, the bungalow became a fashion of the 1890s. The almost extravagant need for land to plant the single-storey dwelling was a visible statement of personal success. Less ostentatious than the two-storey villa, great swathes of suburban Edinburgh around Duddingston, Craigentinny and Corstorphine were built in this style, with smaller estates established in much of east central Scotland. This was housing of the suburbs and once their belongings were unpacked, residents looked to the omnibus and tram to

Figure 4.1 *Back close in Tranent, East Lothian, c. 1880. © East Lothian Museums Service. Licensor www.scran.ac.uk*

take them into town, to work and to shop, ending the reign of the 'walking city'. The middle classes of Aberdeen similarly took this flight path to the suburbs, finding in low densities the environment in which they could use their economic power to create a world of greater privacy and control, leaving the central areas to investment opportunities from which rentier income could be derived. One successful instance of this was the City of Aberdeen Land Agency, formed in 1874 to invest in suburban land and infrastructure with income planned from feuing and reselling the land and from capital gains.

Throughout our period the vast majority of homes were rented. In 1907 about 80 per cent of the Scottish working classes who rented did so yearly, but it was a contract signed in February to begin in May, in effect a commitment for sixteen months, comparing unfavourably with the flexibility of weekly rents available south of the border. Whitsunday was the day of removal, described by urban historian Richard Rodger as a 'day of drama, even farce' for the congestion imposed upon Scotland's streets. To slip under the landlord's eye, the midnight flit was chosen by those unable or unwilling to pay what was due. With rent taking up around a quarter of weekly income in the 1880s, and with around one-fifth of women and one-quarter of men engaged only irregularly in paid work, it meant accommodation was a major financial commitment swelled even further when municipal taxes were added. Excluding London, rent in the Scottish towns was about a shilling a week more expensive than elsewhere in Britain. Building associations operated in the towns; their subscribers drew lots for the right to rent the next completed house. Rent disputes rose in the 1880s with Trades Unions and the Scottish Housing Council (1900) becoming part of the pressure for reform. Monthly rents were introduced for some housing, but difficulties remained as landlords sought to maximise their returns. Of those who did purchase a house, it could be to live in or to rent out for income. In Rodger's study of Edinburgh property developer James Steel in the 1880s, it is found that buyers of his west end townhouses were predominantly lawyers and professionals (43 per cent) and women (17 per cent).

Scots' lower income – at least until the end of the century, when lowland wages had improved – meant a higher proportion of the worker's wage was committed to housing. In the longer term, this drain of housing costs upon the Scots' disposable income contributed to the weakness in the economy at the start of the twentieth century. While other countries were better able to base their post-manufacturing sectoral shift on the service sector, Scots lacked the necessary spending power.

HOUSING DENSITIES

Overcrowding was identified as a major detriment to physical health and moral fastness in urban Scotland. Although the general rate of overcrowding was, if anything, falling, overcrowding was endemic in many streets, courts and wynds. One commentator in 1842, observing the parish of Blackfriars in Glasgow, found that there had been little or no building for ten years, but the population had increased by some 40 per cent.

In some cases overcrowding was attributed to improvements in the neighbourhood – such as pulling down old property to widen streets – leaving those displaced to crowd into the smaller number of remaining homes. The building companies found it difficult to respond to sudden demand, or to remain viable when business was slack. The industry comprised predominantly small-scale entrepreneurs and was vulnerable to bankruptcy and international trade cycles. Rodger's survey found that between 1873 and 1914, 52 per cent of applications to the Dean of Guild Courts in 102 Scottish burghs were to build one house, a pattern that became more pronounced the smaller the town. Even during the peaks in tenement building in Glasgow, in the 1870s and at the turn of the century, the majority were constructed by small building companies. Few of these entrepreneurs were sufficiently capitalised to build rows and streets at a time, but local by-laws enforced uniformity in style and structure. The influx of low-income Irish following the famine of 1845–6 resulted in localised overcrowding, first around the docklands of Port Glasgow and Leith and then spreading out into enclaves such as

the Canongate and the Grassmarket (in Edinburgh), the Gorbals
and east end of Glasgow and east to Dundee. In the 1890s it was
estimated that in 1901 around 15 per cent of Glasgow's population, or 92,000 people, would comprise the Catholic Irish, in
contrast to Belfast, where that community numbered 84,992
people, just under one-quarter of the city's population. Glasgow
extended its boundaries eleven times between 1830 and 1912,
increasing its acreage from 1,864 to 19,183 in the process.
There were 20,000 unoccupied houses in the city in 1914, representing around one-tenth of the city's housing stock, but their
poor quality contributed to the persistence of overcrowding.
Along with municipal expansion there was internal movement
of Scots out of Glasgow to the surrounding towns and further
afield to help lessen the density of city life.

Even with uninterrupted wages it was difficult for the ordinary Scot to afford sanitary housing. If 30s a week was needed
to live in such a home, then whether a labourer earned 12s or
15s would do little to improve his situation. This, however, did
not stop the formation of a powerful and pervasive ideology of
self-improvement, piety and personal obligation, including philanthropic intervention into the housing market. The Aberdeen
Association for the Improvement of the Dwellings of the
Labouring Classes (1863) was part of what have been termed
the 5 per cent philanthropists, who invested for modest returns
into the production of housing for the respectable working
classes. The investment return was deemed fair, undertaken as
a charitable act by the shareholder who spurned higher returns
on, for example, overseas investments. But in Aberdeen, as
elsewhere, the transformative power of philanthropic housing
was small scale compared to the size of the problem, and local
legislation in the form of Improvement Acts were more effective. Scotland-wide Housing Acts from 1875 gave the towns
and cities the power to build houses for those who had been displaced by earlier improvement legislation. With council housing
not a feature of the pre-1918 period, this marked the most inter-
ventionist attempt to recalibrate the private bargain of the urban
Scot and the landlord.

BURGH GOVERNMENT

Scotland gained improved powers to administer its urban areas with burgh police legislation at the end of the eighteenth and beginning of the nineteenth centuries, although Dundee did not acquire these powers until 1824. The Police Acts included provision to watch and protect the population, but they were more widely concerned with by-laws controlling behaviour and urban infrastructure, such as the width of roads and pavements, lighting and the siting of cesspits. Established with a similar but not identical franchise to that passed a year earlier for Westminster, local government was reformed in 1833. Still the reform left intact the police system to coexist alongside the newly enlarged and regularised town councils, giving Scotland a dual system of urban management reinforced by Scotland-wide police legislation in 1847, 1850, 1857, 1862 and 1892. The resulting administrative duplication was sometimes problematic – as were the joint trusts created to deal with cross-boundary utilities from the 1870s. In the 1860s and 1870s towns obtained their own legislation to clear slums, some of the most notable being the Improvement Acts of 1866 for Glasgow, 1867 for Edinburgh and 1871 for Dundee. These were expensive and problematic to obtain, however; in response, there developed a debate centred on the new concept of town planning in the 1880s. Alongside this shift towards systematic intervention into the urban fabric was local authority power to inspect each house – at whatever time of the day or night – to establish how many were resident at any particular time. Drawing on powers granted in the city's Improvement Act 1866, the Corporation of Glasgow took the lead in affirming the limits to overcrowding by stapling 'tickets' – steel plates indicating cubic metres of space and the number permitted to reside therein – outside working-class homes. The practice was extended to the whole of Scotland in 1903.

The move towards municipal government reform in 1833 came from the pressures of 'booming' urbanisation and industrialisation upon an administrative structure that in some respects still followed practices first established in the medieval burghs.

Enacted two years earlier than municipal reform in England, the Scottish local government legislation set in place the £10 franchise, annual elections starting in November 1833 (with one-third of the council retiring each year) and the printing and publication of an annual balance sheet. For each parliamentary burgh there were to be between six and thirteen councillors, with the larger towns divided into wards. There remained a few peculiarities in this structure, however. The Convention of Royal Burghs continued after 1833 to be the dominant force in municipal affairs; and the Scots burghs retained their provosts and bailies rather than creating mayors and aldermen along English lines. As a guiding principle, independence and self-reliance were far more important than paternalism or state 'tyranny' in local regulation. The new town councils were recruited from a much wider base than their rural counterparts, yet political leadership remained a means of achieving social leadership and vice versa.

The historian of Glasgow Irene Maver has pointed out that because the city had obtained the status of royal burgh in the seventeenth century, its pre-reform structure of government was better able to survive the reforms of 1833. Glasgow came out as one of Scotland's few examples of good burgh government in the *Royal Commission into the Scottish Municipal Corporations* of 1835–6. Its town council was relatively continuous and was – perhaps – better able to resist encroachment from the city's police board. Yet the police commission, which had been established in 1800, was to prove a significant alternative power base for the localities, even after Glasgow's police boards had their power curtailed in 1846 following Westminster's eventual acquiescence to the city's wish to expand. This victory for the town council did not stop a ring of police burghs surrounding the city in the ensuing decades. Beginning with Partick in 1852 and ending with East Pollokshields in 1880, a total of nine communities had come to encircle Glasgow in a 'ring of burghs', which made it extremely difficult to claim territorial rights over suburban districts.

By 1871 in Aberdeen, five of the eighteen elected members of

the police commission were also town councillors; and the Lord
Provost was chair. The Dean of Guild took control of the street
committee and the City Treasurer was in charge of watching
and lighting. The dual administration of police commissioners and town councillors continued until the Town Councils
(Scotland) Act 1900 introduced a regular structure. This established a standard constitution for the authorities of provost
supported by bailies and councillors elected from a system of
adult male suffrage, later expanded to include some women in
1907 and power streamlined by removal of the police boards
and many of the joint trusts in 1929. The dual system of local
government was to some extent a point of division, but in other
respects it was a flexible response to the pressures upon urban
management.

URBAN MANAGEMENT

Dundee's population increased fivefold in the period 1820–90,
but until 1871 there was no coordinated attempt to manage the
city's infrastructure. Aberdeen grew at a rate of just under 30
per cent per decade until 1831, and by 1851 the population had
more than doubled. This rapidity of growth outpaced administrative mechanisms and the implementation of infrastructural
reform as the town councils, police boards and joint trusts
jockeyed for effectiveness. The Cowgate in Edinburgh had only
surface drains until the 1840s, with underground piping not
the norm for another thirty years. In the estimation of the city's
waterworks engineer Robert Anderson in 1865, two-thirds
of Aberdeen had no sewers, leaving the water to run over the
streets. Open drains allowed the effluent to be flushed away with
rainwater – but inevitably they would smell and were not overly
effective, leaving basements, closes and cul-de-sacs to suffer
from the path of least resistance.

The supply of drinking water was for urban managers the
more pressing concern. The Loch Katrine scheme for the supply
of water to Glasgow was the most ambitious proposed by any
town council in Britain at this time. In 1855 the parliamentary

power for the necessary municipalisation of the water was obtained, and four years later Queen Victoria inaugurated the new supplies. Municipalisation could bring together the business class, who regarded it as an exercise in the managerial provision of an efficient set of services, and socialists who wanted collective action on ideological grounds. When Victoria returned to open Glasgow's City Chambers in 1888, in addition to the civic and Masonic processions, no fewer than 25,000 representatives of other industrial bodies were present to witness the proceedings and to be recognised.

Expanded town halls were needed in Scotland because local authorities were assuming a new range of functions, providing public utilities in the form of water, gas, electricity, tramways, libraries, art galleries and other services. In Glasgow 'municipal socialism' operated with the municipalisation (1894), then electrification (from 1898) and extension of the tram system. There were other examples of municipalisation: the Botanic Gardens in the 1890s; sewerage purification (from 1894); and telephones (1900). Monopoly services provided by the town councils were promoted for the benefit of the town dwellers and could also allow profits to flood the local treasury and check any rise in the rates.

URBAN SPACE

The red sandstone of Glasgow, the silver granite of Aberdeen, the colourful pantiles of the East Neuk fishing villages, the dark miners' cottages of Lanarkshire. All have at one time or other been immortalised in art and narrative as the Scots loaded their localities with a sense of themselves – finally? – as an urban people. The Scottish baronial style copied from the turrets and peel towers of the bonnet lairds reached the merchant and gentry houses of the city, a fashion that was exported overseas, to Otago in New Zealand and Fergus in Upper Canada. The central area of Scottish towns was a variegated tumult of factories small and large. Not just in the industrial cities of Glasgow, Paisley and Dundee, but wherever railway lines and

stations were established, then carts, hackney cabs and omnibuses vied for space in the downtown core and warehouses
were built adjacent to transportation hubs for the storage of
goods and merchandise. Peppering the landscape with symbols
of economic success as well as pride in achievement, banks,
Exchange buildings, hospitals and dispensaries, literary and
philosophical institutions, public swimming pools, Turkish
baths – and the municipal buildings to administer it all – were
signs of civilisation and the kind of success that invited growth
in economy and people with a corresponding beneficial effect
upon the rates.

Along with the by-laws and regulations imposed on the
urban world by the local authorities and occasionally, but
increasingly, from Westminster, urban space was managed
within its own culture. The town was a mixture of public places
and other spaces closed behind gates or barriers, or as Morris
calls them, 'non-spaces' (open but controlled) such as railway
stations. Men and women, the social classes, different ethnicities, would all learn when a space could be used and for what
purpose. The urban riot, disturbance and protest were always,
first of all, about control of the public street. The rituals that
surrounded the use of urban space were an important means of
confirming urban identity. The descriptions of urban Scotland
by W. P. Alison, Bell and Symons (see pp. 97–9) spoke to
these social demarcations. The cities and towns that expanded
under boundary legislation were about creating communities
where there was much in common, maintaining public order
and public health, and providing a means of resolving disputes
and avoiding boundaries becoming barriers. There were areas
designated for trade and exchange, there was light added from
streetlamps and order was imposed through street design as
much as by the urban policeman. There were divisions in space
between areas for walking and areas for transport. Institutions
for the sick, infirm, ill-educated or irreligious were divided
between the genders. There were areas for shopping, some
more accessible to middle-class women than others. The street
was a formalised place where social groups identified and made

allowances for each other as they used the space for different purposes and at different times of the day. The noise and the rhythm of the urban street grew more regimented as mechanised transportation came into being and railway stations created new bottlenecks of activity from carters, taxis and travellers. This transformation is symbolised by 'going for a walk' meaning a trip to the countryside for exercise and recreation, rather than a means of getting around the town. Just as monuments and symbols of the nation gave meaning to the Scots, so their urban space, contends Morris, forged a social memory and identity no matter how fractured and wide-changing the urban landscape had become.

Historians are still wont to debate whether early-nineteenth-century specialised shops served predominantly the well-off while the working classes used the market halls, a situation that only began to change from around 1850. Retail trade transformed from being scattered and interspersed among the commercial and financial sectors to specialised shopping areas, with the department store at the apogee of this change. Kennington and Jenner took its place at 47 Princes Street, Edinburgh in 1838. Soon known as Jenners, it expanded into neighbouring properties in 1860 and 1890, returning from the devastation of fire in 1892 with a refurbished shop in 1895 and a royal warrant in 1911. This department store was a place for women in the city centre. It was not without thought that Charles Jenner left money in his will for carved figures of women to grace the outside of the shop.

In dark contrast to the welcoming department store, the brothel was a home for some Scottish women, but an unwelcome and unwelcoming place avoided by most. The police knew of twelve brothels in Glasgow in 1889 (compared to five in Manchester and, if it is to be believed, a remarkable 443 in Liverpool). According to research carried out by surgeon William Tait in 1840 it happened, albeit rarely, that there was family succession of brothel-keepers in Edinburgh: mother to daughter, aunt to niece, sister to sister. Most had husbands or 'spoony men' who offered some protection and facilitated the setting-up of the business, while the 'fancy man' was the resident bully for the lower-class establishment. There were 'femmes galantes' who, like their Parisian counterparts, were of a higher social class than the women employed in brothels. They were often part-employed as seamstresses or bonnet makers, and could boast education and musical ability. They used make-up to make themselves appear 'very polished and affable in their manners'. While the department store carved out a place in the industrial city for middle-class women to enter the town, the brothel was a space that had the opposite effect.

URBAN IMPROVEMENT

The sheer difficulty of living in a space where almost everyone is 'other' – because of the rapidity of urban growth fuelled by internal migration and a buoyant natural increase – was a psychological condition rooted in the realities of poor sanitation, a higher death rate, the circulation of disease and previously unknown kinds of crime and disturbance. It ensured that social behaviour was carefully constructed and codified in an interlocking set of ideals against which each Scot was measured. The morality of urban living consumed much contemporary debate. Social reformers ascribed poor-quality housing as detrimental to the righteous mind as well as to the physical health of the city's inhabitants. Why the headline figures debated in Parliament appeared to show the Scots at such a material and corporeal disadvantage compared to English urban dwellers is explained by Devine as being the result of the nation's largest city, Glasgow, being the preferred destination for Irish and Highland migrants, two of the poorest groups in British society. The brooding density of the city as industrialisation developed can be gauged from the descriptions emerging from various public and private inquiries. When Jellinger C. Symons, Assistant Commissioner for the 1839 inquiry into the state of the handloom weavers, visited Glasgow he held little back in his descriptions of St Giles. He found the area with around 15,000 to 20,000 persons living within a labyrinth of vennels and wynds, reached through

various entrances, each with a dung hill 'reeking in its centre'.
Symons' disgust was palpable:

> Revolting as it was the outside of these places, I was little prepared
> for the filth and destitution within. In some of these lodging rooms
> (visited at night), we found a whole lair of human beings littered
> along the floor, –sometimes fifteen or twenty, –some clothed, and
> some naked, –men, women, and children huddled promiscuously
> together. Their lair consisted of a layer of musty straw intermixed
> with rags. There was generally no furniture in these places. The sole
> article of comfort was a fire. Thieving and prostitution constituted
> the main source of the revenue of this population . . .

This description was later reproduced in the tenth edition of the
Historical Gazetteer of Scotland in 1853, an issue that carried
a letter from the historian and sheriff of Lanark Archibald
Alison welcoming Symons' descriptions. It was Alison's brother,
William Pulteney Alison, who had advanced the cause of social
intervention for the relief of poverty and insanitary conditions
through his debates in the 1840s with Free Church leader the
Rev. Dr Thomas Chalmers and the educationalist Sir James Kay-
Shuttleworth. The fear of crime and social unrest was a constant
undercurrent to such investigations, as it was to their readership.
That Symons observed the use of opium amongst the poorest
classes of the city did little to assuage contemporary concern.

Dr George Bell brought his medical training to bear for incur-
sions into some of Edinburgh's most neglected streets in 1849,
contrasting life therein during daylight hours with that once the
sun had set. His observations were encapsulated in a pamphlet
full of hyperbole and moral references verging on the Biblical. It
was designed to shock, but also to show that disease and illness
did not occur randomly: 'everything proves the necessity of sanitary reform'. He showed that of the 14,861 treated by the Royal
Infirmary during the three years leading up to October 1848,
9,148 were the subject of fever and two-thirds of those came
from the same small area of the High Street, Cowgate, West
Port, Grassmarket and adjoining closes. He highlighted illness
affecting the industrious worker: in one case the father, 'a half-
starved mechanic', died and when the wife became ill, resulting

in the children running wild while she slowly recovered, only to return to work before she was fully fit, the family fell into poverty. The telling point for Bell is that the family were lodgers, and when forced to move on were unlikely to find any cheaper accommodation. The lodging class, which was significant in numbers, comprised some of the poorest urban Scots. Lodging houses cost 3d per night or around £3 per adult per year. For the average family it worked out at around £9 per year to 'live in horror . . . in the vilest parts of the city'.

Bell is nothing if not emotive, but he regarded this as the forgotten story of the modern human condition:

> The black-hole of Calcutta, in which men were stifled, has been described, and the hold of the slaver has been described; but no description *has*, because none *can*, be given of the interior of a low Edinburgh lodging house. It defies the engraver of Hogarth, the pencil of David Scott . . .

Bell joined William Pulteney Alison in criticising the argument of Chalmers that the Poor Law should be expunged from the statute books because it undermined the character of the nation. Yet he was not one to dismiss the failure of personal virtue. According to Bell, 'The Scotch are *one-third* more drunken than the English, and *one-half* more drunken than the Irish'. Bell cited evidence given to *The Scotsman* by a spirit dealer who claimed that his sales were £10 more on the paydays of the poor (from the parochial board) than any other day; as an alternative strategy, the poor would attempt to barter what food they had for drink. Here Bell and Chalmers were in agreement, yet for the medical man it was the causes of illness that were of greatest concern and the greatest hindrance to social improvement; for the solution he looked to sanitary reform. Still, the ideological identity of Scots' urban life remained forged in these conditions.

PARKS: THE LUNGS OF THE CITY

An embellishment to the urban world was the public park, introduced in an attempt to improve the air quality of the city for those not able to afford the openness of the suburbs. Land, here, was put not to commercial or agricultural use, but for health purposes.

The anniversary of the birth of Walter Scott was chosen in 1855 as the day to mark the opening to the public of the east side of Princes Street Gardens. In attendance, along with the magistrates and members of the town council, were subscribers to the recently completed Scott monument. The gardens were funded from £4,500 provided by the Edinburgh and Glasgow Railway, following the creation of the adjacent Waverley Station. Amongst the attractions was a small house to be used to help cultivate exotic plants, but commentators made fun of the 'please protect the grounds' sign that was indicative of deeper social tensions. This park was a public space only for those who could afford the entrance fee. Five years later Dr Begg weighed in to the West Princes Street Gardens debate in a lecture to the Saturday Half-Holiday Association in the High Street's John Knox Church, chaired by former Lord Provost Duncan McLaren. Begg argued the parks were indeed the 'lungs of the city' and it was only those who did not know the working classes who would think they would not know how to behave in such a setting.

Perhaps in response to the class demarcation of parks as pleasure grounds debated in Edinburgh, from the 1860s many towns and cities acquired land for the construction of freely open public parks. This was funded from the local treasury, public subscription or the largesse of a benefactor. When the Right Hon. the Earl of Dalhousie was invited to open Brechin's public park for pleasure on 28 September 1867, he pointed out that whereas Montrose, Aberdeen and St Andrews had links for golf and cricket, the inland manufacturing town had had little open public space to offer its people the opportunity of outdoor recreation and sport. The park came about after a long-held gift of £200 from Mr Garden Mitchell was directed toward the purpose. A spectator that day asked the Lord Provost if it was to be open on a Sunday; his answer was 'only after the churches have closed'. The people of Paisley welcomed a much grander public park in 1868, a gift from Thomas Coats, of the threadmakers J. & P. Coats. Estimated to be around £6,000, the donation was sufficient to purchase six and a half acres of land and establish the park's facilities, including a fountain of Franco-Italian design as its centrepiece, with herons and dolphins decorating its four basins. A new park could also be the occasion for social renewal in the community. The inhabitants of Grangemouth were gifted a public holiday in 1882 on the day that saw the opening of both new docks and a public park, the latter donated by the Earl of Zetland. In a similar vein of inclusiveness, Lord Provost Mearns closed Duthie Park in Aberdeen to host a garden party in honour of Queen Victoria's diamond jubilee in 1897, at which a thousand guests of all classes in the community enjoyed the hospitality despite the wind and rain doing much to dampen the day. In 1899 the park hosted 'Hospital Saturday Sports' between the New South Wales Lancers and the Fife and Forfar Light Horse in front of 3,000 people. As well as used for sporting occasions, parks were also envisaged as cultural hubs. Kirkcaldy's Beveridge Park came about from the donation of £50,000 in the will of linen manufacturer and former Lord Provost of the town Michael Beveridge, who died in 1890. Seeking to stimulate the physical and cultural strength of the town, the philanthropist made provision for the establishment of a library and hall (now an art gallery) as well as a park covering over 100 acres of land. After much debate it was decided to redevelop Robbie's Park and adjoining lands on Southerton farm, yet not all were pleased. As befits the 'lang toun', the inhabitants of Pathhead in the east held an 'indignation meeting' to protest at this site so far to the town's west. But the vision was realised two years later when the park was opened, and the Beveridge family motto 'Up and be doing' adorns the Raith gates, the pillars for which were made from Carlisle granite and sculpted by a local man.

ORGANIC MODERNITY

There was a growing realisation, then, of the need to recalibrate the urban–rural balance. When the urban planner Patrick

Geddes (1854–1932) purchased a six-storey building next door to Edinburgh Castle in 1892, he acquired a building that had previously been used as a public observatory. Geddes installed a camera obscura to allow visitors to have a panoramic view of the city. The symbolism was clearer than the weather would often allow: that to understand the city it had to be seen in the round. Geddes was acutely aware of urban growth, coining the term 'conurbation' and nicknaming Glasgow 'ClydeForth', with its resource needs stretching from the Firth of Clyde to the Firth of Forth.

Geddes lived in Edinburgh's St Giles parish and encouraged the students of the University to live in this poor area. To support his ideal of inter-class mixing, Geddes worked with the Edinburgh Social Union to manage affordable housing, following Octavia Hill's 5 per cent philanthropy scheme. In a lecture given in Edinburgh in 1902, Hill had stressed the need to be a strong landlady but also a compassionate one, to find the sober, thrifty and industrious to rent and, if they fell behind with their payments, to remind them that credit cannot go on forever. Geddes's vision of Edinburgh was as a 'region-city', combining fully functioning civic, cultural and spiritual institutions. Unlike the garden city movement that was to bring the best of the countryside to the city, Geddes wanted the rural hinterland to benefit from the best of the city. He was particularly attracted to the idea of citizenship. Historian Helen Mellor has pointed out that Geddes's first planning report, for Dunfermline in 1904, placed great emphasis on female voluntary labour for leading the civic culture of the town. Any solution to the ills of urban mismanagement throughout the Victorian years was not to come without government engaging the urban dweller in the project. The town planner Raymond Unwin persuaded Geddes to show his Outlook Tower work to the first International Town Planning Exhibition at the Royal Institute of British Architects, which then turned into a travelling exhibition and led to a commission by Lord Aberdeen, Lord Lieutenant of Ireland, for plans to improve living conditions in Dublin.

Geddes planned but never built similar structures for other

cities. Perhaps Edinburgh was just too good an example and others, such as the special hardships Glasgow endured from its migration, just too challenging. Some towns and cities had no wish to re-energise past urban structures so decrepit had they become. For some, the urban world was all about modernity. In contrast to Geddes's vision of mixing the new and the old with 'empathy', the vision of Dundee town planner James Thomson was to dispense with the city's building stock and convoluted transportation system and build anew. The growing town and city, in Thomson's view, required an influx of new technology to allow people to work and live without hindrance. Getting around the modern city, and across the nation, is our next concern.

5

Getting Around

It is difficult to estimate just how often Scots journeyed across their nation, or how far they moved to new lives away from home. They were certainly to be found moving home, and how long they remained in any one location is an interesting question of 'place'. Getting around Scotland, moving around the nation, serves as a useful metaphor for human agency. It speaks to fluidity in the national self that objectification is wont to overlook. Individual movement highlights, further, that national identity is no inert slice in time, but rather a relationship between ourselves and others that is continuously in flux. Migration to elsewhere in Britain and to settlements overseas has shaped Scotland's domestic history, as Chapter 11 will show, but the present discussion is framed around questions of everyday mobility at home, of trade and travellers, canals, railways, bicycles and motorised transportation, and the societal fluidity that personal mobility engendered.

Walking, of course, was not just a stand-by. It was the primary means of getting around, even for quite long distances. Tramping has become a reference to those who wandered from place to place with only the stars (or more usually cloud cover) above their heads at night, but in Victorian Scotland one tramped to get around, for example the three hours needed to walk from Tain to Thurso, or the overnight tramp from Nairn to Dundee. When historians refer to the 'walking city' it is no futuristic sobriquet but a reflection on the ordinary Scots who had little option but to walk around their towns and cities and the fact that town growth was initially constrained by human puff. Few other than the wealthy owned a horse or carriage, and cabs were a luxury. Towns reflected this reality, and stores, public houses, churches and places of work were all, if possible, close to home. It was one of the explanations for the heavy concentrations of people, the intermix of people and economic activity, the communities of people that made the streets busy places and the high demand for the services of the cobbler. Indicative of the later spread of the town and city on the back of mechanical transportation – to the extent of Glasgow's conurbation – walking had become associated with a healthy outing by the last quarter of the century, a beneficial tour of the countryside rather than a means of conducting the business of the day. When Charles Dickens wanted a 'breather' he walked a few miles, but if his mood called out for a 'buster' then he would traipse for up to thirty miles.

Mechanisation in transportation came first to longer distances. The first railway lines in Scotland opened in 1810 between Kilmarnock and Troon, later part of the Glasgow and South Western Railway, built to move coal and minerals, not people. Scotland's first locomotive trains for passengers travelled along the Monkton and Kirkintilloch Railway. Opened in 1826, the year after the Stockton to Darlington line in England became the inaugural passenger line, it was another year before a passenger carriage was added behind the coal wagons.

The new fad of the railway had its enthusiasts from the start. Charles Maclaren, the editor of *The Scotsman*, embraced the noisy urban interloper, penning a series of articles in its favour in 1825. Impressed at the Stockton and Darlington's speed of twelve to fifteen miles per hour with a locomotive pulling thirty-six vehicles, Maclaren's vision was to move 600 people rather than coal with such rapidity, perhaps even reaching twenty miles per hour on favourable stretches. Addressing a Glasgow audience in January 1837, Sir Robert Peel argued the railway meant more than the facilitation of moving goods and trade around Great Britain; it meant more than shortening the time it took to travel any distance: the railways 'are creating new demands for knowledge, they are fertilising the intellectual as well as the material waste'. It was perhaps inevitable that before long 'railway speed' came to describe any movement that was thought remarkably fast.

BEFORE THE RAILWAY REVOLUTION

When Scots did use more than their own two legs to get around, and before the steam locomotive took them at such a giddy pace, their standard recourse was to make use of the natural waterways and seas that crisscrossed the mainland and surrounded the nation's many islands. When nature's waterways could be improved upon, then the canal was dug and the harbour was deepened by dredging or was protected by lighthouses and sea walls. With its paucity of flat land Scotland was not the most auspicious location for this form of transportation, but by 1832 the Edinburgh and Glasgow Union Canal had been in operation for a decade, linking the two key cities. Canal traffic in the 1830s was served by seven canals: the Caledonian Canal (Inverness to Corpach near Fort William), covering over sixty miles and making use of the deep waters of Loch Ness, Loch Oich and Loch Lochy; the Forth and Clyde Canal, connecting Grangemouth to the Clyde, dug to link coast with coast in 1790; the Monkland Canal, which skirted Glasgow; the nine-mile-long Crinan Canal, opened in 1801 and linking Kintyre to the Atlantic Ocean; the Aberdeenshire Canal, traversing the valley of the Don; the Glasgow, Paisley and Ardrossan Canal; and the Edinburgh and Glasgow Union Canal.

For those who looked for a return on their investment, canals were not always great earners in the post-1832 years. Revenues of £1,903 for the Crinan Canal in 1838 set against expenses of £1,671 meant a surplus of only £232. Even with the waterway being shared with steamboats, over the next fifteen years the canal never earned more than £200 or £300 per annum. It was Scotland's smallest canal, but its profit levels were similar to the significantly larger Caledonian Canal, which was struggling to maintain efficiencies over its sixty-mile route. Yet the

Caledonian is remarkable not only for being funded as a government project, but for being wider and deeper than any other canal in the world save the Great Ship Canal in the Netherlands. Describing it in 1877, the contemporary T. A. Croal claimed 'there is probably no artificial channel in the world so well known to travellers for pleasure as the Caledonian Canal'.

Scotland's industrial Lowlands maintained a need for affordable, regular and preferably speedy transportation between east and west. The Forth and Clyde Canal was joined by a junction canal in 1839 allowing access to manufacturers from Paisley, helping build upon impressive revenue that totalled £95,475 8s 7d that year. But that growth quickly retracted with the inception of the Glasgow to Edinburgh railway in 1842. It was an unwinnable battle, hastened in favour of the new technology by the railway companies buying up the canals to integrate their ability to move goods around the country, but also to stifle competition. The Railway and Canal Traffic Act 1854 was designed to ensure that each railway and canal company provided 'reasonable facilities' for through traffic as well as its own, enforceable by the Court of Session. Legislation was also put in place to stop the railway companies controlling canal traffic without permission of the Railway Commissioners, and, if they did own canals, to keep them in good working order.

Disputes continued between the various transport operators, although often the interests of competition won out. The complaint that railway journeys in 1855 between Edinburgh and Glasgow cost 2s but the fare from either city to the intermediate stations was higher was dismissed for not being an issue of competitiveness. In another example, one ship owner (Napier) complained to the Court of Session in 1865 that while the Glasgow and South Western Railway Company once provided through fares for passengers who would then take his steamer between Ardrossan and Belfast, this was no longer the case. A rival was afforded the benefit, including advertising, whereas his service was excluded from notifications and his passengers were obliged to pay local rates at a higher overall cost.

Notwithstanding the bickering, the extent of integration in

Scotland's transportation network is shown by these links. The railway was the new and eventually dominant form of haulage and passenger transport in the Victorian years, but road and water remained in use. In the 1830s Tay Ferries offered a daily service between Forfarshire and Fife and the Tay Steam-Packet Company plied its trade daily between Perth and Dundee. In the same decade, two stagecoaches a day left Perth for Dundee, Dunkeld and Glasgow, and three for Edinburgh. Carters would leave Perth daily for England, and for Glasgow and the Borders on Mondays, Wednesdays and Thursdays, with arrivals on the same days. Trade and information flows followed these routes as business, families, letters and newspapers circulated short and medium distances. Access to a port remained vital in these early decades and would remain important, if less essential, for the remainder of the period. Listed were seventy-four ships belonging to the port of Perth, a small facility on the River Tay thirty miles distant from the North Sea. The average ship docked in Perth in 1837 was ten years old and weighed seventy tons. The larger harbour at Dundee, serving the textile and engineering firms of the city, was haven to 284 vessels in the same year, totalling 36,473 tons at an average size of 128 tons. Two 280-horsepower steamships – 'the largest in the kingdom' and 'two of the most powerful steam vessels in Europe' – were in place to connect Dundee with London and, it was further boasted, take passengers to Paris in the same time it previously took to get to the English capital. In 1871 Dundee's port was home to 163 vessels with a registered tonnage amounting to 55,531, an average of 341 tons. The west coast port at Greenock was always one of the busiest on the Atlantic side of the country. Its port could boast a long list of shipping companies, shipping agents for steam and sailing vessels, agents for ferry boats and licensed deep sea pilots: regular vessels headed for Bristol, Glasgow, Leith, London and Liverpool. Steam vessels were scheduled to Arrochar (daily), Ayr (three times a week), Belfast (three times a week), Campbeltown (twice a week) and then on to Port Rush and Londonderry once a week. Daily steamers would also make their way to Glasgow ('every lawful day') and to Helensburgh, Islay, Stornoway, Skye, Tobermory, Dunoon and many places besides. Weather permitting, steamboats and omnibuses were timed to meet the trains to take passengers on the next leg of their journey.

Despite the many and increasingly game-changing developments in transportation, travelling around Scotland in this period was rarely straightforward and contributed to the trope of highland backwardness. Miscontrol by drunken Captain Gillies of the steamer *Inveraray Castle* resulted in the death of a man mid-century and become a police matter with charges laid. The Rev. J. Calder MacPhail of Pilrig wrote to complain about the ferryman at North Connel in October 1890 who was 'tipsy and unable to manage the boat alone; he fell off his seat, dropped his oar overboard and my daughter had to take one of the oars for a time'. A corn miller from Liverpool, Mr J. Wilson, complained to the Secretary of the Board of Trade that the man in charge of the Ballachulish ferry in August 1898 was 'much the worse for drink'. And the state of these boats, let alone those in charge, was also of concern. Survey work was not always easy in some of Scotland's more remote coastal areas, with W. H. Sitewell describing the problems faced with this work when attempting to sail in a sloop from Crinan to Isleornsay. Such were the dangers involved with a far from seaworthy vessel, his sailors frequently crossed themselves and recited Gaelic prayers. Once safely on Skye Sitewell found hospitality was seldom extended, his lodgings were dismal and, despite the offer of 'liberal money', few were willing to enter his employ.

RAILWAY LOCOMOTION

Whatever others thought of the poor quality of some of Scotland's provincial seafarers, investment flowed into the nation's nascent railway network after a hesitant start. When railways started to attract large numbers of passengers and goods traffic in the 1840s and 1850s, the journeys were made city to city with few stops in between. It was an expensive and sometime difficult process to get railway legislation enacted:

£25,000 was expended getting the Edinburgh–Glasgow Railway Bill through Parliament in the 1830s and still the proceedings stalled upon the King's death. Railways were not always directly cheaper than alternative forms of transport. James Grierson, the general manager of the Great Western Railway, envisaged Scotland and England together as an island not just for the operation of the steam train, but for the competition his company faced from the sea: Aberdeen on the east coast; the west coast ports of Glasgow, Liverpool, South Wales and Bristol; and between London and Yarmouth in the south. If the railways did not compete with sea traffic, Grierson argued, they would be of little attraction to manufacturers and merchants. The railway companies also debated the practice of grouping prices, where manufacturers in Scotland would pay a certain amount to places in Yorkshire, for example, and a certain price beyond there. By the 1880s the practice of fixed prices irrespective of journey length was deemed illegal although still followed on the Continent.

Provincial railways came to be regarded as vital to regional economies we have already seen to be diverse (see Chapter 4). Aberdeen was linked south with the east coast main line in 1844 and north to Banff and Buchan in the 1860s and 1870s. The Highland Railway Company was formed in the second wave of activities that brought together several smaller companies to provide a main line from Perth to Forres and then a connection to Inverness. The main activity of the Highland Railway Company was to move produce from the Moray Firth, an area that exported fish, cattle and sheep, to Perth, avoiding a sixty-mile detour via Aberdeen. A report by Captain Tyler to the Board of Trade describing the Duke of Sutherland's railway in 1870 noted that its terminus at Dunrobin was connected to a temporary station at Helmsdale en route to Golspie where the line ended. Funded by the Duke, the line was serviced by one engine, one carriage and four goods wagons, the whole ensemble costing an exorbitant £3,700 per mile to build and run.

Between 1825 and 1844 the number of Acts that had been obtained to build the railways in Britain was 120, with twenty-

Figure 5.1 *Fishwives at Buckie Railway Station, c. 1890, ready to send the gutted fish to Aberdeen and on to the rest of Scotland.* © *Moray Council (Elgin Library). Licensor www.scran.ac.uk*

two of them begun at a value of just under £6m in Scotland, compared to nearly £70 million of activity in England and £3.7m in Ireland. To service this expanded network, and to cater for local and more distant travellers alike, publishers produced standard railway timetables and visitors' guides while local newspaper offices advertised the *A B C Railway Time-Table and Diary*. Great care was being taken to provide the traveller with all manner of information to eliminate any uncertainty in the journey, yet life in a railway carriage was not always the best of modern experiences; Jane Welsh Carlyle told her husband of a closed carriage in 1857 where she feared her death would be assigned to 'bad air'.

It was not only the canals, the coastal shipping trade and the horse trade that lost business to the railways; between 1834–5 and 1848–9 turnpike trusts that were competing with railways experienced a fall in income more than twice as large as that for the Scottish turnpikes as a whole – and this relative decline continued into the 1850s. Several coach owners found the best means of maintaining custom was by running coaches in connection with the railway services or by giving up direct routes where the railway was so much faster and concentrating instead on serving the rural and generally more inaccessible towns and villages. The Royal Mail steamer doubled up as a pleasure cruiser sailing daily around the Kyles of Bute, Tarbert and Ardrishaig, returning in the afternoon. David Macbrayne of Hope Street in Glasgow promoted a steamship tour from Glasgow to the Highlands as the 'Royal Route' via the Crinan and Caledonian Canals. Tourists' Special Cabin Tickets cost £3 for one week, £5 for two weeks or £3 10s for six separate days. Macbrayne knew his local and international market for consuming Scott-land, romantically naming his ships *Iona*, *Columba*, *Cavalier* and *Staffa*. 'There is not perhaps in broad Scotland,' ran the publicity, 'any trip so well calculated to interest and delight the tourist as a trip to the Western Highland, by way of the Clyde'. It was a journey of great magnitude, now not so far thanks to the steam engineering of Watt and Bell – 'almost to their doors'.

MASS TRANSPORTATION

The railways were responsible for the mass transportation of Scots around their nation. From its inauguration, the Edinburgh and Dalkeith railway had passengers flocking to make the journey: in August 1832, 32,367 enjoyed its 'delightful and invigorating experience'. Even regional lines could be inundated. In 1839 the Arbroath and Forfar railway counted 6,083 passengers in one week; 3,600 in one day. What is remarkable is that previously the traffic was thought insufficient to maintain even one stagecoach. In the six months to 30 June 1847, the Arbroath and Forfar line carried 52,673 passengers. That accounting period saw significant numbers on other lines, too. The Dundee and Arbroath railway carried 139,503 passengers; the (new) Dundee and Perth line transported 24,214 people; the Caledonian (Glasgow, Garnkirk and Coatbridge line) sold tickets to 202,068 passengers; the Edinburgh, Leith and Granton line sold 258,570 tickets; and the Edinburgh and Glasgow line carried 515,155 passengers.

The speed of the railway made it possible for the Edinburgh tradesman to be in daily communication with his counterpart in Newcastle, York or London. For the Aberdonian trader, business was connected to Inverness and the hinterland, as well as to the markets of the central Lowlands. The parochialism of the local market was now much less a constraint and, in turn, railway companies enjoyed healthy profits. This growth in the number of journeys increased railway company revenues (for Britain) by 2.5 times over the twenty years from mid-century, with a total of 506 million passengers, while revenue from goods traffic increased threefold.

While not common, injury and even death accompanied railway travel. The disorientation and confusion caused by the speed and noise was frightening and inexplicable to many; it resulted in new kinds of accidents being recorded. In 1832, for example, a young man had his body mutilated underneath six coal-laden wagons he was driving, having caught his foot while jumping off. A man dressed in the garb of a sailor died after jumping from the fourth-class carriage as the train from Glasgow was arriving into Falkirk, falling beneath the wheels. Other deaths involved trespassing or accidents affecting railway workers such as Alexander Lyne, a brakesman, who missed his footing while trying to stop the wagon, fell and was run over. When something did go wrong, the calls for enhanced inspection were heightened. The government report on railway accidents in Scotland in 1864 recorded a number of examples of regulatory failure.

The great disaster of the period was the failure of the Tay Bridge in 1879, just one year after its opening. There was a loss of seventy-five crew and passenger lives when the bridge collapsed during a storm. The designer Sir Thomas Bouch had planned to repeat the design for the railway crossing from South Queensferry to Dalmeny in Fife, but it was shelved. His death soon after the public inquiry implicated him in the disaster merely served to confirm the need for a new approach and pushed Scotland's engineers into something both ingenious and dramatic. The redesigned plan for the Forth crossing became a major triumph and created an icon for the nation. The cantilever solution covered more than twice as long a span as any previous and led to an increase in orders for Scotland's engineers.

CONGESTION

Railways brought bustle and noise to Scottish life. A youth named Robert Kidd, charged with stealing a purse from a women travelling on the Edinburgh to Dalkeith railway in November 1832, was probably not the first but certainly one of the earliest pickpockets who made use of the heady confusion of mass transportation in order to better ply his trade. Agents, shopkeepers and wholesalers were also attracted to the termini as places to establish their businesses. The arrival of long-distance passengers, with their mountains of luggage, caused a disproportionate amount of confusion and congestion on the approach roads to these main-line terminals. With Queen Victoria's sixty-fifth birthday celebrated as a public holiday in Scotland in 1884, around 24,000 people booked to depart from Waverley, Haymarket and Caledonian stations and the tramway system was fully used, including extra cars that ran to Portobello and Musselburgh. Holidays were similarly observed in Glasgow, Perth, Dumbarton, Dunfermline and elsewhere.

The attraction of the railway was more than just the moving of people and goods around the country, as Prime Minister Peel has already reminded us. It transformed the nation by reducing the effective distance between regions of Scotland and Britain and increasing knowledge and comparison. The use of fixed prices irrespective of distance was part of this process. The railways were significant investment opportunities, consistently offering some of the best returns. The railways were also at the technological forefront of the day, the economic potential of new innovations being suitably strong to drive research investment with Glasgow's North British Railway Works in 1903, the largest of its kind in the world. The fashion, profitability and leading-edge technology were all part of the reason why railway development around the world was of interest to Scots, not forgetting the international reputation of the Scottish railway worker, a confidence maintained by Sir David Hunter's successes in building the railway infrastructure of the Cape Colony.

The newspapers in Scotland carried all kinds of news of the colonial railways. Investment opportunities for speculators or feats of engineering ingenuity were standard fare. It was reported that McGill University in Montreal was offering a curriculum in railway management, with $5,000 subscribed each by the Grand Trunk and the Canadian Pacific Railway and $2,000 by the Canadian Northern. Under the heading 'Victoria's Successful Scottish Railway Manager', Scots read about John Mathieson, Railway Commissioner for Queensland in 1900, who for many years previous had been employed by the Glasgow and South Western Railway Company. Credited with numerous positive reforms of the system over the last three years, he was leaving for America to learn about the grain elevator system: 200 officers of the Department waved him off.

TRAMS AND THE SUBURBS

Until the late 1880s, rail journeys taken by the working classes were generally reserved for holidays, longer distances and the occasional excursion: the steam railway was not a major influence in Scotland's suburban transportation. The advantage of the tram over the omnibus was the greater load that could be pulled by the two-horse team: fifty passengers instead of twenty-five allowed cheaper fares to be offered. Glasgow was first to obtain the relevant legislation in 1870, but all the Scottish cities opened tram routes within ten years. Serious congestion of horse-drawn tramways was limiting its effectiveness and investment was needed to move them to electrification. Because of its steep hills, Edinburgh relied on an awkward but cheap cable network literally pulling the trams along. Portobello would then grow as the city's seaside and Musselburgh in East Lothian was made accessible for commuting. In Dundee the solution was to use steam traction for the hillier routes and horses for the level ground until electrification at the turn of the century. Dundee's poor urban management in the first half of the century had the knock-on effect of streets being too narrow for trams and contributing to congestion as urban traffic increased. Horse-drawn trams started in Aberdeen in 1872 with the move to electrical trams beginning in 1899.

In 1891 municipal councils began to take control of the trams in order to avoid uncertainty in fixed-term leases so that investment in electrification might be made over the next decade. To show the interchange of information, the *Glasgow Herald* reproduced a letter sent to *The Times* which highlighted the international interest in Glasgow following the report of the Tramway Commission of Glasgow, '"that municipal authorities in all parts of the world were watching with great interest the experiment of the Glasgow Corporation" in working their own tramways'. A profit of £8,260 for the eleven months ending 31 May 1895 recorded by the Glasgow system was used to supplement the common good with the expectation that greater profits would come in the future. By the first decade of the twentieth century the trams were travelling through sparsely populated countryside to link up with what were to become commuter towns and suburbs. After a difficult start, the electrified and extended tramway in Dundee was travelling along Perth Road to Maryfield in 1900 with plans in place to open lines via Constitution Road, Infirmary Brae and Constitution Street to the top of Hilltown and thus provide relief to congestion in Seagate and Blackscroft Street.

It was not just the railway that was prone to causing accidents; the tram was in even closer proximity to pedestrians. Following a steam tram accident on Govan Road in Glasgow in April 1889 involving a horse-drawn removal van, the Vale of Clyde Tramway Company was fined £15 for not giving enough room to the restive animal when overtaking. Incidents relating to passenger etiquette also resulted. Tensions could run high, and Dundee tram conductor James Smith was convicted of assaulting passenger John McIntosh one Saturday night in 1894 when too many people rushed to get on board. In a humorous commentary called *Tram Etiquette for Women*, published in Dundee in 1897, we learn a little about what a tram journey was like. A local by-law states that trams are only to stop on the upper side of a crossing in the direction of travel. Women, we are told, tend to ignore this and simply smile or glare at the conductor to get the tram to stop, risking the wrath of the police by crossing the road to board it.

Only Glasgow successfully developed an underground rail system, the first carriages running in 1896. It was Britain's second subway system after the London Underground, which opened in 1863.

A BASKET, A BELL THAT RINGS: THE BICYCLE

The steam railway transformed distance travel for goods and passengers. For personal travel with a degree of freedom then an equally transformative development was the introduction of J. K. Starley's 'safety' bicycle in 1885 aided by John Boyd Dunlop's pneumatic tyres, patented in 1888. The adoption of the safety 'machine' was consistent with a fad becoming an everyday necessity, giving rural Scots especially an inexpensive means of leaving their immediate vicinity. With versions of tandems known since the 1810s, and some precursors even before then, Dumfriesshire-born Kirkpatrick Macmillan invented the first pedal bicycle in 1839. It was a difficult machine to master and when in 1842 Macmillan pedalled the seventy-seven miles from Dumfries to Glasgow it took him two days, which was no quicker than had he walked. The bicycle or velocipede, sometimes called a cycle, but never a bike, was confined to a few enthusiasts until the 1870s. By the 1880s the middle classes as well as competitive and endurance bicyclists had taken it to their hearts, showing off its potential and the extremes the body could endure. By the 1890s bicycling had become a national pastime for all social classes: 'What the locomotive has done for man travelling in companies the bicycle has accomplished for the individual' was one reflective summary of its development in 1897. The appearance of a number of French ladies arriving in London to exhibit their skills on 'the bicycle' got the *Dundee Courier* rather excited in 1869. The novelty of the new machine and the gender of its operators carried a greater sense of 'the foreign' than the nationalities involved. Bicycles from Glasgow and Carlisle were displayed at the annual Spring Show of the Ayrshire Agriculture Society in 1869: 'the latest innovation'. The bicycle was hailed for inspiring the health of the people and was described as a new development of 'Muscular Christianity' following the success of four members of the Middlesex Bicycle Club who completed the journey from London to John O'Groats in 1873, led by Charles Spencer, the author of *Modern Gymnast*.

RACING MEETS SCOTLAND

Such was the interest in the new phenomenon that even terribly mundane journeys were reported over these early years: William Lapsley's ride from Edinburgh to Cockburnspath in 1873 recorded the times passed en route through Haddington, East Linton and Dunbar. By the end of the decade Scotland had found its place, and then its passion, for bicycling. Around 4,000 turned out to watch the second annual Scottish bicycling meet in 1878, stopping the traffic to get the best view. A Saturday gathering of 250 cyclists who gathered on the Mound in Edinburgh in 1879 represented twenty-three Scottish clubs and thirteen English clubs, the riders then making their way to Powderhall grounds for races. The next June, Glasgow held its first six-day professional contest with the competitors enduring twelve hours each day in the Burnbank Drill Hall surrounded by spectators coming and going throughout the event with the hall being near filled in the evenings.

The Scots had by now acquired a cycling hero for themselves: the Royal Scottish Cycling Clubs representative A. G. Rennie was praised for his 'plucky' performance in following home the 'English cracks', not dismounting for 188 miles other than to tighten his machine. Interest in competitive cycling had grown

Table 5.1 Cycle clubs at the North of Scotland bicycle meet, 1882

Name of club	Date of formation	Number present
Royal Northern	1882	10
Aberdeen	1880	10
Rangers	1881	11
Blue Ribbon	1882	12
Speedwell	1882	18
Peterhead	1881	5
Forfarshire	1881	3
Dundee	1881	3
Fraserburgh	1882	4
Western (Glasgow)	1881	2
Dowanhill (Glasgow)	–	1
Stonehaven	1881	8
Tricyclists	–	7
Unattached bicyclists	–	67
Total		**161**

and in June 1880 upwards of 300 cyclists in brightly coloured uniforms representing thirty-five or forty clubs in Scotland and England gathered at St Andrew Square in Edinburgh before heading off to Powderhall for races. For the six-day bicycling competition in Edinburgh in October that year the long-distance bicycle champion of the world G. W. Waller was on hand to distribute prizes totalling £170: the professional winners were all from the south, from Wolverhampton, London, Newcastle and Birmingham, but the midweek amateur prizes saw J. B. Tierney from the Bicycle Touring Club of Edinburgh defeat Mr Davies from Tynemouth and J. H. A. Laing from the Edinburgh University Club. Aberdeen hosted local bicycle races in 1880 and the next year the city secured the 'best of the world's bicycle riders' for a twenty-six-hour contest for the bicycle championship of Scotland held at the Recreation Grounds in September. More interest than ever was excited for the event, especially the attraction of G. W. Waller, 'the man who maintained the prestige of England and gained the championship of the world'. The only stimulants were hot coffee and cool or warm milk. The victorious Waller received a prize of £30 and the 'champion belt of

Scotland'; the crowds had been sufficiently enthralled to return the next week to bid farewell to the champion.

The competitive spirit was always in evidence: Waller wrote to the organisers of the 1883 Aberdeen cycling meet to challenge the winner to a race over any distance, and for any sum, either in Aberdeen or Newcastle. Local rivalry was equally forthright. In 1887, Forfar cinder track was the venue of a race-off between Scotland's bicycling champion Jim Young of Aberdeen and Forfar's champion George Douglas.

The endurance bicycles were large and difficult to control, but there were other options over the next decade for those who just wanted to get from one place to another: 'sulkies', 'sociables', 'the traveller', tandems, tricycles, 'four in hands' as well as 'crypto-dynamic two-speed gearing' to help get up hills. The 'coolie cycle' was a tandem arrangement, worked by a servant sitting in the after part, that well might have elegance, but was socially divisive as well as negating the exercise of the owner. Extremes were sought, and the Barnes Bicycle Company produced a machine for ten riders in 1896, known as the 'double quint'. For everyday use, newspaper advertisements and trade shows kept Scots up to date with the technology. When Lord Provost McGrady opened the Dundee cycle show at Kinnaird Hall in 1897 it was because of the great popularity of cycling in the city and surrounding district. There were forty stands to show off the latest bicycles and accessories, with the spectacle enhanced by singers and musicians. The Eadie Cycle Company of Dundee secured a prime spot with twelve machines to display, including the Elswick Roadster and the Elswick Lady's Cycle, of which over 200 were sold to England each week. After success the previous year, the traders of Glasgow organised a second cycle exhibition in the city in 1897, with Sir John Stirling Maxwell MP opening the proceedings. Bicycling, once a pastime, was now a necessity of life for all classes and for both sexes. The show was open for a week. The same year Edinburgh held an exhibition promoted by the Edinburgh Cycle Trade Association. In a British industry valued at £20 million of invested capital, thirty-six exhibitors were on display with 600 cycles. The bicycle accessory would also make it into the fashion world when the redoubtable Mrs Bygrave sailed to America and within four days had sold the design for her Bicycling Skirt for $5,000. Employing a system of cords, the woman was able to produce three different styles of skirt to satisfy all her cycling and walking needs. Design excellence was part of any competitive advantage. The Howe Machine Company from Glasgow won an honourable mention for its bicycles at the British section of the 1889 Paris Exhibition (plus a gold medal for its sewing machines).

THE LAW AND THE BICYCLE

Although Kirkpatrick Macmillan was fined 5s for a minor collision with a child during his inaugural journey to Glasgow in 1842, the initial interactions between bicycle users and the law were concerned mostly with the sharing of road space with horses. A deputation of bicyclists went before the Local Government Board in 1878 to insist that, under the Highways Act now going before Parliament, bicycles should be as free on the highways as carriages, receiving a satisfactory response. The Sheriff of Lanark was asked in 1883 to decide on certain by-laws respecting the use of bicycles on the roads in the Upper Ward of Lanark in a court case that pitted the County Road Trustees against 400 bicyclists who had signed a petition on the subject. The Trustees wanted bicyclists to use lights in the hours of darkness (although no such laws were in place for carts) and to dismount when passing a horse and carriage (whereas in England such a by-law only applied when the horse became restive). The English practice was followed for fear that some evil-minded driver might put his hand up to stop a cyclist simply out of spite. Under the newspaper heading 'Sensational Bicycle Cases at Banchory' a number of gentlemen were charged with riding around the district without lights on in 1895. One of those charged was the Hon. Mr Fielding, brother of the Earl of Denbeigh. They were each to pay 5s or face three days in prison. Fielding opted for the latter and made the journey to Aberdeen to begin his sentence where, upon observing the outside of Craiginches Prison, he paid his fine and went home – all the while laughing and enjoying the whole rigmarole.

Once the bicycle became cemented in ordinary interaction, it made its way into the courtrooms as a carrier of indiscretion and then reckless enthusiasm. The bicycle was cited as part of a divorce case in Langholm pursued by Henry Graham against his adulterous wife, and there were numerous examples similar to the case of a Banff man who used a bicycle to commit fraud in various Scottish counties. Not only was he able to get around, but having stolen the bicycle he then sold it for funds. Accidents resulting from increasingly confident bicyclists riding 'furiously' marked the 1890s. One Kirkcaldy blacksmith sued for £12 damages after his son was knocked down and injured. Treating the bicycle on a par with a horse vehicle, the court decreed that the mere ringing of a bell 'gave no right to run down any person who might be in the way'. Aberdeen Sheriff Court attempted to define dangerous bicycling under section 58 of the Local Government Act 1898 but it was not the speed that was of concern so much as the offence of riding in a furious and reckless manner. One parish minister wrote to *The Scotsman* to complain of the number of bicyclists he had observed with their dogs struggling to keep up with their masters as they made their way to town. Bicycles were then seen to clog up the railway carriages. In 1898 the Great Eastern Railway booked 9,700 bicycles on other companies' lines and there was much debate about how bicycles should be carried on trains.

The bicycle was feted for its mix of glamour and practicality: bicycles appeared in circus shows for popular entertainment and the British army experimented with their use in a 'horseless cavalry', contemplating their deployment during the Anglo-Boer War. Sunday bicycling for pleasure and golf were the new and increasingly popular forms of 'Sunday breaking', noted the United Presbyterian Church Synod in 1896. Similar upset was recorded at the General Assembly of the Church of Scotland, at which the bicycle was said not to take people from rural areas to church, as might be expected, so much as to take them past

Figure 5.2 *Bicycle rally around Falkirk, c. 1910, joined by a motorcycle rider with sidecar.* © *Falkirk Museums. Licensor www.scran.ac.uk*

the church on excursions. The bicycle was a great service to the rural population, 'relieving the dull monotony of rural life', while also enabling the urban dweller to get the fresh air of the countryside. Such movement contributed to economic diversity and increased choice in marriage partners, relieving the reliance upon cousin marriages that Stark had worried contributed to higher than expected levels of insanity in the Scottish population (see Chapter 3).

MOTORCYCLES AND MOTORCARS

As early as 1832 the failure of the great mechanical talents of the land to produce steam carriages on a par with the 'miraculous effects produced by steam power on Railway' was lamented. The motorcar started to be seen on Scotland's roads during the 1890s. The first commercially available motorcar manufactured in Britain came from the Daimler Motor Company in

1897, following on the success of the Brighton to London road
trip on 14 November the previous year. That experiment also
influenced the outcome of the legislation governing vehicles
propelled by mechanical power on highways, allowing them to
go above 3mph and not have a man waving a red flag in front.
There was much discussion about whether motorcars would be
of any greater commercial use travelling at 10–14mph rather
than the notional maximum of 25–30mph. By 1896 electricity
and oil were confirmed as the two likeliest means of propulsion,
with steam out of the running. In 1903 the arrival in London
of twenty-one motorcars that had left Glasgow was deemed
a more successful trial than motor enthusiasts had dared to
hope for. Motorcars were offered for tours of the Highlands
in 1904, including a regular service to the Lochaber ferry. The
Edinburgh Motor and Cycle Exhibition held at the Waverley
Market had some eighty firms selling their wares: it was clear
that the bicycle was now a 'mere supplement' to the motorcar.
There were still around 500–600 bicycles on display, compared
to around 250 motorcycles and 150 motorcars, but motorisa-
tion was the new fashion. It was for the middle classes that the
motor vehicle was marketed, including the commercial traveller
and especially the doctor: 'It is the doctor who has cast aside the
bicycle and before then the brougham to embrace the motorcar'.
Appraisals and modifications of the technology helped advance
reliability, reduce costs and encourage sales, but the motorcar
remained out of the financial reach of the masses during this
period. The ordinary Scot could instead look forward to riding
the motorbus, which had successfully completed its trial phase
in 1911, and the motorcycle following the ninth annual London
to Edinburgh motorcycle reliability trial which had roared into
the city in May 1912, this time including some cars.

TAKING FLIGHT

The American aviation pioneer Wilbur Wright's interview in
The Scotsman of 1908 followed his success in covering sixty-one
and a half miles and clearing 330 feet while remaining in the

air for nearly two hours with a passenger accompanying him. Flying was a firm crowd-puller in Scotland; immense numbers came to see Cattaneo's long flight reach Lanark Aerodrome in 1910, which represented 'the national life in every department'. After 2 p.m. five special trains were still on their way from Edinburgh and Glasgow, and benefiting from the 'un Scottish brilliance of the weather' Cattaneo stayed in the air for three and a quarter hours, a British record. To inspire Scottish and English engineers to explore the potential of flight, a prize of £250 was offered by Messrs Pettigrew and Stephens of Glasgow for a cross-country flight to Glasgow and back. The British aviators Dickson, Grace, McArdle and Radley declared they would attempt to be the first to fly around Glasgow University without touching the ground, and with a 10mph wind behind him, Radley flew straight at 70.52mph, impressing the crowd estimated at 40,000–50,000.

The identity of the nation as a landmass and as a people of the land – what was termed 'being Scotland' in Chapter 1 – could never remain fixed as it became easier and quicker to get around the country. Developments in transportation gave fluidity to Scots' lives, helping them experience other Scots and other parts of Scotland. Nor was the journey one-way. Others – outsiders – came to experience Scotland and the Scots, just as Victoria had done to such great renown. Entrepreneurs, too, could better ply their trade as consumer demand slowly widened. Mass transportation helped business move goods and supplies throughout the nation and to trade in distant markets. The Scots' working lives is the subject of the next chapter.

6

Working Scots

The story of Scotland's economy throughout the century from 1832 is one dominated by the sights and sounds of mechanisation. It became the machine age, with all manner of inventions, automated processes and developments in older technology bringing light and speed but also darkness and tumult to the lives of the Scots. There were simply more ways to make a din and while contemporaries proclaimed proudly the transformative prospects mechanisation brought, hardship, ill health, dirt and social dislocation were never too far away. The Victorians first peered with candles and ended bathed in gaslight and then electrical light; they rode horses and shipped by canal, then transported themselves by locomotive, motorcycle and motor-car. They pictured themselves in silhouettes, oil on canvas, and then in photographs and moving images. Machine-formed brick and steel replaced hand-cut stone as the building material of the house and factory. Wood and sail, later iron and steam, transported their industry, their emigrants and their tourists. It was the people who led this transformation: more Scots were in paid employment than ever before, but still they emigrated and still they lived in poverty and still they consumed alcohol copiously and still they sought God's redemption.

Where engineering skills first made their impact, and where mechanisation was introduced, was in the countryside of the eighteenth century. Here spinning and weaving was done in the corner of the room and can be regarded as the earliest and predominant experience of modernity, rather than the equally transformative but not yet widespread factory experience of the cotton mill such as that at New Lanark. But with dwindling order books in the face of international competition, Scotland's handloom operatives saw their piece rates deflate and then their workload diminish from 1860 without it completely disappearing: textile manufacturing maintained a presence mid-century in the Borders and the islands. The industry still provided employment in the 1880s to 100,000 workers, two-thirds of whom were female, but their average wage had dropped. The second large contraction of employment was in agriculture and on the land. In that sector the number of Scots in employment declined from 316,000 in 1851 to 218,000 in 1911. What was underneath the ground, rather than what grew upon it, fuelled the shift in the economy towards industrial activity. In west Fife, the Lothians and Lanarkshire, around 8,000 coal miners were employed at the start of the century and nearly 47,000 by 1870. Nor was that a peak: coal output in Scotland increased threefold from just under 15 million tons per annum in 1870 to 42.5 million tons per annum in 1913. The growth in demand for coal came from the heavy industries of iron, steel and shipbuilding. Between them 300,000 jobs were added from 1851 to 1911. Along with this new demand for workers, there were an extra 200,000 jobs in transport and commercial activities, around 200,000 in the professions and 100,000 general manufacturing jobs added to realign how Scots made a living.

The 1830s had opened with a new phase in industrial-fuelled economic growth that carried through strongly for the next four decades. Scotland was well placed for this development, with a strong banking system supporting a motivated business class linked to both town and country, a labour force with experience from a rage of proto-industrial enterprises and a strong tradition of exporting to mainland Europe as well as to England, with no part of the nation too distant from water. Scotland's shipbuilders employed 4,000 in 1841, 51,000 in 1911 and 122,000 in 1921. The Clyde produced less than 5 per cent of Britain's shipping output in 1835, but advantage came with the confluence of a skilled workforce allied to a thrusting and entrepreneurial group of masters so that in the four decades after 1870 one-third of British shipping and, by 1913, 18 per cent of world shipping, launched from its docks. With new work practices came new social relationships. A hardening of time-discipline, a greater demarcation between work and non-work time and a widening conflict between wage and capital followed as general although not uniform changes. This was a noisy century and a hard century, where reliance upon the cash wage meant physically tiring and dirty work. Was this work any more arduous than life in the fields? Perhaps not if we take as a measure the number of Scots who chose to migrate to the towns in search of this work, but then industrial pay was better. Certainly the work they did was exhausting and unhealthy, six days a week, long days with little time off – creating the conditions that helped Engels source Marx's study of capitalism. The imposition of work discipline took many forms for those who were irregular, tardy or too fond of St Monday: docked pay, physical and verbal punishment and the rise of the worker-turned-manager – the supervisor – to see that discipline was implemented.

In 1834 Ours-Pierre-Armand Petit-Dufrénoy, Engineer of Mines in Paris, contrasted the use of cold air in the fusion of iron in Wales with the use of hot air in Scotland, both rivals to English production. The new Scottish technique using the coal in its natural state enabled iron for castings to be sold at £4 15s per ton compared to £6 per ton in Staffordshire, hitherto the standard of quality and price. When Petit-Dufrénoy and others overcame their doubt that the cheaper Scottish iron was as durable, then demand grew along with consistently impressive output from Scotland's blast furnaces.

The iron industry was one of a series of interconnected headline successes that made Scotland the place from which new technology flowed to Britain and the world. T. M. Devine lays the figures bare: by 1913 one-third of British marine-engine horsepower, one-third of all railway locomotives and rolling stock, one-third of shipping tonnage and one-fifth of steel production came out of the Glasgow production lines and those of the surrounding towns. Not only was Glasgow the second city

Table 6.1 Blast furnaces and output in Scotland, 31 December of each year, 1849–55

Year	Furnaces	Tons
1849	112	690,000
1850	105	595,000
1851	112	760,000
1852	113	775,000
1853	114	710,000
1854	117	770,000
1855	121	825,000

Source: *Merchants' Magazine and Commercial Review*, 34 (January–June 1856), p. 385.

of Empire, it was the 'workshop of the world', with one-fifth of the world's tonnage sailing forth from the yards located along the river Clyde. The North British Railway Works, a merger of four of Britain's largest railway works created in 1903, had the largest output in Europe. These were national industrial realities that shaped the home life as well the town and city of Scotland; they also confirmed the centrality of international trade to the historical development of the nation. Selling 960,000 tons of steel in 1900 was assuredly an international endeavour and there is evidence of the Scottish steel rail manufacturers colluding with their counterparts in England, Belgium and Germany to fix prices and, to some extent, regulate output.

MADE IN SCOTLAND FROM REGIONS

For all the dominance of the west coast industries and Edinburgh's knowledge creators, and while internal migration to the central belt fed the growing workforce, the overall Scottish economy remained a regional one. As we saw in Chapter 4, the nation's towns and districts were distinguished by their sectoral activities: the metal towns of Coatbridge and Clydebank, the textile towns of the Borders, the linen towns of Brechin and Forfar, the tread-making dominance of Paisley and the leisure towns of St Andrews and Dunoon. Despite its overall decline, agriculture and fishing still accounted for around half of male employment in the Highlands and one third in the Grampians and western Borders at the end of the nineteenth century. Whisky production sustained pockets of employment throughout much of highland and island Scotland, with blended production mostly taking place in and around Glasgow and Leith, the latter home to the port trade.

Of Scotland's regional cities in the east, Dundee sustained six large shipbuilding yards in the 1830s, alongside a series of manufacturers fitting out those vessels, but the spinning of cotton, once the business of seven large companies, had all but disappeared by mid-century. Yet in May 1833 Dundee boasted an increase in its trading activities with 15,010 tons of flax imported along with 3,082 tons of hemp. Exports from the docks totalled 356,817 pieces of linen amounting to 50 million yards, 85,522 pieces of sailcloth amounting to 3.5 million yards and 62,199 sacks totalling around 4 million yards. Exports raised double the cost of the raw materials (which came mainly from Russia), and local trade benefited from the city's port being the transfer point for materials coming into Forfarshire, Carse of Gowrie and Fife. The manufactured linens from these smaller centres would then be sold back through Dundee's port, notably to the US, again to the benefit of the city's workforce.

In 1895 the import of flax to Dundee totalled 30,643 tons but this had more than halved to 13,792 tons by 1900 when the price had risen greatly on the scarcity of the crop (despite demand fuelled by the Anglo-Boer war). Earlier Dundee's jute manufacturers had sent their product off to Kirkcaldy to be treated with linseed oil to manufacture linoleum. To avoid crack-ing, sufficiently large warehouses were used to roll and store the flooring, and barges were employed rather than the railway wagon or cart to transport the finished product to London. The jute industry had brought wealth to Dundee. Employing 34,000 people at its peak, women outnumbered men by a factor of 4 to 3. But by the second half of the century those jobs had largely left the city as the Calcutta mills increased production and domi-nated the markets, although with a predominantly feminised workforce the wage rate was low enough to keep the industry going. The attraction of this work contributed to only 3.4 per cent of married women in the city being employed in domestic service compared to the Scottish average of 21 per cent. In 1895 Sir John Leng MP sent back a series of letters (with illustrations) to the *Dundee Advertiser* from his tour of India that described the 'Indian Dundee' and the 'Manchester of India'. The affinity between the Scottish and Indian cities was not just because of the jute industry, he maintained, but because so many Dundee men were involved in its manufacture in Calcutta; otherwise he found their topography, atmosphere and climate rather different. One count indicates the Indian city had thirty-eight mills in 1914, employing around 38,000 workers, of whom 1,000 were Scots. Jute was in demand the world over for sandbags and all manner of sacks to transport produce and goods, as well as for military uniforms. The municipal leaders of Dundee had made some attempt to diversify the city's economy, however. A dedicated fish dock was built at its harbour in June 1901 to help expand the fishing industry. Shipbuilding, too, continued as the century turned, although never approaching the level of the Clyde yards. The *Discovery*, built by the Dundee Shipbuilders' Company, was launched on 21 March 1901 for Robert Falcon Scott and Ernest Shackleton's Antarctic exploration.

When the British Association for the Advancement of Science reported on Aberdeen's economy in 1859 it summarised the city as being dominated by open mining, fishing and marine work. Aberdeen had gained an industrial niche in the excavation and export of granite. With new techniques for polishing developed in 1832, this hard stone defined the silver grey architecture of the city as well as its economy. So dominant was the city in this finishing work that it had to import the stone.

Aberdeen's shipbuilding successes were in the 1840s, 1850s and 1860s, with its output of clipper ships for fast trading with North America especially contributing to this success. The city was also at the centre of Scotland's white fish trade with a new fish market that opened in 1899, while steam trawlers especially, and the application of deep-sea nets, continued this emphasis as the century turned. As the city furthest away from the concentration of the Scottish population in the central Lowlands, and thus also from the markets in England, Aberdeen's merchants had much to gain from the connectivity of the railway. The city acted as service centre for its rural hinterland, for the linen, wool and spinning workers who combined mechanised employment with craftwork, as well as for the paper makers of Inverurie.

THE INDUSTRIALISTS AND THE CAPITALISTS

Sectoral changes in the Victorian economy removed working Scots from the life their parents or grandparents would have known, although continuities persisted in aspects of workplace customs and employee expectations. For all that Scots were engaged in local employment away from the industrial heartlands around the Clyde, these regional economies maintaining their own distinct specialisms, the Scottish worker as 'engineer' followed on from the rise of an industrial economy to become entrenched as the key sense of ourselves as a working people. Work is readily associated with the construction of self, unsurprisingly so when we think of a working day that lasted anything from ten to fourteen hours, not including the opportunity for overtime. There may have seemed to be little time for anything else but other chapters show otherwise. The trope of the engineer was no better imagined than Rudyard Kipling's evocative placement of the male worker within a national ethos of Presbyterianism in M'Andrew's Hymn (c. 1890):

> Lord, Thou hast made this world below the shadow of a dream,
> An', taught by time, I tak' it so – exceptin' always Steam.
> From coupler-flange to spindle-guide I see Thy Hand, O God –
> Predestination in the stride o' yon connectin'-rod.
> John Calvin might ha' forged the same – enorrmous, certain, slow –
> Ay, wrought it in the furnace-flame – my 'Institutio'.

What carried this vision out from Scotland was the role of industrialist, the 'captain of industry', where a few key individuals contributed to Scotland's version of the 'great men' of history.

Whereas in 1825 Scotland's pig-iron output measured around one-twentieth of Britain's output, the endeavour of William Baird and his company helped raise that figure in 1837 to around one-sixth of the British total. William and James Baird formed the company in 1830 and had already begun to 'purchase every foot of ground' to bring the Lanarkshire coalfields under their control to supply their iron-making furnaces. Importantly for this industrial venture, Bairds' profits allowed them to invest from their own resources rather than use bank loans or external investments, only moving to become a limited company in 1893. Research shows that in 1836 the selling price of Gartsherrie no. 1 'pig' (the name coming from the shape of the ingots) was 338 per cent above production cost, and although the price had dropped by 44 per cent from that peak in 1840, the profit was still £54,855. In 1843 the works had sixteen furnaces and a capacity of 100,000 tons per annum, making them at that point the largest single pig-iron producer in the world. By 1870, in just forty years of operation, Bairds had built forty-two furnaces with a capacity of 300,000 tons per annum, the profit for that year alone put at £1 million. The brothers between them chaired five companies and sat on the board of twenty-nine railway companies. With economic success came political influence. Rather than the Free Church or the dissenting religions, William Baird was a strong supporter of the Established Church of Scotland. Politically, Baird eschewed the Liberals for the Conservative and Unionist Party.

The Bairds were part of a new breed of Scottish hero. More grudgingly admired than worshipped, the Scottish capitalists shaped their industries through their own endeavours to the extent that their personal success (or demise) was associated with the fortunes of their industry. This was a cohort connected by industrial sector but also through family, marriage, friendship and directorships. Both Dumbarton-born David Napier (1790–1869) and his cousin Robert Napier (1791–1876) were leaders in marine engineering. David worked on the first steamboat, the *Comet*, in 1812 and went on to develop the twin screw propeller. David Napier built and invested in the *United Kingdom* to link Leith and London, while Robert had worked for Robert 'Lighthouse' Stevenson but made his reputation on the quality of his marine engines. To maintain his success Robert purchased the Barrowfield coal works to supply the coal he needed and a share in the Muirkirk Iron Company to acquire iron at the best price. An investment in Cunard's British and North American Steam Packet Company in 1839 led to an order of engines for their large transatlantic ships, establishing Robert Napier and his works as the leading providers of marine engines.

Perhaps the greatest Scottish factory since the Carron iron-works in Falkirk (1759) was the massive St Rollox chemical works outside Glasgow, established by Charles Tennant (1768–1838), that was producing one-third of Britain's alkali by the 1920s. His son John Tennant (1796–1878) continued his work and Sir Charles Tennant (1823–1906), John's youngest son, after training in Liverpool joined his grandfather's company in 1843 and by the 1850s had boosted its fortunes by combining with companies in England to mine overseas. As an example of how he diversified to expand, in 1876 Sir Charles led Britain's exploitation of Alfred Nobel's advances in explosives.

Archibald Coats was another who drove his company to international dominance. Known as the Napoleon of the thread-making world, he was always aggressive: when he came up against prohibitive American import tariffs, he established sufficient factories to become the leading manufacturer of threads in North America. Similarly, James Templeton (1802–85) gained his experience in England and overseas (Liverpool and Mexico), before returning to Scotland to work in Paisley's shawl industries. Using that knowhow, he moved into carpet manufacturing, patenting chenille carpets as a machine-made alternative to the more expensive handcrafted Axminster carpets and, from the 1850s, the 'Brussels' carpets. With American investment, Templetons had become Britain's largest carpet manufacturer by 1914.

Homegrown partnerships could reap great success. Along with William Young, known as 'Paraffin Young', who exploited shale oil in West Lothian, Sir George Beilby (1850–1924) developed the extraction of ammonia from the distillation of shale that was then used as fertiliser. Beilby's opportunity came from the short supply of guano. Scottish industrialists were also making an impact in the economy of Belfast. Charles Allan (shipbuilding), James Mackie, who travelled around Russia and Eastern Europe to gain orders for his machines and engines, David Duncan Leitch (linen and flax merchants) and William Cleland (stationer) were all visible in that community.

The personal role in Scottish manufacturing remained entrenched in these late Victorian years and so the actions of industrialists (themselves perceived as 'the Scots engineer') stoked Victorian conceptions of self-improvement and industriousness. By 1914 over a quarter of shipbuilders' boards of directors were still run by a single family. And these companies worked together. The majority of the Clydeside steel industries were contained within four trade federations by 1918: the Scottish Steelmakers' Association, the Scottish Ironmasters' Association, the Scottish Bar Manufacturers' Association and the Scottish Black Sheet Metal Makers' Association.

LOOKING OFFSHORE

Individual Scots, too, made their contribution to Scotland's economic influence by living a life overseas. The Kirkcaldy-born engineer Sir Stanford Fleming (1827–1915) learned his trade surveying railways, harbours and canals from the age of fourteen before completing his training as a surveyor, an educator, then a leader of railway development in Upper Canada. First crossing the Atlantic as an eighteen-year-old, Fleming later became a director of the Hudson Bay Company and a director of the Canadian Pacific Railway, developing lines connecting the east and the west of the nation. His international reputation came with the push to link the trans-Canada telegraph across the Pacific to Australia and New Zealand (completed in 1902), and for the instigation of Universal Standard Time, adopted from 1885, with mean time running through Greenwich, London.

Figure 6.1   *Steam locomotive pictured in 1889: made in Scotland by*
Neilson and Co, it was one of four ordered and operated by the Chile
State Railway. © *Glasgow City Council. Licensor www.scran.ac.uk*

Scotland's economic transformation was sustained by the
overseas demand for what its people extracted from the ground
and what they manufactured in their factories. Around 38
per cent of Scottish coal left the nation's ports for England or
for overseas and two-thirds of the mid-century pig iron was
exported, dropping to around 50 per cent in 1860. The creation
of the Steel Company of Scotland (1872) under the ownership of
Sir Charles Tennant headed Scotland's industry reaching out to
the world. Coats of Paisley amalgamated with Patons in 1896 to
create the world's biggest threadmakers. Along with the North
British Railway such massive economic plant came to define
Scotland's place in the world in the second half of the nineteenth
century. The North British Locomotive Company sent around
half of its locomotives to operate throughout the British Empire.
As Devine concludes of the Scottish industrial experience: 'the
international market was king'. Specialisation allowed this to
be so, but regional economic diversity accompanied these transformations. There was always movement of workers between

the four main cities and their hinterlands, meaning that the Scots themselves were not straightforwardly of any one industry. So while 'being Scotland' was to others fixed by industrial specialism – dominating the outward face of Scotland to the world – to themselves the Scots were more diverse.

INCOME

With this level of industrial success it is no surprise that the wealthiest Scots were to be disproportionately found within manufacturing. In the period 1876–1913 of the seventeen personal millionaires who died in Scotland, ten were in manufacturing or industry, three were merchants, three were landowners and one was a brewer (see Table 6.2).

The Scots' record level of contribution to British income tax occurred in 1851 when they supplied 15.7 per cent of the national total. Thereafter it fell back to between 9 per cent and 11 per cent of that aggregate. With a smaller share of income liable for assessment, Scotland, it would appear, was becoming relatively poor compared to the rest of Britain despite growing employment. Nor did increasing opportunity for skilled employment secure either a sufficiently high wage or a sufficient number of openings to stop people emigrating. Scotland was working hard, but cash was not being bandied about. With the outflow of Scottish capital hastening throughout the 1870s, it can be seen that even the modest amounts of income saved by the middle classes mirrored the emigration of the people in being put to work in another land. As the economic historian Clive Lee makes clear, it is evidence that investment opportunities were not sufficiently attractive at home, and therefore a sign of weaknesses in the economy.

The cotton spinners were probably at their peak in the spring of 1836 when they bargained successfully for a 16 per cent pay rise, payback on general wages that had not risen since 1827. But such gains were not to be sustained for long following the almost immediate collapse in the American market; despite extensive strike action, and financial hardship to maintain the

Table 6.2   Top ten probate returns in Scotland, 1876–1913

Name	Age at death	Location of probate return	Occupation	Value of probate return
James Baird	73	Glasgow	Ironmaster	£1,190,868
George Smith	72	Glasgow	Merchant and shipowner	£599,130
John Buchanan	68	Glasgow	Shipowner and foreign merchant	£371,259
Thomas Houldsworth	48	Glasgow	Ironmaster	£221,483
Archibald Finnie	62	Kilmarnock	Coalmaster and merchant	£213,924
George Hay, marquess of Tweeddale	89	Haddington	Landowner	£209,502
John Mudie	64	Forfar	Landowner	£172,979
Alexander Pirie	63	Aberdeen	Paper manufacturer	£169,393
William James Lumsden	81	Aberdeen	Landowner	£120,875
Henry Dawson		Edinburgh	Manager of Carron Co., ironmaster	£124,000

Source: W. D. Rubinstein, '"Gentlemanly Capitalism" and British Industry, 1820–1914', *Past and Present*, 132 (August 1991), pp. 153–4.

dispute, the power of the union was broken. Wages were reduced back to the previous level or even further, with some rates down by a quarter. Many unionists were victimised. Writing of 'The Practical Working of Trade Unions' in *Blackwood's Magazine*, the Tory lawyer Archibald Alison regarded trade unions as promoting a civil war of the worst kind. Combination was not illegal in Scotland, however. In January 1834, 300 delegates representing as many as 50,000 weavers throughout Scotland and Northern Ireland gathered in Glasgow with the aim of establishing minimum wages. The urban craft workers contained what were probably the strongest groups of unionised workers: in carpentry, boilermaking, printing and shipbuilding. Contemporary evidence indicates it was near impossible for Irishmen to get a job in the almost entirely Protestant Clyde shipyards, although work was found in the yards that struggled to offer regular employment. These artisans were willing to strike, not just for wages, but also to reduce the working day and in opposition to the more pernicious clauses within the Factory Acts of the 1870s. They were predominantly Scottish, not British, unions at this point, focused on the local shop floor. Both Scotland and Ireland record wider skilled/unskilled pay differentials than England in 1905. Highland and Irish workers were used as strike breakers, prepared to work for lower rates and as outsiders not so wedded to the social relations of the local community. Although Scotland's lowland wages had generally caught up with comparable wages in England, a Board of Trade report in 1912 estimated that incomes in urban Scotland were still 10 per cent lower than in England once the more expensive foods such as beef, eggs, cheese, butter and tea were accounted for.

Women similarly gained status at work, meaning that paid employment was not just an interlude before marriage. For single women and families this income was vital to escaping destitution. Around 90 per cent of working women in 1841 were employed in the agriculture, textiles and clothing sectors, or in domestic service. In 1839 girls and women made up two-thirds of Scotland's textile workforce, and most of them were unmarried. By 1911, 65 per cent of working women were still concentrated into these four occupational groups.

Much of a woman's work was 'broken', or casual, meaning she was not consistently employed. This is a major factor behind the underestimation in the historical record of their contribution to the nation's economic output. Unpaid work in the home is also difficult to discern, and the 5 per cent of married women returned as being economically active in 1911 is almost certainly a significant underestimate. From this we begin to see difficulties with the rhetoric of domesticity. Research by historians Gordon and Nair has shown that domesticity was only one among several values such as individualism and Christian duty held by women, along with the practical reality of maintaining these ideals in face of economic and time restrictions. Women's lives were not so segmented that the private and public worlds were divided, for either the middle or the working classes. While working women predominated in four key sectors, other sectors existed in which there was a notable predominance of women workers. The teaching profession was feminised, with female teachers increasing as a proportion from 35 per cent in 1851 to 70 per cent in 1911. Retail was also a growing field of employment for women, and the department store had a particular focus on its female customers.

Retailing was a changing presence in the town. New technologies were part of the appeal, such as when J. Robertson, a tailor, clothier and ladies' outfitter in Motherwell, advertised shirtmaking as 'scientifically accomplished' in 1896. Shops were also under pressure to expand their services, yet two merchants in Glasgow who were not members of the Early Closing Movement had their plate glass windows smashed in order to put a brake on such growth. The multiple retailers made the most of technological and social changes, many trading under the name of their entrepreneurial founders: William Low (1864) in Dundee, Galbraith and Son (1894) in Paisley and the Glasgow grocer Thomas Lipton (1871). Lipton, a millionaire by the time he was thirty, expanded his business into England and New York by buying direct and maintaining close supply links in order to maximise profits. Tea would become the symbol of his success, and in 1889 Sir Thomas Lipton purchased his first plantation in Ceylon.

To feed the industrial city any advantage was sought to encourage both the poor and the respectable customer. Cooperatives have been part of the supply of food and rural manufacture to the cities and wider markets since the eighteenth century. The Scottish Cooperative Wholesale Society (SCWS) was formed in 1868, five years after the CWS opened in England. It internationalised the import of food, looking for the best deals for butter, flour, bacon and other mainstays of the working-class diet, invested in manufacturing foodstuffs to avoid the cut of the middleman and regenerated many of the struggling cooperatives that had been serving the provincial towns during the 1830s and 1840s. One of the new breed of cooperative grocers was Edinburgh's St Cuthbert's Cooperative Society, formed in 1859 on the back of £30 capital and sixty-three members. A later addition was the Scottish Women's Cooperative Guild, opened as a branch of the English movement in 1892. Its quick growth suggested support of the working classes with its guild members becoming role models for the progress of women. Its buying power threatened to undermine the independent retailers and a Scottish Traders' Defence Association was formed in 1888 to try to claw back lost business, with a campaign of opposition to the cooperatives in the mid-1890s.

A range of smaller economic activities continued to mark the industrial landscape, supporting Scots' livelihoods and contributing to the heterogeneity of experience. Research by Ronnie Johnston has pointed to both rural industries and, importantly, the smaller craft and engineering industries operating within Clydeside, industries the historical record is wont to downplay in comparison to the headline-grabbing titans. In the decades after 1840 small craft producers remained vital to the manufacturing economy of rural Perthshire, for example, yet their fragility meant company turnover was frequent. The small business owners were their own retailers and at the lowest level had income and control of their work processes little improved upon that of waged labourers. Craig Young's study finds low levels of capitalisation within this group, with average assets of only £246, mean liabilities of £645 and usually fewer than five people employed, who tended to be family members. Small amounts of funding were all that was needed for quite respectable capitalist endeavour, however. A watchmaker in Blairgowrie was able to start up his own business in 1839 with less than £25 to see him on his way. James Brown, flesher and dealer, established himself with £7 in 1840, and Henry MacMillan set up as a carrier in 1855 with £8 of assets, the value of his horse and cart. Female business owners predominated in garment making and were located mainly in urban locations. As business owners, females predominated in garment making and were located mainly in urban locations. In 1891 women made up around one-third of all Edinburgh business owners who employed others in the manufacture of clothing, with around 600 business in the city owned by women. These entrepreneurs tended to be in their thirties or forties and to be spinsters, working off family capital. In Edinburgh at that census date, 14,000 workers were involved in the manufacture of clothing, of which 65 per cent were women. Of this number around 1,000 were employers, a third of them women. Clothing was a business that involved as much retail as manufacturing, and relied upon a great deal of subcontracting before the mass production of lines in the 1890s. Fashion and individualism dictated demand, resulting in uneven sales. Many of the girls were lodgers, providing free labour in return for what Scottish historian Stana Nenadic concludes was no more than a nominal apprenticeship, allowing the employer to get the low-skill work done without having to pay more experienced staff.

LIQUID CAPITAL

Later economists in search of the benefits of a laissez-faire banking system drew attention to the lending institutions of Scotland in the eighteenth and early nineteenth centuries as examples of how it might operate successfully. But the system had drawbacks. Without extended credit lines, it was very difficult to become a master: blood family and the reinvestment of profit were the principal sources of investment income. After 1856, and the Joint Stock Companies Act, non-familial ties grew along with shareholders and the size of small businesses. Yet banks and financial institutions were slow to lend to other than the high investors, leaving Scotland's smaller entrepreneurs to use credit on purchases, trade credit and bills of exchange to infuse liquidity into their businesses. Scotland's three public banks, the Bank of Scotland (formed 1695), the Royal Bank of Scotland (1727) and the British Linen Company (1746) were centred on Edinburgh. The stock market began operation in Scotland in 1844. As the lender of last resort, the Bank of England maintained a fixed exchange rate between the English and the Scottish pound; this also meant the policies used to administer Scotland's money supply were those of London. The strength of the Scottish banking industry came from its interlinkages with industry. In Edinburgh, management of the Bank of Scotland and the British Linen Bank overlapped in the boardroom with the North British Railway, while in Glasgow, the Clydesdale Bank was similarly linked with the Caledonian Railway and the Tennant family. Sir Charles Tennant was a director of the North British Railway and chair of the Union Bank of Scotland.

Scotland's wealth relied significantly on overseas investment, with estimates suggesting that this increased from around £60 million in 1870 to £500 million in 1914. Approximately 8 per cent of Scotland's income came from investment and business ventures overseas in 1910. This was a higher proportion than found down south, equating to £110 for every person in Scotland compared to £90 per person in England. With the unavailability of capital elsewhere, Clive Lee explains that the North of Scotland Mortgage Company undercut high interest rates to invest in Canada, where land was available, to secure loans. Likewise, 74 per cent of shares in the Texas Land and Mortgage Company were held in Aberdeenshire. The Dundee Mortgage Company and the Dundee Investment Company were similarly active in the world of investment trusts. Land prices did fall in the 1880s in Canada and America, as did income, but this remained a strong investment opportunity for some of Scotland's cash-rich industrialists.

By contrast, at the end of the nineteenth century external investment came into Scotland from international companies seeking to establish subsidiaries, the creation of the 'branch plant economy'. Scotland had long experience of investment from English industrialists, and now international trade brought investment from America and elsewhere. The Singer Sewing Machine Company established its first factory in Clydebank in 1884, attracted by a culture of low trade unionism and peaceful work relations (Red Clydeside did not come until later). Within six years the company had obtained 90 per cent of market share, continuing to dominate thereafter. While another American company, Bissell, was manufacturing its carpet sweepers in Scotland from the 1890s, it would be the twentieth century before doubts were cast on the efficacy of this kind of exogenous employment.

HUMAN CAPITAL

We know that in the 1830s children worked because of the pressure on all to contribute to the family's finances, but also, importantly, that there were many children for whom work could not be found. The most extensive research has been done on England, where it was determined that children in rural areas would enter service aged around thirteen or fourteen, with only intermittent work available for them before those ages. The evidence for Scotland has not been so comprehensively gathered, but there are nonetheless some striking examples. Of the nearly 41,000 women working in the Scottish textile industry in 1839, 43 per cent were under the age of eighteen, with most aged thirteen or fourteen. The youngest children were tied to the local job market and movement to other districts to enter service or an apprenticeship was only possible once they were in their early teens. With the move to larger spinning mules there was less work for spinners but more for children who, as piecers, would dive under the machinery to repair broken threads.

For all the importance of technology, inventions and machinery, Scotland's industrialisation was predicated throughout on the men and women who worked in those industries. Coal mining remained primarily back-breaking work with a shovel; with cutting machinery only coming into use near the end of the nineteenth century, the difficulty of operating in confined and combustible places was a constraint. It was the industrial skills of the workers, the riveters, wroughters and beaters, that gave the Clyde its place as the pre-eminent location for shipping companies and the British navy to place their orders. The industrial workplace was otherwise generally small, with half of all urban shop floors comprising five workers or fewer in 1851. Where we get our industrial image from is the large textile then ship-building employers, in part because compared to the machinery in use, the investment in human capital was proportionately large. As late as 1910 the value of machinery at John Brown's shipyard was only £200,000, such was its dependence on its workforce. In the Census of Production Act 1906 the Board of Trade was authorised to collect industrial data from throughout the UK, separating Scottish evidence from that of Ireland and of England and Wales. The survey found the human/technology balance was tipped towards flesh and blood: while 58 per cent of the Scottish workforce had a net output of less than £100, this compared to 52 per cent in England and Wales and 82 per cent in Ireland.

We should remember also that individuals having multiple and consecutive occupations lasted well into the machine age. Despite the general success story of Scotland's industrial output, trade cycles and slack periods had a negative effect on the regularity of employment. Trade downturns in 1903–5 and 1907–10 impacted across the shipbuilding and engineering unions, for example. Tailoring had its slack months from January to April, while the Jewish 'sweaters' – those who worked long hours producing low-paying piecework – maximised their output by relying on unpaid female apprentices in the period May to August. In those months of underwork tailors could pick up wages in the ready-made clothing workshops or in the production of uniforms, but it was not always straightforward to align working lives between industries.

Cabinetmakers had their 'dull' period in the winter months, but when busy they could be found working on Sundays. Washerwomen and street sellers also suffered a downturn in business in the winter months and colder spells and would have to look for income elsewhere. Dockers and quay workers had daily fluctuations in the demand for their labour. Even the most industrial of workforces in Scotland, the Glasgow engineering and shipbuilding workers, were to be found on the move as

*Figure 6.2   Jewish immigrants working at a cap factory in Glasgow,
c. 1910. © Glasgow City Archives. Licensor www.scran.ac.uk*

demand varied throughout the year. Shipbuilders would travel
from the estates of inner Glasgow to the Upper Clyde, while
engineers from Bridgeton travelled the dozen miles to Clydebank
for employment with Singer's sewing machine works. Economic
historian J. H. Treble suggests the interrelationships between
communities in the west were often quite dense, covering what
were significant distances before the adoption of the motorcar.
These were moves forced by the particular industrial economy
of the region, where a downturn in orders would impact the
local supply companies, obliging workers to look further afield
for continuity of income.

More widely known as economic migrants are the highland
Scots who had a long history of securing urban employment
during the winter months, sometimes for significant periods.
Of the Glasgow Highland Society's 735 members in 1861, out
of those who stated an occupation, 26 per cent were classed as

intermediate non-manual workers, 23 per cent held managerial or professional positions, 7 per cent were skilled and only
1.5 per cent were semi-skilled and 0.1 per cent unskilled. More
broad census-based evidence from historical geographer Charles
Withers finds Highlanders in the managerial and professional
class in 1851 ranging from 2 per cent in Paisley, 7.6 per cent
in Perth, 10 per cent in Dundee to what appears to be an exaggerated 22.4 per cent in Stirling. From the same source the
distribution of highland workers within skilled occupations is
seen to range from 23.5 per cent in Dundee and 26.3 per cent
in Aberdeen to 31 per cent in Stirling and Paisley. As might be
expected, in both Paisley (34 per cent) and Dundee (24 per cent)
significant numbers of Highlanders secured employment within
the textile industry in 1851, with the proportion staying similar
in Dundee through to 1891.

Highland Scots, like all Scots, continued to be disproportionately represented in the British army. Of all those who
volunteered in 1911, 26.9 per cent were Scots and 24.2 per cent
were English, despite the latter's larger population. It tended
to be the poorest sections of society who saw most value (and
economic reward) in recruitment. It was not just in the institutional settings of the universities and the fee-paying schools
that patriotic volunteers were mobilised at the start of hostilities
in 1914. The most celebrated today were the Hearts football
team, for once in their history leading the league in November
of that year, when the entire first team left for a deadlier field
of conflict. Amateur clubs and supporters joined the rush, along
with transport workers, municipal workers and whole neigh-
bourhoods, answering the call for pals' and workers' regiments
to be formed. Scots overseas joined the recruitment drive, too.
In Australia, New Zealand, South Africa and Canada, Scottish
regiments swelled in number as men and women returned to the
auld country to help with the cause and temporarily (at least)
regain employment at home. The Scots who had left for a life
overseas, or whose families had done so a generation or more
before – the 'other Scots' – were now as much part of Scotland
as they had ever been.

Following the lead of Clive Lee, three important conclusions follow from this analysis of the Scottish economy and workforce as it developed in the 1832–1914 period. The first is that Scotland's experience was not too different from that of the rest of the UK. Where the difference was greater, however, was that Scotland's economic growth was insufficient to keep its rising population in gainful employment, despite the growing number of jobs and the relative wealth of the nation. Second, the result was that emigration – both temporary and permanent – became an experience common to many Scots although for others it remained a backdrop to their personal political economy. The third conclusion, connected to the structure of the economy, is that Scotland's wealth was unevenly distributed. Banner success was found in a few industries, but not all contributed, and Scots invested a higher level of savings abroad than did their southern neighbours. The Scots' disposable income was also less than that of the English. The result here was that many Scots remained in need, and economic and social inequalities persisted. To explore this consequence, the focus shifts to the Scots with the least money, those in poverty, before attention transfers to consumption and how income was spent on necessities, sport and leisure.

7

Poverty, Spending and Sport

Strategies for money management throughout the life cycle – 'getting by' and the use of the informal economy, of borrowing and sharing skills – were all necessary pathways to navigating Scottish life in a century of industrial transition. Within their homes, Scots gathered a broadening range of material possessions, but this varied greatly between the social classes and over time. Social class was also reflected in what Scots wore and how fashion dictated they accessorise their appearance. Festivities, drink, gaming and gambling were regularly excluded from self-help budgets for misdirecting scarce resources away from clothing, food and rent. Realignment in the way credit was used, pawning and the way that the shop, shopping streets and markets developed all changed habits of consumption. While the development of leisure and sporting attractions explains how Scots structured their time when not working, participation and spectating drew down further on the family budget.

A 1907 Board of Trade enquiry into living standards recorded that Scottish farmworkers received around 30 per cent of their income in kind. The cash economy that had advanced for more than two centuries was not as all-encompassing as we might have believed. From historical distance the Victorians and Edwardians more than most were concerned with the morality of poverty. Where once land reigned as the purveyor of power, now liquidity, credit, stocks and investments were taking their place. The landed dominated those whose probate returns edged above one million pounds, but a new and advancing breed of

half millionaires was fashioned from commerce. The morality of
money also consumed the lives of the majority who had insufficient value in their property, goods and cash to register their
successes at death, as well as those who had no regular income,
let alone savings or investments. Independence of action was
key to a Presbyterian religion that placed no barriers between
humankind and God, where there were no earthly controls
to the pathway to spiritual redemption, or at least fewer than
there were in other religions. 'Out of debt, out of danger' was
a favourite maxim in the family of Free Churchman Robert
Candlish. Keeping out of debt, as much as debt itself, was the
cornerstone of family life, yet Candlish's theological preaching was dominated by atonement: sinners – including debtors
– would be welcomed by God and not lost to hell. It meant
that personal harmony could be achieved immediately after
conversion, whether the debt was cleared or not.

The greatest of all Scottish, if not British, nineteenth-century
churchmen, the Rev. Dr Thomas Chalmers, invested his energy
and that of his churchmen in communitarian action and the
promotion of voluntary charitable relief. Edinburgh University's
William Pulteney Alison challenged this approach for being
insufficient to meet the prevalence and depth of poverty that
Scotland was enduring. The difference between absolute poverty
and relative poverty was a case made most completely by
the English Quaker confectioner Seebohm Rowntree in 1899.
Absolute poverty is constructed as an estimate of a family's
minimum consumption needs and is measured without reference
to the income or consumption levels of the general population;
as a baseline for personal intervention, the concept of absolute
poverty dominated the self-help guides and diet manuals produced in the first half of the nineteenth century. The concept
of relative poverty was set against the average income or consumption of the population as a whole (generally and with
appropriate adjustments for family size). It was this difference
that challenged further those opposed to state intervention in
the budgets of the poor, and also undermined the argument that
poverty was immoral. Relative poverty was quite a leap from

blaming poverty on personal failings such as fecklessness, lack of personal industry or intemperate behaviour. It was a move away from financial economy and the better management of scarce resources; it was an acknowledgement that Scots' wages were simply too low no matter how virtuous and economical was the worker. By moving poverty away from personal failing towards inadequate wages and societal segmentation, the endemic persistence of inequality and concomitant fears of unrest and political challenge were firmly in the sights of the reformer.

POOR RELIEF

The Poor Law as it existed in Scotland before 1845 placed fiscal responsibility for the relief of poverty on the landowners and heritors of the parish, with administration assigned to the Church of Scotland. In the parish of Humbie at the start of our period, for instance, it was

> expected that each resident heritor or elder (having a district under his charge) shall make himself thoroughly acquainted with the characters and circumstances of all and each of the poor resident in the district under his care and be able to report the same to the heritors and Kirk Session.

The responsibility for the poor in their locality of those with means was central to the system. Contributions in Humbie were voluntary and not to exceed £100 a year for the whole parish with the heritors meeting in the schoolhouse of Upper Keith on the first Monday of every month at 12 noon to discuss the districts under their charge. The parish contained eighteen paupers, each receiving between 6s and 10s monthly out of a yearly total cost to the 'casual' charities of £40.

Responding to a worsening depression in the textile industries in the early 1840s, and the undermining of administrative coherence following the Disruption in the Church of Scotland in 1843, reform was enacted through the Poor Law (Scotland) Act 1845, eleven years after reform in England. Both Acts must be contextualised in the long-held reluctance to countenance public expenditure or intervention in the labour bargain of the individual. With a growing population, any plans to relieve poverty had to deal with a population displaced by the opportunities and challenges paid employment offered.

The legislation in England allowed relief of the able-bodied, but only in the workhouse, and was designed to rein in costs. In Scotland the workhouse system was not a requirement, facilitating relief to be more widely distributed including to the able-bodied if illness stopped them working or, for women, if they had young children under their charge. The Board of Supervision was established in Edinburgh to oversee the operation of the new parochial boards in the parishes. Anyone receiving aid from the poor rates was classified a pauper and with it a clear designation of Other. In the decade from 1850 the average rate of paupers per head of the population in Scotland was just over 4 per cent while in England for the same period it was 4.7 per cent; in the immediate post-famine years, with so many of the destitute having already emigrated, the number of paupers in Ireland stood at 1.5 per cent of the population, or 226,452 being relieved (a figure that fell further to 43,272 in 1860).

Scotland maintained a higher level of outdoor relief than did England. The Scots were less worried than their southern neighbours that the policy was open to exploitation by employers as a regular subsidy to keep wages low. Some suggested it was the lack of a sufficient workhouse test that had contributed to the increase in pauperism. But with 80 per cent of Scottish parishes having no access to poorhouses, this inevitably lowered the numbers who could go there.

If the Scottish pauper was deemed Other and therefore outside the mainstream values of Victorian society, then the Irish pauper in Scotland was doubly segmented off from any virtuous ideal. The Scottish Poor Law Commissioners noted in 1857 that one in thirteen of the Irish population in Scotland was a pauper. The disparity with the number of paupers in Ireland vexed the Commissioners, who stated that there are 'in any given number

Table 7.1   Census of paupers, Britain and Ireland, 1859

	Indoor	Outdoor	Total
Scotland	8,678 (7.1%)	113,335 (92.9%)	122,013
England and Wales	121,232 (14%)	744,214 (86%)	865,446
Ireland	40,369 (97%)	1,248 (3%)	41,617

Source: F. Purdy, 'The relative pauperism of England, Scotland, and Ireland, 1851 to 1860', *Journal of the Statistical Society of London*, 25, 1 (March 1862), p. 30.

of the population, more than 12 paupers in the Highland counties for every 1 pauper in Ulster and Connaught'. The availability of outdoor relief compared to the immediate harshness of the workhouse in Ireland was the explanation. Mr Briscoe, an Irish Poor Relief Commissioner, observed the 'demoralizing effect' of outdoor relief amongst the Scots in 1862, claiming it undermined 'self-respect, self-reliance, the natural affections'. Rather than bringing poverty-stricken Scots into the norms of society and avoiding the creation of what later theorists would describe as an 'underclass' or the 'ghettoisation' of the poor, the very relief itself, according to some Victorians, fractured the society it was designed to soothe. The admittedly slow and uneven improvement in the Scots' standard of living sustained by the sectoral changes and increase in paid employment outlined in the previous chapter was also responsible for growing inequalities within Scotland. Yet the Scots ensured maximum value for the cost they bore. Whereas in England much of what was raised on the poor rates was used for other purposes, in Scotland the whole rate went towards relief.

Over the decade from 1861 the poor rate increased in Scotland by 25 per cent compared to 10 per cent in England and Wales and a decrease of 60 per cent in Ireland. Notwithstanding this growth, it remained a proportionately cheaper burden in Scotland than it did for its southern neighbour because low

Table 7.2   Expenditure on Poor Relief in Britain and Ireland, 1861

Scotland	£5,917, 634	3s 11¼d per head of the population
England and Wales	£54,767,542	5s 9½d per head of the population
Ireland	£6, 656,745	2s 11¾d per head of the population

Table 7.3   Paupers per head of the population in selected locations, 1859

Edinburgh	1 pauper on the parish roll for every 15 inhabitants
Lanark	1 pauper for every 16 inhabitants
Caithness	1 pauper for every 21 inhabitants
Aberdeen	1 pauper for every 27 inhabitants
Argyll	1 pauper for every 29 inhabitants
Orkney Islands	1 pauper for every 36 inhabitants
Shetland Islands	1 pauper for every 38 inhabitants

remuneration was doled out: 'greater parsimony rather than less poverty'.

Pauperism was highest in the areas with greatest manufacturing and commercial activities, showing not only that the poor migrated to the towns in search of work, but that living costs were probably higher in urban areas where alternative means to finding food and warmth were limited when a wage was lost, reduced or interrupted. It also suggests that the new urban industrial centres that were home to over 80 per cent of Scots were also some of the most fractured communities.

What these figures do not show, however, is that more women than men were receiving poor relief, at a rate of about 3:1. That the experience of poverty was gendered is further evidence of how quickly relative poverty can slip into absolute poverty, leaving large sections of society on the margins. Scotland continued to offer more outdoor relief than the English, even when numbers in the poorhouse peaked in 1906. The limited introduction of the old age pension (1908) and associated national insurance reform (1911) established the beginnings of a structure for dealing with poverty which the Beveridge Report (1942) moved further away from means-tested relief. Not until 1948 was the Poor Law (Scotland) Act repealed.

HELP THE POOR

One symbol of rural poverty was the tramp, but he (or occasionally she) was a confusing character to contemporaries, varying between social outsider and public nuisance, oftentimes described as vagrant. Many tramped between places of work, but there was also the tinker who was found more permanently traversing the highways and byways of Scotland. In 1840 the local police constable at Dunoon waited at the pier to ensure no vagrants would enter the county from the incoming ferries. Evidently these outsiders circumnavigated this watchman, for five years later the Superintendent of Police read a report to the police committee on the local increase in vagrancy. His advice to his constables was to take tinkers and vagrants directly to the nearest magistrate and not take on the cost of ferry money or ailments. The few beggars found populating Ross-shire in the 1880s were described as 'generally lowland tramps of the drinking class'. In contrast, tinkers rarely begged but set up stalls offering to repair tin pans.

Where the old and new Poor Law left gaps, and there were plenty, then contemporaries turned to the voluntary society to deal with the social ills that industrialisation seemed to exacerbate so acutely. The registration of friendly societies in Scotland began in 1829 as a response to fears that political societies were structuring radicalism (a bureaucratic process that became the responsibility of Whitehall in 1875), but by 1832 the focus fell firmly onto philanthropic and cultural activities. The early to mid-Victorian voluntary society was a means of class formation and a vehicle for class influence to develop. Typical was the presence of a patron, usually honorary but sometimes more practical and chosen to reflect status and public approval, a religious leader or an industrialist being customary selections.

Edinburgh provides evidence of the range of philanthropic agencies that structured civil society: a house of refuge for the destitute and their children; the Maiden Hospital fund founded by the craftsmen of the city; a local committee on pauperism; educational help for apprentices; a dispensary and

vaccine institution; a society for the suppression of drunkenness; another for the promotion of total abstinence; a society
for relief for the industrious blind; a Magdalene society; and
various dispensaries and missions for seamen, Highlanders,
fallen women and orphans. This was generally replicated in the
other cities and the larger Scottish towns as help for the poor
was sustained through voluntary action. In some of the smaller
towns, however, this kind of institutional help was not always
welcomed. The burgh of Oban, for example, was served with
a petition from the inhabitants of Tweeddale Street against the
conversion of an existing dwelling into a poorhouse.

The citizens of Aberdeen had no such qualms and that city's
House of Industry and Refuge provided help for those who
were unable to get relief from the parish. At times, however,
no amount of help would be sufficient, such as in the case of a
young servant (case no. 1593) who in 1840 died in the House,
aged twenty-three:

> Destitute; admitted from the infirmary in consumptive condition.
> Relatives at a distance corresponded with, and promises made to
> remove her and pay board, but never removed nor board paid. A
> small sum received from a more distant relative. Claim attempted
> on parish, but failed to be established for want of evidence, and in
> consequence of changes of residence. Remained five months in the
> House; was visited by her clergyman and by others who took an
> interest in her spiritual welfare. Died.

Piety was important to health provision but this was not
allowed to interfere with secular provision. The infirmaries were
the greatest beneficiaries of the practice of ritual giving while the
dispensaries may have been the most effective part of the system
in cost-benefit terms. Criticisms were made that they patronised
and manipulated the poor. The infirmaries were also thought by
some to be unclean and unsafe centres for the propagation of
disease. Typically the philanthropists took the prevailing form
of society for granted, along with its gross inequality of incomes.
Their energies were devoted not to remaking society, but to
alleviating the condition of its current casualties and repairing

the gaps left in social provision by the market system and state support. Their preferred solution was to build cheaper houses and teach the working class to budget better: higher wages for the poor was not regarded as a legitimate concern of the philanthropist.

SAVING MONEY

The Scots, as we saw in the previous chapter, earned on average less than their English counterparts and their spending power was further weakened by comparatively higher costs for food and rent. The ordinary Scot was rarely, if ever, sufficiently well off to go through adult life without the spectre of poverty becoming an unpleasant reality at some point. Yet some Scots were excellent savers. The means to save had first to be achieved: a place that could be trusted, and which allowed for funds to be withdrawn upon request since the fragility of working-class budgets meant there was often little time to navigate through the peaks and troughs of employment; more importantly, the culture of thrift had to be sufficiently strong to make this both a rational and an emotional desire.

Formed in 1836, the Savings Bank of Glasgow was not untypical in the preponderance of small savers amongst its customers. By 1881 the bank had over 11,000 customers with a sample of one day's deposits showing an average of 2s but reaching as high as £14. In one year the equivalent of about a week's labouring wages would be saved, around 15s. So while the deployment of savings was an important means of flattening out income lows, the equivalent loss of more than one week's income each year would place the family in some difficulty. An examination of labourers who opened accounts in the same east end branch in 1881 finds that 36 per cent had been born in Glasgow, 10 per cent were Scots-born from outside that city and the remainder were born in Ireland. This study of this branch by Gordon Pollock also unearthed over 800 women depositors, around half of whom were 'general labourers' through their own or their husband's occupation. Widows were also to be found and the general cross-class composition indicates that the culture of saving was fairly broad, although the majority could not call upon (sufficient) savings either for future planning (including one's funeral) or for easing out times of financial shortage.

SPENDING

With annual savings no more than a week's income, and with around 60 to 70 per cent of expenditure going to food and around one-quarter going to pay the rent, there was little money to be spent on acquiring goods or clothing. Expenditure on alcohol and gambling was an obvious target for those who scrutinised working-class budgets and who considered intemperance a drag on industriousness. Beer lost out to tea as the beverage of choice during the first half of the nineteenth century on account of the temperance campaigners' message holding sway. The consumption of spirits also appeared to decline over this period, although a combination of tax initiatives and changes in the methods of collection make the data imprecise, and contemporary rhetoric was more concerned with the ease with which bars and drinking dens were opened. Greenock's John Dunlop was the leading campaigner, taking inspiration and practical examples from the American Temperance Society. Working with the Glasgow publisher William Collins, the West of Scotland Temperance Society was formed in 1830. As the movement developed – to the extent that some burghs declared themselves 'dry' – alcohol-free boarding houses, hotels and meeting rooms offered a change to the Scottish cultural environment where the consumption of alcohol was frequent and pervasive. Taking 'the pledge' to change one's own and others' intemperance was a personal commitment. In turn customs developed around the popularity of coffee, although even when coffee's delectation in Scotland peaked mid-century, this was still only around one-sixth of tea consumption and its attraction faded thereafter.

Clothing, as evidence of consumption, shows thrift in the decision to patch up rather than purchase anew. While the kilt might be taken as the national dress of Scotland, what Scots wore every day was much less colourful. Two bodies washed up from the Clyde near Rutherglen in 1874 provide some description of ordinary wear. The first, a man aged between forty and fifty, was dressed in well-worn black clothes, a mauve-coloured shirt and a pair of old socks and shoes. The second, a female child, was wearing yellow wincey petticoats and was wrapped in a black coburg jacket.

There was not much colour to be found in working-class clothing, and for the mourning widow black was the expected dress for the remainder of her life, a custom epitomised by Queen Victoria after the death of Albert. Fashion did have its place, argues W. H. Fraser, with grooming and hats playing a part in courtship rituals. Most clothes were altered and repaired to ensure long use. Hosiery was stitched and skirts were revamped. Frequent changes of underwear, rather than washing, was the response to personal smells. From the 1840s men would wear a coat, waistcoat and trousers, generally all dark with the occasional spark of colour in the waistcoat. From mid-century most Scots would have a second set of clothes, although the 'Sunday suit' was frequently pawned for six days each week, and shoes would be preserved for when needed most. By the 1890s even the evangelical press was carrying advertisements for the latest fashions, highlighting how pious heroines could be appropriately dressed.

As producers, the Scots were known for their hosiery, their knitwear, their shawls and their tartan. The provision of goods was generally local until the railway made available fashions from outside the community. Shops offered some specialisms. Paisley's Department Store in Beaconsfield, Greenock, advertised gentlemen's and crews' yachting outfits in 1900. Their service extended to measuring the crew at mooring for estimates for items including apprentice seamen and engineers' outfits. In the same year, the Greenock Rubber Company branched out into mechanical goods, ladies' and gents' waterproofs, as well as travelling trunks, portmanteaus and bags.

For more decorative needs, the production of Paisley shawls in Scotland in the period up to 1840 was part of an international interchange between England, France, India and Kashmir. Making use first of the harness loom, then the Jacquard model, Scottish producers sent their agents to London to keep up with the latest designs, copying the best from Kashmir, using the buta style. Paisley shawls of average quality were selling for £3–£9, good-quality ones for £20–£25 – expensive even for middle-class budgets, yet significantly cheaper than Kashmiri shawls which would fetch £200 or more. The fine goat hair patterned in triangles and worn as a shoulder mantle became a great European fashion in the early nineteenth century. Kashmiri shawls were favourite wedding gifts. The European imitations were prolific, and the 'Paisley design' – as it was known in North America – had taken the name of the town from mid-century. Winter fashions for the ladies of Aberdeen in 1833 included an evening dress with very full short sleeves, a gauze ribbon cincture of the scarf kind, a head-dress of hair ornamented with a bouquet of larkspur, offset with diamond earrings and a large pearl necklace. This was very different from the morning and promenade dress featuring sable fur, amadis sleeves and a bonnet of green satin, the body wrapped in a scarf of white cashmere with embroidered ends.

FURNISHING THE HOME

Just as clothing was an outward expression of self, and of success, so cleanliness of the home was a personal achievement when the supply of water was too haphazard for it to be taken as a matter of course. Clean steps, doors and window ledges, polished brass and starched curtains were all symbolic of con-quest over public squalor, of money for 'show' over absolute poverty. For those who could furnish their home with more than furniture recycled from storage boxes or passed down through the generations, then the early-nineteenth-century penchant for lightness and space gave way to the heavy upholstered clut-tered effect of the mid- to late-Victorian taste. There was the omnipresent piano, the ornate fireplace, large mirrors, wall-to-wall bookcases, wall hangings, curtains for the backs of doors, comfortable chairs, tables for eating from, tables for bridge, side tables for displaying the best china or cutlery, and all requiring dusting. Only the well-off could afford rooms given over to specific functions, and we have seen the predominance of Scottish families living in housing of one of two rooms only. A sign of respectable working-class living was the parlour, kept 'good' and generally free of use. For those who could afford to embellish their homes, walls would be decorated with 'Non-Arsenical' Artistic Wall Paperhangings in early twentieth century fashion, including Tynecastle Tapestry, Cordelova, Anaglypta, Lincrusta Walton and Japanese Leather Papers. The retailer Thomas Lynch advertised in 1896 to the people of Motherwell the cheapest prices for wool beds and mattresses. In Dumfries W. M. Wilson sold a variety of furniture at 'tempting prices' in 1911, ranging from cheap kitchen chairs to an entire household of furniture.

THE MATERIAL CULTURE OF CHILDHOOD

As material goods slowly entered the home, and personal possessions filled more than a trunk or comprised more than a trousseau, so age-specific and gender-specific consumption followed. The idea of childhood as a period of life distinct or at least shielded from that of the adult is a contradictory one for this century. According to Philip Ariès, admittedly analysing an earlier period although his argument was relevant to later times, children were best understood as little adults, dressed as such and framing expectations as to their behaviour and contribution to the household economy. Critics paint this as an argument that lacks precision in class and is not sufficiently robust to stand the test of time: in any case the concepts of parenting and good mothering are socially constructed ones. In term of popular culture, sociologists have dated the creation of youth culture – of older children with money of their own to spend and of symbolic and group-formed identities – as a product of the second half of the twentieth century. Children's dress in the period covered in this volume did mirror that of adults. It makes them look much older to later generations who scan the photographic record. The short waistcoat for boys and the pinafore dress for girls were part of a limited wardrobe in which there was no distinction between everyday wear and leisure wear, with the Sunday outfit, or the ballgown, of whatever standard and age, being all that was different. Nor were children shielded from the hardships of life and the inevitability of death. Research from religious historian Callum Brown has shown that until 1860 not only did the evangelical press lead with stories of death but early children's magazines would also have as much as half their content devoted to obituaries, each with a strong message of how the young reader should live his or her life.

Of the balls and hoops, cards and rattles, wooden instruments and fabric dolls, draughts and chess pieces that made up much of a child's pastimes, none would unduly drain the working family's budget in the early to mid-nineteenth century. Where we see a reimagining of childhood comes in the mass manufacture of bespoke toys and dolls in the Edwardian years when levels of consumption increased. More affluent women in 1908 were advised on the purchase of gifts for a child's Christmas, learning that children preferred gifts that helped them see themselves as grown up. Sewing machines, in various sizes ranging in cost from 2s 3d to 6s 11d, were said to be excellent options for a girl. For boys a soldier's helmet, lead soldiers or sets of pyramid picture blocks were thought acceptable to a future territorial, and the budding engineer could learn from the mechanics of the jack-in-the-box.

The representation of animals in toy form came out of literature in the final decades of the nineteenth century in which nature was idealised as rejuvenating and morally pure compared to urban life and in which the natural environment had value over economic gain alone. Kipling published *The Jungle Book* in 1894, but it was about more than humans as animals; it was animals with their own complex set of emotions. The Germans Adolph Gund and Margarete Steiff, a disabled seamstress, each shifted production to newly styled teddy bears in 1903 while others, mostly small, family-run companies, used their cutting

Figure 7.1   *An early Victorian, German-made jack-in-the-box.*
© *Victoria & Albert Museum. Licensor www.scran.ac.uk*

and sewing machines to produce toys as sidelines. Through
trade journals such as *Playthings* and *Toys and Novelties* Steiff
built up a substantial market for the teddy bear by 1914. Much
of the cultural penetration of these toys into Scottish society,
as elsewhere, links back to American president Theodore

Roosevelt. The cartoon produced from a hunting trip he undertook in 1902 brought the teddy bear into American popular culture, confirmed when the New York shopkeepers Morris and Rose Michtom renamed a stuffed bear 'Teddy's Bear' and displayed it alongside the cartoon.

In Scotland the teddy bear was sold alongside the golliwog and the doll, each in its own way a reflection of contemporary perceptions of childhood, race and motherhood. Dancers were dressed both as teddy bears and as golliwogs at a charity matinee at the King's Theatre in Edinburgh in 1912, promoted by Lady Dunedin to raise £400 for Edinburgh Day Nurseries. Hodder and Stoughton advertised *The Cockyolly Bird* to readers of *The Scotsman*, including the adventures of 'Kit, his Cockyolly Bird, his Teddy Bear, and his black doll Jum-Jum', which was also performed on stage. A 'live teddy bear' was employed to encourage the crowds into a toy bazaar in Glasgow's Union Street in 1916. The representation of the new fashionable toy in jewellery and ornamental objects offered manufacturers new market opportunities. 'Teddy Bear' was the name given to a racehorse that competed at Musselburgh and throughout Britain in the Edwardian years, as well as a name used by an entrant to a bowling competition for the Thornhill Tournament in Dumfries and Galloway. The loss of a baby's silver teddy bear rattle in Stockbridge made the classified advertisements in 1911 with a reward offered for its recovery. In the golfing world girl caddies brought variety to the Scottish ladies' golf championship with the novelty found in the mascots, including the white teddy bear Miss Cecil Leitch carried attached to her golf bag by a pink ribbon. Teddy bears were used as good luck tokens during the First World War, and photographers posed the new toy with children.

Perhaps it was because of climatic concerns that fashionable Scottish ladies wished to see themselves wrapped in plush: 'teddy bear cloth' was the autumn fashion in 1913. In Jenners' 1914 sale, a coat of copper-coloured teddy bear cloth, with seal musquash collar and lined squirrel lock could be bought for 13 guineas. For those wishing the same look at a lower cost, then Robert Maule and Son on Princes Street sold an evening wrap

Table 7.4 Toys for sale from the Professional and Civil Service Supply Association Ltd, 1913

Toys	Price range	Toys	Price range
Undressed dolls	6d, 1/, 1/6, to 15/6	Cinematographs, generating electricity	37/7, 70/
Dressed dolls	6d, 1/, 1/6, 2/, to 15/	Mechanical trains, complete with rails	1/, 1/3, 1/9, 22/6
Baby bumps, unbreakable heads	4/6	Mechanical boats, all the latest	2/6, 4/, 6/, to 22/6
Wool animals (assorted)	1/, 1/6, to 3/	Mechanical motor cars, very fine models	1/, 2/6, 3/3, to 27/6
Cinematographs, complete with slides and films	4/6, 7/, 10/6, to 22/6	Rocking horses	8/6, 17/6, to 30/
Teddy bears	1/9, 2/6, 3/, 4/6, to 15/	Aeroplanes	1/, 1/6, to 12/6

in teddy bear plush at 6½ guineas, highlighted during a special evening fashion event. The George Street auctioneers James Harvey were advertising a 'Fashionable Fawn Teddy Bear Coat' and singled out by the Professional and Civil Service Supply Association Ltd were new wrap coats in teddy bear cloth.

At this time in Scotland's history, the fashion for mechanised toys as well as for stuffed animals was to the fore. Lamley's in Leith Street were selling dolls in a range of highland regimental tartans, as well as growling stuffed animals. Edinburgh's Robert Maule & Co.'s Toyland was a 'Children's Eldorado' with its mechanical devices, toys and games.

Without a doubt the teddy bear was an international plaything now indigenous to the Scottish nation. So when the striking stuffers at the Bruin Manufacturing Company in New York became a cause célèbre in 1907, despite the manufacturer's insistence there was 'no liability of a Teddy Bear famine', *The Scotsman* reported in all seriousness that blackleg bears were on their way from Europe. And with the approach of war in 1914, attempts were made to encourage the purchase of shares in British companies to make dolls in particular, but also wooden toys and stuffed goods that included cats, dogs, camels 'and the popular Golliwog'. These goods had hitherto been manufactured almost entirely in Germany, but this trade was now blocked. The high-end work was to be done by women in factories while the cheaper items were to be outsourced to women in their own homes. In a world of international consumption, toys were part of Scotland and Britain's home front.

FROM LEISURE TO SPORT

As with clothing and personal goods, the quickening commodification of leisure and sport can also be dated to the two decades before and after 1900. Pleasure seekers in the last quarter of the nineteenth century enjoyed more regulated but also more sophisticated amusements. The Royal Aquarium and Pleasure Grounds at Rothesay offered visitors the living wonders of the mighty deep, trained seals and, to further connect the land and the sea, a camera obscura. Leisure also included personal grooming. Edinburgh's first Turkish baths were in Rose Street Lane, with Dr G. E. Allshorn overseeing the treatment. The baths' proprietor, A. H. Allshorn, a homoeopathic chemist, moved his operation to South Clerk Street in 1865 and offered a central hot room and a room for bathers separated from the cooling room by a glass screen. It was claimed that Turkish baths, rather than offering 'cures', were 'beneficial' in cases of colds, influenza, bronchitis, rheumatism, sciatica, dyspepsia, indigestion, lumbago, gout, stomach disorders 'and all nervous complaints'. Both the notional healthy Highlander and the clean-living novelist Jane Porter were used to advertise their benefits. Although he agreed that hydropathy had welcome properties, its proponents were nonetheless criticised by chairman of the Board of Supervision Sir John McNeill for claiming universality 'as wide as that claimed by the Church of Rome'.

The towns offered a range of regulated leisure activities. Mid-century Dundee had public baths, a bowling club, a cricket club, a golf club and a curling club to help keep its people active. There was also a chess club, a sketching club and a phonetic society for those looking to be intellectually challenged. For the musically inclined, there was a choral society and an instrumental and brass band. For the associative there were two lodges of Free Gardeners and two Weaver lodges. By 1871 Dundee had expanded its associational opportunities, adding the YMCA, the James U.P. Church Literary Society, the Society for the Prevention of Cruelty to Animals, the Dundee Band of Hope, an amateur choral Society, the Band of the Dundee Rifle Volunteers, a whist society and three cricket clubs. For the city's incomers from the south there was the St George's Society of English Residents in Dundee and Neighbourhood, with John Lang as president and the Rev. Charles Short as vice-president.

In 1872 Perth could boast two curling clubs, two golf clubs, a bowling club, an anglers' club, a regatta club and horse racing. By 1912 the sporting options had expanded to include a civilian club, a miniature rifle club, whist and lawn tennis clubs, two swimming clubs and two public baths, Perthshire Football Association and St Johnstone Football Club, plus six golfing clubs to be enjoyed.

The attachment to self carried by Scots' leisure and sporting activities was nothing if not diverse. Scots tennis players were doing particularly well at Wimbledon in the 1880s, although this remained a sport limited to the middle classes. In 1883 not only was Scotsman Captain Young of the 2nd Renfrew favourite for the top competition (the Queen's Prize), the Prince of Wales Prize of £100 was won by Sergeant Lawrence from Dumbarton, the China Cup was won by a team from Forfarshire, a Scot was second in the St George's vase and a team from Edinburgh was second in the Belgian Cup competition. Golf, tennis, running and swimming were not the spectator attractions of football, but all formed part of Scots' liking for physical activity and their fascination with feats of human endurance. The Arlington Swimming Club raised £50 in subscriptions in 1874 for the purchase of a cup named the Championship Cup of Scotland given to the winner of a competition open only to Scots. The

Associated Swimming Clubs of Scotland was established in
Perth in February 1875, but it was the Associated Swimming
Clubs of Glasgow that dominated swimming in the west of the
country. Swimming was an important part of bringing health
to the cities, with public baths a priority for local authorities.
The ability to swim also mitigated against accidental drown-
ing, yet complaints were made that girls lost out to boys in any
encouragement to learning strokes.

Curling was a sport that developed out of doors and has
a history dating back to the sixteenth century. Following a
meeting held in the Waterloo Hotel in Edinburgh, the Grand
Caledonian Curling Club of Scotland was formed in 1838 with
the aim of standardising the myriad of rules that had emerged.
The club gained a royal charter in 1843 after which one prominent member, Scottish papermaker and Edinburgh MP Charles
Cowan, travelled to London's Great Exhibition of 1851 to present
two curling stones to Prince Albert. Notably, Scottish emigrants
to North America, especially to Canada, carried with them a
deep appreciation of the game. Meanwhile, in contrast to curling
on the frozen lochs of the Highlands, professional quoits was
being played in the central Lowlands during the 1860s. Bowling
greens remained well used throughout the period, not experiencing the dip in popularity of greens in England at the start of the
century before a later revival. Golf was at a low point in the 1830s
because of gambling and associations with the lower classes, but
grew in popularity mid-century, as the town directories have
shown. In 1896 there were sixteen women's golfing clubs, all
links courses; the North Berwick course had women members
from London. Local newspapers would try to promote their local
sporting events, with both the *Dundee Evening Telegraph* and
the *Glasgow Evening Times* sponsoring golf tournaments in the
1890s. The same newspapers would also try to internationalise
the sport, giving coverage from around the world.

Most cricket clubs in Scotland were organised from mid-
century, but enthusiasts had developed the game in earlier
decades. The 'invincibles' in 1834 were Perth Cricket Club, but
their loss to Glasgow Cricket Club at the North Inch in Perth

allowed the west coast club to name themselves champions of Scotland. It was a noisy social occasion and several parties of ladies joined the gathered crowds to admire the 'tough customers' from Glasgow. In 1846 the Perth club were described as the 'first' (i.e. best) cricket club of Scotland for a near innings defeat of a representative all-Scotland side which would have been completed had the rain held off. Amongst a 'host of gentlemen' attending the match in Perth were Lord Mansfield, who immediately joined the local club so pleased was he with the proceedings, as well as Lord Ruthven and the Hon. Fox Maule.

Perhaps the quality of Scottish cricket at this time can be gleaned from a series of matches played between eleven 'of the most celebrated' English cricketers and twenty-two Scots. After two innings in May 1849 the Scots, with twice as many batsmen, had lost by 166 runs. The next year rain saved the Scots, with sixteen wickets down for twenty-four runs in the second innings; they remained 188 runs behind even with a number of itinerant professionals from the north of England swelling their ranks. Yet this was no national disgrace, or nationalist touchstone, with the match 'looked forward to with so much interest by lovers of the game' and the celebrated cricketers of England fawned over. In a low-scoring game in 1851 the Scottish twenty-two came within twenty of the English eleven. And the losses continued for the Scots throughout the decade. Success did come when the twenty-two of club side Clydesdale beat the English eleven by twenty-one runs in Paisley in 1859, celebrated by the music of the band of the Royal Sussex Militia and the many spectators in attendance. Undaunted, the English team went on to beat Kelso on their tour.

Ball games have an ancient history in Scotland as in other parts of the world. The world's oldest football dates from 1540 and was found at Stirling Castle, and the accounts of James IV in 1497 show the purchase of 'fut ballis'. Shinty was long part of highland culture, but it was not until 1893 that the Camanachd Association was formed and the game's competitions formalised. Ball or ba' games of all forms were popular in localities in the Borders and Orkney especially. The Jedburgh

Ball Game, like its Kirkwall counterpart, was contested between the 'Uppies' and the 'Doonies' of the divided town. The Orkney version dates from the mid-seventeenth century, although its origins are unknown. In 1800 the game moved to the centre of the town and by 1850 the ball was picked up as it was in rugby football. Later in the century there was a Youths Ba', and women-only encounters began in the twentieth century.

Out of the YMCA developed Queen's Park Football Club in 1867 and the popularity of associational football from the 1870s was confirmed with the first formal international against England in 1872. The Scottish Football Association was formed the next year, nearly a decade after the Football Association emerged without the need for a national moniker in England (in 1863). Three of the cities – Glasgow, Edinburgh and Dundee – each sustained two major clubs but were also home to a number of smaller sides. The Scottish Cup (1873) and regional cup events was the standard fare along with friendlies. Scottish teams were banned from playing in England in 1887 and it was not until the 1890–1 season that a Scottish league was formed to rival that in England, with a second division added in 1893. English-based Scots were excluded from representing their nation during the 1890s until poor results dictated their recall in 1896. Nor were Scots always accepted in England. Sunderland's employment of the northern nationals was met with opposition cheers of 'Play up Scotland' and 'Well done imported goods'. Yet Scots did achieve success in promoting football when working or serving overseas, such as in India (Figure 7.2).

Celtic Football Club was formed specifically to raise money for the Catholic poor. With the growth in popularity of the game, the potential revenue that could be raised helped focus the more expected benefits of community involvement. Clubs began building stands to protect spectators from the weather and made much of tram and railways links near to the grounds. The cost to enter a game in the 1890s was 6d, with free entry offered to servicemen in uniform and to women, and a discount given to children. With all that investment in infrastructure, clubs attempted to boost their revenues in the close season with

Figure 7.2   *The Royal Scots football team proudly showing their trophies after becoming champions of India in the 1894–5 season.* © *National Museums Scotland. Licensor www.scran.ac.uk*

the installation of athletic and cycling tracks or by hiring out their ground to the SFA for representative matches. There was no maximum wage in this period and the more successful clubs paid more, with Rangers' second team being paid more than the first team at Partick Thistle. Some clubs kept fairly uniform wages for their players during the season, but these varied during the close season or when footballers were not playing because of injury.

There were some major developments in this period that would continue to shape the game into the late twentieth century. A riot at the semi-final of the Renfrewshire Cup between Greenock Morton and Port Glasgow in 1899 showed some of the tensions that large gatherings could engender. Upon victory for Morton, the Port Glasgow fans broke through and assaulted other fans, players and the police, a disturbance lasting two hours and causing much panic in the town. The nine arrested all came from Port Glasgow. More seriously, the collapse of the stand at Ibrox Stadium in 1902 killed twenty-one and injured another 300. The Press Association story describing the tragedy made its way by telegram to New Zealand and elsewhere, raising concerns worldwide about spectator safety.

The willingness of the working classes (chiefly) to follow the game continued to impress contemporaries. Special excursion trains left Scotland for the Crystal Palace in London, with around 45,000 from Scotia and places in England outside the capital swelling the crowd to 100,000 who watched the 1902 championship match between Southampton and Sheffield end in a score draw. Nor was it simply the 130,000 who turned up at Hampden to see the Scots defeat the English 3–1 in April 1914 that evidenced the continued growth in crowds, but the 'thousands of enthusiasts' who were turned away. Worldwide enthusiasts enjoyed the game. A report on the 50,000 who witnessed Celtic defeat Rangers 4–0 in the New Year's Day derby that same year to remain top of the league with thirty-eight points was enjoyed by some, if not all, of the *New York Times*'s readership.

Rugby football developed along similar timelines to those of the round ball. In 1878 Scotland and England began their international competition for the Calcutta Cup donated by exiles in that city of the Empire. The New Zealand rugby footballers expected to clear £1,100 for their match against Scotland as part of their triumphant tour of 1905. When the tourists came close to losing to an Edinburgh club side, it was because the rugby footballers of the mother country (it was said) were more used to the frost upon the ground than the colonialists. The international match against Scotland was watched by 25,000 spectators brought by special trains from throughout Scotland and the north of England. Among them were a number of Australian and New Zealand students at Edinburgh University who waved the blue flag with the silver fern and sang out Maori songs. Earlier in the week some 10,000–15,000 spectators turned up to a wet and windy Hampden Park to see the tourists easily defeat the West of Scotland.

The Scottish Rugby Union (SRU) cancelled its annual encounter with England in 1909 over accusations that the English Rugby Board had paid the New Zealand team 3s per day (supposedly to cover drinks and meals) and thus had broken the amateur rules. It caused the Australians to predict that no team would tour Britain again because of the Scottish decision. The Scots were unbending upholders of fair play, and the actions of the Bordeaux club advertising in Scotland for a half-back led to the cancellation by the SRU of an international match against France with encouragement that England, Wales and Ireland take similar action. In both forms of football, national character was signalled to other nations through the amateur ideals of the representative associations.

In contrast to the spectator sports of football and rugby, and the personal endurance sports of swimming and tennis, competitive and social chess played in most of Scotland's towns developed from earlier literary and social clubs. The Aberdeen Chess Club was formed in 1853 from the ranks of the University's professoriate while representative matches between the East of Scotland and the West of Scotland commenced in 1871. Scotland already had a healthy number of clubs in its towns before the Scottish Chess Association, the world's second oldest national association, was formed in 1884 and well before the British Chess Association was formed in 1904 to administer the game in England. Clubs formed in Fort William (1818), Edinburgh (1822), Glasgow (1840, 1860, 1870, 1873), Dundee (1847), Aberdeen (1853, 1859), Falkirk (1863), Hawick (1878), Berwick (1880), Wick (1880), Elgin (1885) and Perth (1885) provide evidence of the growing popularity of the game. There were also a couple of clubs on board the steamers *Clansman* and *Claymore* to cater for enthusiasts and gamblers. European international masters visited Scotland to partake in simultaneous displays and promote the game, including the German Richard Teichmann (1894, 1901, 1902, 1905), the Englishman Joseph Blackburne (1893, 1895, 1902, 1903, 1904, 1905) and the German Jacques Mieses (1895, 1900, 1934), who took British citizenship in 1938 following persecution because of his Jewish faith.

All sports were of potential interest to the gambler. Despite inclement weather, hundreds came to watch a challenge cricket match between the gentlemen of Edinburgh and the city's garrison in 1849, lost by the military along with the wager of £200. There was some attempt to protect the unwary, and a gamester who fleeced an unsuspecting innocent over a game of chess during a railway journey between Edinburgh and Glasgow in 1860 was brought before the magistrates and forced to return the ill-gotten winnings to the Kirk Session for the benefit of the poor. Before 1874 Scotland's laws on gambling were less robust than those found in the rest of Britain; they were tightened in the 1910s and 1920s amid concern that the football pools along with gaming machines were criminally controlled.

IN THE BOOK

Scotland was not simply North Britain, the poor relation of England. Poverty and hardship was great, spending power was weakened, spirit consumption higher and part of a diet that was more restrictive than south of the border. Against their southern Other, the Scots had a history of negative contrasts upon which they could draw, but their first concern was to look around them. Victorian and Edwardian Scots found it difficult to construct adverse perceptions of self from otherwise strong evidence of industriousness and individualism, but the pauper, the drunk, the criminal, the migrant, the tramp and the tinker forced them to face up to their nation full of Others against which they measured themselves. And it was not just absolute poverty, but secondary poverty that compartmentalised Scots into internal Otherness. When Scots did have disposable income then they could tell stories of their spending that followed individual, family and community interests: clothing, fashion, soft furnishings, childhood toys and leisure. The age of mechanical reproduction bound Scots together but also enabled them to express incremental individualism as funds allowed. Nor was sport simply a ball game between two nations or two religions; instead it encompassed many different encounters. Celebrating the amateur rugby footballer as the essence of Scottish fair play went along with welcoming the crack Newcastle cyclist G. W. Waller or the feted English cricketers. Scotland's variegated sporting and gaming history is one more example of narratives that cannot be essentialised into dichotomies of them and us. The reciprocity and the stigmatisation of ourselves and others started locally from within the nation.

8

Reading, Writing, Talking and Singing

Whether we kick with the left or the right might determine which football team we support, and we might well be what we eat, but culturally we are what we read. One gain from the printing press and the publishing trade was the opportunity for Scots to read their way into a shared identity. The concept of an imagined community talks to this and is a useful way of thinking how the evidence presented in this book – of how Scots objectified an everyday reality of themselves as Scots, and of Scotland as nation – made the people more than a group of individuals rattling around in some kind of national container ship. Our identity is not just from what we read, but how we read. It is also what and how we wrote, how and what we spoke. And when the feeling calls, it is what we sang and what we listened to.

EDUCATION: LEARNING TO WORK

Most workers, as a rule, did not need literacy for their jobs. For manual or simple repetitive machine work, such as that carried out by the young women who went to work in mills and factories around Dundee, or the young lads circling the Lanarkshire mines, education was simply a delay or restriction upon paid employment. In 1837 around 90,000 out of 400,000 Scots aged between five and thirteen did not attend school.

Yet few Scots over this period had no ability to read or write. Estimates from 1871 indicate that only 6 per cent of Protestant men and 16 per cent of Protestant women signed their marriage register with a mark, with the remainder able to sign with their name. The comparable rate for Catholic marriages was 46 per cent and 62 per cent. The difference, though, was less a religious boundary than the consequence of the many illiterate Irish migrants who out of economic need were less likely to send their children to school, especially in the industrial west. Few children avoided schooling altogether, and while it may have been interrupted most experienced six or seven years of education, and some as many as ten. This refers to the length of time children were registered as pupils of the school and not the actual time spent in school, with attendance dipping during harvest time or other periods of economic pressure. In weeks of heavy rainfall attendance would drop either because it was just not worth getting the few clothes owned soaked or because no shoes were available. The 1872 Elementary Education (Scotland) Act did not introduce free or compulsory education, but it made both conceivable. Nor did it supersede the voluntary schools and religious schools, for a number continued, but paved the way for their decline. The legislation brought the state into a child's life to an extent not seen since civil registration in 1855. A more unified and consistent experience of schooling was on its way and a new structure of local administration was put in place. The Act was a key component in the creation of a national narrative of ourselves as a unified Scotland, but its results were more complex than that, and to varying degrees ethnic, gender, class and religious segmentation continued.

Historians talk of elementary rather than primary education in the decades prior to 1872, with schooling experienced at different ages; the term primary education was, however, used informally from the 1860s. The cost of sending a child to be educated pre-1872 was generally one penny a day along with fulfilling the request that suitable clothing be worn. Part of the push for elementary education for the masses came from those who recognised its importance to the maintenance of social order in a society that was industrialising and urbanising at rates Parliamentary Papers informed them was unprecedented. The

second reform of the electoral franchise in 1868 further dem-
onstrated the need to educate the working man in the towns.
Starting at age five (rather than the more usual six, seven or
even eight), compulsory up to the age of thirteen, with exemp-
tions from the age of ten (raised to eleven in 1893 and twelve in
1899), national education was a new experience, but with strong
antecedents. National education had been much debated since
mid-century, but whose religious instruction was to be used
stalled any resolution, and for longer than in England. Most
Scottish children grew up reciting the Westminster Confession
of Faith through heavy exposure to the Shorter Catechism, for
which they learned the answers by rote. To move away from this
would present evidence that secularisation was creeping into
Scottish society. When agreement coalesced, it did so around the
Cowper-Temple clause that required that 'no religious catechism
or religious formulary which is distinctive to any denomination
shall be taught in the school'. This was a compromise between
the Established, Free and United Presbyterian churches, while
from the Catholic Church and the Scottish Episcopal Church
there continued to be opposition.

National education had been a long time coming with
attempts in 1854, 1855, 1856, 1862, and 1869 derailed in
Parliament. Only as recently as 1861 did the state remove the
insistence that parochial teachers be members of the Established
Church of Scotland, such was the system of recruitment obli-
gated to pre-1843 patterns of adherence. The report of the
Argyll Commission (1865–8) had shown that the management of education by the churches was failing. The 1872 Act
brought a least a dozen different schools under state control,
but Roman Catholic and Episcopal schools continued outside
the state system with only nominal grants to defray their costs.
The newly established School Boards instituted to manage the
regulations of the Act varied in size from five to fifteen elected
people. All ratepayers could vote and stand for election, including women. Among the wider changes this signalled, it ended
education administered by the parish in favour of the ratepayers
and ultimately by local government itself.

In the towns and cities the burgh schools were rivalled by fee-paying adventure schools for the middle classes, plus industrial and factory schools, reformatory schools and endowed schools, with predominantly parish or parochial schools found in the countryside. Here the local minister took an important role, and for him it was a means to supplement a modest income. The Disruption in the Church of Scotland in 1843 resulted in over 500 of these parochial schools being separated from national educational provision. Some of these schools were good, but many were isolated, struggling with inadequate facilities and underpaid masters or over-committed ministers. Parish schools did not operate in the city; instead there were burgh schools, some run by the heritors – the elites of the town – most by the town council.

CHURCH SCHOOLS

As with the provision of urban churches there was an imbalance between where the population lived and where the educational provision was delivered. The Evangelical leader Robert Candlish was very much in favour of bringing religious education into schools and he was appointed to head the Free Church's education committee in 1846. The great advantage of the Sunday schools was that they educated the largest number at the smallest cost by locating the school in the church or other similarly cheap premises. Voluntary zeal allowed a large teacher supply and low teacher/pupil ratios. The staple of instruction was reading, with writing considered a luxury the poor did not really need. Reading was prioritised because it was a means to provide religious instruction. Religious schooling aimed not to adapt people to new conditions, but consciously to warn against social and moral dangers in order to reinforce traditional codes of behaviour. Some factory owners opened Sunday schools in their works and factories and encouraged their workers to attend, such was the advantage of linking religious education with social and economic order.

Catholic elementary education carried the benefit of exposing children to the teachings of the church while instructing the young on the benefits of civic culture. In 1825 there were only five elementary schools, teaching 1,400 pupils between the ages of six and twenty in Scotland. By 1866 this had risen to sixteen elementary schools and over 2,500 children under instruction. Nuns rather than priests took on elementary education in most of the seven parish schools in Glasgow in 1851. Edinburgh's seven schools in that year also relied on the work of women, but made greater use of pupil-teachers. In a church that struggled to maintain a Scottish identity in the immediate post-famine years, it was the women-religious, historian S. K. Kehoe has argued, who led the way in Scotticising the church through education. When the new system was introduced in 1872 there were sixty-eight Catholic elementary schools receiving some state finance. The reform did not bring the Catholic schools into the system, but the School Boards were points of influence for Scottish Catholics, although their elections did at times descend into sectarian conflict. One further hindrance to bringing Catholic education into a Scottish national system was the lack of a Catholic training college for teachers until 1894, meaning that training had to take place in England.

The Roman Catholic schools were integrated into Scotland's public provision in 1918, with the church still able to manage and appoint the teachers. But this separate experience is evidence that national reform cannot be said to have had a national effect on the Scots. There was segmentation in the system that undermined unity of socialisation just as it kept the faith traditions separate. Catholic education also had the counterintuitive impact of splitting Protestantism. Those who had feared 'Catholic advance' in Scotland from the 1840s had become ever more extreme in their rhetoric, and while this language had the effect of heating up anti-Popery activity, on the whole it blindsided the zealots from the passive Protestant majority. Sir Robert Peel's reaction in the House of Commons to the suggestion that the Roman Catholic youth ought not to hear lectures about geology or history except from Roman Catholic professors fitted those fears. He asked, somewhat mischievously, if

Charles Babbage's 'calculating machine was a miracle' might it not 'lead the mind to an infidel bias'? The answer from the educationalists of 1918 would surely be in the negative.

INDUSTRIAL AND RAGGED SCHOOLS

If the Scots were very much a working people, as Chapter 6 argued, then one safety net in educational provision were the industrial and ragged schools. The term 'ragged' refers to the appearance and clothing of the children and youths who were brought into this care. The British ragged school movement began in the early 1840s and had firm Scottish roots. Aberdeen's House of Industry and Refuge, founded in 1841 and under the leadership of Sheriff William Watson, was hailed as an example of social intervention relevant to all towns and cities in Britain. Watson persuaded the police to sweep the city of all its street urchins and bring them to the school where they were offered food and clothing if they came back the next day, but threatened with prison if they did not. In Bath in 1847 and in Birmingham in 1851 the success of this northern effort was proclaimed: it was reported in the Bath newspapers that 'Aberdeen had become more celebrated for Industrial Schools than for anything else she possesses'. Aberdeen and then Edinburgh were the main centres of activity with the hope of converting criminals to Christianity and industriousness, part of Thomas Guthrie's *Plea for Ragged Schools* (1847). Some of the schools lodged the children; most fed them. Reading and writing and some kind of musical skill were encouraged alongside training in basic industry for the boys and the skills of domestic service for the girls. The operatives of the school sought out vagrant children and used whatever makeshift accommodation they could find if a dedicated Home was not yet established. The work of these schools was formalised within the Youthful Offenders Act 1854, which established state reformatory schools, and the Industrial Schools Act 1854. Some of the ragged schools requested the School Boards take over their operation, but others existed as Sunday schools thereafter. Industrial schools more generally provided basic education or preparation for emigration. Such schools were funded, in part, by the sale of crafts produced by the children, an entrepreneurial activity followed by the Society for the Industrious Blind in Edinburgh, amongst others. Success was measured by how many children could be placed in the workforce, or who safely emigrated, and it was a vigorous response to vagrancy amongst a population whom we have already seen (in Chapter 3) was predominantly young.

The school was only one influence among many in the child's life. Parents and other adults in the home, the wider family and the community would be charged by reformers with inculcating improvement in the few spare hours at the end of each non-Sabbath day. Once into adulthood, newspapers, clubs, pubs and societies would then alter the child's perception of self. The spreading of literacy was perhaps the greatest achievement of education, more so than providing any notion of social or political stability. Education is a great source of socialisation, especially for the very young, but the schoolroom was just one influence of many.

By the 1840s the teaching of political economy and a practical education became fashionable as the best means for Scots to advance the nation economically. To this end, the labouring and skilled classes were to be taught how to shop in economical ways, to keep out of the hands of the pawnbroker and to look after their health in order to remain able-bodied workers. Demands for a secular as distinct from a denominational solution to the perceived crisis in elementary education came from the industrial and commercial middle classes who called for an efficient, coherent and uniform system of national education: it was termed 'useful' knowledge.

To better meet the requirement of skilled industrial work, scientific knowledge could be obtained from mechanics' institutes which offered adult education classes in the evenings to avoid interrupting the working day. In 1844, for instance, after nineteen years of operation, the Mechanics' Institution of Aberdeen had built up a well-rounded diet of instructive courses for its members.

Table 8.1 Mechanics' Institution of Aberdeen courses and costs, 1844

Natural philosophy	6s
Chemistry	6s
Mathematics	5s
Drawing (pencil and chalk)	7s
Drawing (architectural, mechanical and perspective)	7s
Modelling	7s
French	6s
English grammar and composition, reading and elocution	4s
Music (singing)	3s

Henry Craik, Secretary of the Scotch Education Department in 1885, was one who added his voice to the call for technical schools in Scotland, a plea met by various philanthropists. The Allan Glen Institution in Glasgow, founded in 1853, was aimed at the children of the industrial classes in the city from 1853, and in the 1880s various other institutions were formed, including the College of Science and Arts, the Glasgow and West Technical College and Robert Gordon's College in Aberdeen. Edinburgh's mechanics' institute became the Watt College and later Heriot-Watt University. Such schools were in the same situation as the more general secondary schools in that it was not until the Education Act 1908 was passed that the state produced central funding for their provision.

SECONDARY EDUCATION

Secondary and university education in the nineteenth century was primarily education for the middle classes and thus catered for those who had a different set of values. Both a cause and an effect of changes in higher education was a concern with training for the professions, principally in service to church or state. By making potential recruits sit exams and by rewarding with certificates those who passed, professional associations such as accountants and lawyers controlled access to income and thus status in society; the prerequisite of accreditation expanded from the 1880s.

Secondary schools were variously named grammar schools, academies, institutions or higher class schools (or higher grade schools). They were funded by charitable monies and relied on endowments and fees for their existence. After 1872 there was no immediate state funding, resulting in an ad hoc spread of provision and wide variation in standard. At their best, secondary schools provided an education that embraced the teaching of science and classical subjects. At their worst they were burgh schools similar to poor parochial schools, with little or no pretension to teach the higher branches of education. In the last quarter of the nineteenth century the dismal supply of secondary schools in Scotland did not go unnoticed. It particularly affected the universities; the Scottish universities had long been in the practice of admitting schoolchildren as undergraduates to make up the numbers, but they objected to being forced to provide remedial secondary education to their students.

At the time of the 1872 Act there were twenty-three educational 'hospitals' (charitable schools) where boys (and a few girls) were boarded, usually between the ages of eight and fourteen. A few of the bright ones at George Heriot's stayed on as scholars before going to Edinburgh University on a bursary, but most went into the trades. The boys from George Watson's mostly went into shops and merchants' or lawyers' offices. The girls became teachers and governesses. George Heriot's drew on the artisan and the lower middle class, with preference given to orphans. After 1872 the Commissioners on Endowed Schools (Scotland) insisted that they take in more pupils and the School Boards undertook their management, revamping the hospitals mainly as day schools, while ensuring their endowments were recognised and their independence maintained. A few, like Fettes College (opened in 1870), became public schools on the English model.

ACCESS DENIED

The state view was that as secondary education was a preserve of the middle classes, so fees should be charged – a philosophy that excluded the mass of the population who could not pay. The first preparatory boarding school for girls was St Leonards in St Andrews, founded in 1877. Thus Scots who secured secondary education were in a minority, and were from a narrow socio economic spectrum and predominantly male: the result was to segment national education further, making this segmentation the universal experience for the Scots.

Highlighting the variety of public and private educational provision does not negate the conclusion that Scottish education was broadly based in curriculum and sustained by open if not universal access. The Scots' emphasis on 'general', not specialised, education offered choice and the opportunity for anyone of any class, if they had the ability, to aspire to further or higher education. In the world of parish schools, the village dominie (minister or schoolmaster) and the lad o' pairts (the boy with ability) had leading roles. Education was the universal route to self-advancement, no matter one's class; if one had talent, the system would allow self-improvement.

The work of educational historian R. D. Anderson has shown that the majority of those who went to university from a parish school were not poor boys but the sons of the rural middle class – of the minister, of the schoolmaster himself, of the farmer – and only rarely did the sons of labourers or ploughmen make the grade. As for the artisans and tradesmen, they were mostly in the schools of the small towns. Nor was the lass o' pairts found in any number, despite the strong presence of girls in the elementary schools. No girls at this time were admitted to Edinburgh High School or Academy, Glasgow High School or Academy or Aberdeen Grammar School. It was generally thought that girls in the burgh schools were from a lower social class than the boys, since the upper middle class disliked mixed education and some schools responded to this by segregating the sexes. Yet no matter how we stack up the evidence, the numbers carry insufficient power to undermine the construction of the national self. The ideological power of 'openness' in Scottish education trumped contemporaries' experience of personal segmentation and its contribution to otherness.

THE UNIVERSITIES

The 1831 Report of the Royal Commission on the Universities confirmed that Scotland's universities were no longer 'ecclesiastical' institutions and the break with the Church of Scotland was confirmed in their legislative reform of 1835 and 1836. John Stuart Mill expressed the view in 1867 that 'youths come to the Scottish Universities ignorant, and are there taught. The majority of those who come to the English Universities come still more ignorant, and ignorant they go away'; but the quality of instruction and the size of classes was mixed. The state met only a fraction of the costs of running Scotland's universities pre-1858, and as late as 1895 provided less than 40 per cent of the monies needed to run Glasgow University. By 1872 the ratio of those at university was five times higher in Scotland than in England: the Scottish universities were open to all levels of society, without entrance qualification, and the degree structure was distinct – offering some strong evidence for the democratic narrative. Further, the system was sufficiently open, ironic as it might seem, to borrow from England. Because the two countries faced similar problems, and the Scottish middle class wanted the top jobs administering Empire, they were seduced by the prestige of the English public schools and universities. It was just as patriotic to bring Scottish universities up to English standards, which were believed by some – if not by Mill – to be superior, as to develop Scotland's own universities independently.

University life was a difficult existence of struggling along on a bursary or modest family support, living in lodgings in the town. The Scottish student took the Master of Arts, in which moral philosophy was the mainstay of the curriculum, and then might take specialised training for the ministry, medicine or law. At the same time as an entrance exam was introduced in 1892, the Scottish universities allowed women to gain degrees, some fifteen years after the University of London had first done so. This had been confirmed in the Universities (Scotland) Act 1889, which allowed, but did not insist upon, the acceptance of women. The legislative change was loose enough to allow the instructor to decide whether a woman be accepted into the classroom.

It was the skill, endeavour and resources of Sophia Louisa Jex-Blake (1840–1912) that had led the campaign for women to be educated and admitted into the medical profession. Sussex-born, this one-time boarder of the housing reformer Octavia Hill in London lived and worked in Germany and the Unites States, publishing the essay 'Medicine as a profession for women' in 1868. That year she was accepted into Edinburgh University's medical faculty. Her place was initially blocked by the university court, but with four other women, quickly rising to seven in total, Jex-Blake continued her studies, surviving the barracking of her male counterparts in 1870 – the 'Surgeon's Hall riot' – and a block on the opportunity to undertake clinical training at the city's Royal Infirmary. What she could not overcome was legal confirmation of the University's decision not to award women a medical degree even if they passed all their examinations. Jex-Blake continued her campaigning and in 1877 obtained her medical degree in Switzerland just a few months before women gained legal entitlement to train and be registered as physicians. Having allowed women to attend since 1892, in 1916 Edinburgh University's medical faculty allowed women to become full members of the University, still significantly earlier than Oxford, which had allowed women to attend classes since 1870 but did not allow them to matriculate until 1920, and Cambridge, which had allowed women to attend from 1881 but did not allow them to receive degrees until 1948.

READING AND WRITING

The Sunday schools, the parish schools, the philanthropic institutes and the universities were all contributing structures to the inculcation of self within the young. Free from such control, reading was a universal world that was, nonetheless, also personalised. A variety of reading material was available at little or no cost. Religious and moral improvement literature was distributed free from those whose aim was to reform minds and

behaviour. Chapbook literature was still popular, available for
a penny or two and containing stories that were read aloud and
passed around family, friends and the workplace. Newspapers
were publishing only two or three times per week until in 1855
they were freed from all the costs imposed by the Stamp Office
and moved to daily issues thereafter.

Pleasure in reading was a major contributor to the development of literacy. Reports on unusual deaths, workplace
accidents, and descriptions of crime were the standard fare
of early newspaper coverage. News from the royal court and
the Westminster Parliament, and major events from overseas,
particularly when the British forces were in action, was joined
by recirculated stories from London or provincial papers, or
literary periodicals. Rarely frivolous or salacious, reading was
fun and a favoured pastime for many. Local papers would carry
anecdotes and fiction penned by its readership, with Dundee's
People's Journal carrying fiction, some of it in vernacular Scots,
to a circulation of 220,000 people in 1890. Kailyard literature
was one version of Scotland, but the use of everyday vernacular
was an important alternative that gave plentiful prominence to
local and regional news as well as to national and international
events. Reading opened up new worlds and experiences as well
as providing knowledge of far-off places. Whether a conscious
objective or not, self-betterment was an outcome of reading
widely.

It was not difficult to envisage some sort of future economic
reward from the skills of reading and writing. Signage, street
names, house names and then numbers in the growing towns
and cities, as well as increasingly regularised carriage and
postage rates detailed in post office and trade directories, as well
as the need to be able to read the time to ride on the railway or
to meet passengers or goods from a train, all made it a society in
which the written word, numbers, dates and times were essential
to daily life.

In this period that embraced the European age of modern
nationalism, the formation of Scotland's national literature
relied on Scots and others celebrating the insight and reflections

of Robert Burns and Walter Scott. When Captain Burns, son of the great poet, attended the Shakespearean Club meeting in Edinburgh's Waterloo Tavern in December 1831, around 140 gentlemen drank his family's health along with that of Walter Scott and Mr Murray of the Theatre Royal. Scott had recently returned from Malta and a southern European diet in an attempt to improve his health, but nine months later, in September 1832, his life ended. As a man who had attained such renown in so many aspects of national life, it was no surprise that Scott's novels continued to sell strongly throughout the century after his death. His impact had been to historicise Scotland in an international imagination. Scott was Scotland's favoured literary son, with his romantic descriptions ranging from highland Scotland to the English Middle Ages in the much-read Waverley Novels (including *Rob Roy*, *Ivanhoe* and *Redgauntlet* as well as the first in the series, *Waverley*, published in 1814), his political support for the Union, his rediscovery of Scotland's crown jewels in 1818 and his stage-managing of George IV's visit north in 1822. For contemporaries in the 1830s, and for the Presbyterian Church in particular, Scott was much less problematic to appreciate than the memory of (republican-leaning and morally questionable) Robert Burns, although this would later switch as the sentiment of Burns melded with that of Wallace in a Victorian cult of individualism and universal rights.

Along with Scott's Jacobite heart and Unionist head, the Anglo-Scot Jane Porter had an important role in the nation's nineteenth-century fiction. Like Scott, Jane Porter was a borderer, but from the southern side. She qualifies as an Anglo-Scot through her childhood stay in Edinburgh, during which she befriended the young Walter, and her (unsubstantiated) claim to having created the historical novel before Scott with *Thaddeus of Warsaw* (1803) and her seminal Scottish national romance, *The Scottish Chiefs* (1810) – both of which were continually reprinted over the century.

The Scottish Chiefs contrasted the domestic bliss of its protagonists Sir William Wallace and the English king Edward with the Union of Scotland and England, making the story one of feminine intrigue and revenge. The novel was transported overseas and was the literature of choice amongst the reading public of the nineteenth-century diaspora, with booksellers and circulating libraries targeting their subscribers with low-cost companions to the Waverley Novels. In the lead-up to Christmas 1854, for example, Aitken's Circulating Library advertised the work of Jane Porter in the southern hemisphere. To some, the name Jane Porter had become shorthand for Scotland. When the Duke of Edinburgh visited Wellington in 1869, the transparencies created to mark the occasion immediately brought some hazy recollection of *The Scottish Chiefs* in the newspaper article penned by a reporter placed to cover the event. Unfettered, its market penetration reached out among readers of English literature in Europe, North America, India, Australia and New Zealand. Adding to its place in the popular mind, *The Scottish Chiefs* was serialised in the San Francisco weekly *The Golden Era* in 1871 and 1872, a marketing ploy copied by others. To the people of the Taranaki region of New Zealand, Porter was remembered because '[h]er brain has been called the mother of the Waverley Novels', while in Otago this same description was given under the heading 'Famous Old Maids' in the *Tuapeka Times* in 1894. That this historical romance was taken to be the spirit of Scotland was thus evoked with some diverse allusions.

The rumbling cultural relevance of the story continued into New Zealand's North Island in 1899 when it was pointed out that *The Scottish Chiefs* had been the 'weighty authority' that Mr Wilson, MA, had relied upon to suggest the need for a Burns Day celebration in Dunedin. The critic poured scorn on the suggestion that Wallace, or Douglas, or Bruce, were able to outdo Samson in putting so many pitiful English solders to death 'like so many sheep'. The letter carried sufficient scorn to prompt the editor of the *Otago Witness* to append the comment that one should 'not take Burns and such like celebration speeches in quite so serious a light'. It was not an isolated example: the novel was highlighted in such obverse settings as a Burns celebration in Chicago in 1894 and a Scottish-themed evening of the

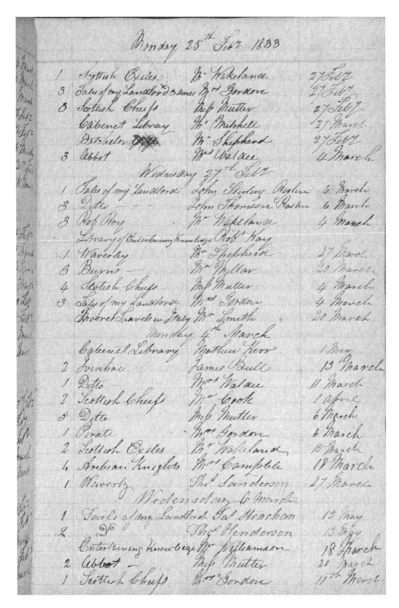

Figure 8.1 *Subscribers to the Loanhead Subscription Library signing out Jane Porter's* The Scottish Chiefs *in 1833. © Midlothian Council, Local Studies Library. Licensor www.scran.ac.uk*

Ipswich Literary Society in March 1896. It is one example, but a strong one, of how a Scottish identity was consumed in the diaspora, and with these events and whimsies reported in the Scottish press, it helped connect the Scots at home with those abroad.

The increase in Porter's readership benefited in part from the growing prevalence of advertising in newspapers and the circulation of comment through the postage system. The costs involved in sending letters, however, tended to rein in working-class use. Postage rates in the 1830s were liable for an extra halfpenny for mail travelling through Scotland, and doubled or trebled for 'double' (two sheets of paper) or 'treble' (three sheets) letters. The base price of posting a single letter from Perth to Aberdeen was 9d, from Perth to Dunblane 7d, and to Peterhead 10d, Edinburgh 7d and Glasgow 8d. Indicative of the care taken with this new speedy and increasingly bureaucratic service was the list of non-permissible uses of the Royal Mail, the first being: 'No indecent or obscene print, painting, photograph, lithograph, book, card, or any article having thereon, or on the cover, offensive material'. This warning was put ahead of posting explosives, dangerous substances, filth and livestock (except bees). Special rates were offered for books and papers impressed for the use of the blind. Telegrams from Greenock in 1900 cost 6d for the first twelve words, then ¼d per word thereafter with free delivery within a three-mile distance, then 3d per mile thereafter. Non-European or Latin words were assumed to be five letters per word, and profane or offensive words were not transmitted. Foreign and colonial telegrams cost 2½d per six words and ½d per word thereafter, or 1d and ½d for British possessions and protectorates.

TALKING AND SINGING

The telegram rates make no mention of the cost or permissibility of Scots words. Yet the path of Anglicisation was not smooth. Despite the decline in the use of Scots in some sections of society, it was, as we have seen, revived as a literary form in the provincial newspapers. Yet the objectification of Scots in the national narrative takes its lead from Walter Scott, who wrote in English but used Scots to linguistically signify the presence of a Scottish character. It was a common trope, used by *Punch*, diasporic associations and those living in and out of Scotland. Here Scots was employed as an ethnic marker that did not give agency to the Scottish people who spoke it.

Gaelic was less easy to present in this way, but some did try. Queen Victoria's diary entry for August 1849 recounts her rudimentary familiarisation with the language, noting that '"Hamis" is Gaelic for James, and is pronounced "Hamish"'. In return, the locals offered some German for the benefit of Albert. Lowland urban Gaelic societies feared that if the Gaelic language was not cultivated, many Highlanders would lose out, with the census of 1881 providing statistical evidence of the language's decline from earlier estimates, data brought into visual focus by Friedrich Bosse's mapping of Scotland's languages for John Bartholomew and Son in 1895.

The village of Ford in the west Highlands is an example of a predominantly Gaelic-speaking settlement, according to the Statistical Accounts in 1845, that lost that distinctiveness just as it lost its population through migration to America and job opportunities in the enlargement and improvement of farms elsewhere in Scotland. Yet in the last third of the nineteenth century it was the development into sporting estates of part of the area around Loch Awe and the Ederline Estate that created employment for the Gaels. The steamers arrived, bringing well-heeled visitors to indulge their interest in fishing and shooting built on a Walter Scott-inspired awareness of highland scenery. And despite the increasing frequency of the steamer to Gairloch, and the arrival of the steam train within five miles of the village, Gaelic was the language of communication round the fireside and in play, although in 1886 few were able to write it and the children's lessons were in English. Gaelic bibles ranged in price from 2s 3d to 3s 6d or a large-print version for 6s; Gaelic psalm books from 1s 4d to 1s 10d. *The Celtic Garland* offered translations of English songs in 1886 and *The Harp of Caledonia* and the *An T' Oranaiche* Gaelic songbooks were available. The consumption of the 'domesticated picturesque' brought new jobs that helped sustain the old language of the Gael but did so by allowing the new language of English to penetrate.

MUSIC

At the start of nineteenth century the Scots had well-established aural signifiers to their understanding of self. Scottish snaps and drones were well known and there was a particular emphasis on melody using fiddles and bagpipes that could be replicated by orchestra. The nation was represented by musical clichés that were readily reproduced. Purcell, Field, Haydn, Beethoven, Schubert and Berlioz were some of the composers who consciously included Scottish motifs in their work. Two of the most internationally recognisably pieces of 'Scottish' music, Mendelssohn's *Hebrides Overture* (1830) and *Scottish Symphony* (1830–42), inspired by the composer's visits to Fingal's Cave on the Isle of Staffa, became the influential British style of the period. James MacCunn's *The Land of the Mountain and the Flood* (1887) and Learmont Drysdale's *The Spirit of the Glen* (1905) both give a firm nod to Mendelssohn, the latter representing Scotland at the Festival of Empire Concerts held at the Crystal Palace in 1911.

   This reflection of Scottish music through a British prism developed from Scotland's major composers spending time in London, notably Hamish MacCunn (1868–1916), Sir Alexander Campbell Mackenzie (1847–1935), William Wallace (1860–1940) and Sir John Blackwood McEwen (1868–1948). Mackenzie was overt in the homage he paid to home, writing *Rhapsodie Ecossaise* (1879), *Burns* (1880) and *Tam O' Shanter* (1911), as well as the distinctly Unionist-Nationalist *Britannia Overture* (1894). One example of the more blatant merging of Scotland's classical music tradition and the national narrative came in 1905 when William Wallace took the opportunity of the 600th anniversary of the death of his famous namesake to compose the symphonic poem *William Wallace*. He concluded with the refrain from *Scots Wha Hae*, celebrating Scotland's contribution to Britishness.

Non-classical music equally followed Scottish motifs. Flute music written by Dundee flautist James Simpson mid-century mixed Scottish reels and strathspeys with marches, waltzes and quadrilles that could equally have been played in Dundee or elsewhere in Britain. Music would be played on board ship, with pipes and fiddles and 'Scottish concerts' most nights on board the *Southesk* in 1883 en route to Australia. Ballads became a popular mix of lyric and music. With overt sexual reference hidden by contemporary prudery, the reworking of Burns by Carolina Oliphant (Lady Nairne) being the most loved, comic songwriters had to become inventive in how they conveyed the humour their audience expected. Riddling, punning and multiple rhymes were all used. There were strong regional overtones to this music. One of the earliest collections of ballad songs, the *Glenbuchat Manuscript* collection, made some time before 1818, is confined to the north-east. Scott's *Minstrelsy of the Scottish Border* collection was published in 1802 and 1803, and in the 1840s Oliphant published her remarkably successful Jacobite romances, *Charlie is my Darling* and *Will Ye No Come Back Again?* being her most enduring. A quintessential Scottish tale rewritten in the 1880s, Englishman Harold Boulton's *Skye Boat Song* romances the glorious defeat at Culloden by recalling Charles Edward Stuart's escape across to Skye and his self-sacrifice of exile. The sentiment of the song helped form the 'saviour narrative' of the Jacobite story that was institutionalised in organisations such as the Legitimist Jacobite League (1891), the Order of the White Rose (1894) and the Society of King Charles the Martyr (1894): it brought complexity to a national identity that otherwise proclaimed unswerving loyalty to the Hanoverian line and to Queen Victoria.

Most of the bothy ballads of the nineteenth century were composed in the 1820–60 period, with the second half of the century repeating and disseminating songs written to reflect previous working lives. Bothies were in part rough and masculine accommodation, but women not only sustained notions of

love but also kept in sight domestic and public gender divisions.
The bothy songs came to reflect the all-encompassing regularity of work and time management. Unsurprisingly, perhaps,
their lyrics recalled better times and celebrated fair and generous employers. Whereas later generations might venerate the
ballad as spectacular, to contemporaries it was the seamlessness
between working and singing that was important.

Other social groups, like the itinerant tinkers, had their own
music that similarly referenced their place in Scottish society.
The Trespass (Scotland) Act 1865 was the legislative response to
society's demand of controlling the tinker as the urban worker
was legislatively and socially managed. In practice, it meant
tinkers were removed from campsites long used and forced to
search for alternatives, further hindering their known grounds
for work, but they remained part of Scotland's cultural landscape just as they remained a menace to the local parochial
boards and magistrates.

MUSIC HALL AND HUMOUR

Whereas in much of England the music hall was a challenge
to middle-class sensibilities and the structured respectability
of leisure, in Scotland the range of acts that were featured was
much closer to the variety performances popular in London
with the added counterpoint of local entertainers performing
in the vernacular. When Glasgow's Gaiety Theatre, founded in
1874, transformed into the Empire Palace in 1896, top of the
bill was Miss Vesta Tilley (1864–1952), best known for her
masculine (and English) 'Burlington Bertie' routine. Mixing
English stars such as Tilley (born Matilda Powles) with local
talent exposed Scottish audiences to the humour and cultural
references of London's west end alongside local patter. The
introduction of fixed seats in rows for families and the middle
classes brought some order to the audience's behaviour, but
still social divisions were retained through pricing and heckling.
The Edinburgh audience attending the Empire Palace Theatre
in April 1910 gained a wide exposure to world cultures and at

lower cost if they took up of the offer of using the new technology of the telephone to make the booking. The acts offered some rich clichés masquerading as internationalism: the 'Favourite Drury Lane Comedienne Marie George' was joined on the bill by Sahib Gustave Fasola, famous Indian Fakir (from the London Coliseum), the vocal skills of Stewart and Morgan, twelve real Moorish artistes going by the name of the Abdulah Arabs, plus Harvey's American Boys and Girls whose act included Frank Victor's latest popular cowboy ditty, 'Santa Fe'.

'Human-animals' were also much in vogue. In the circus the dancing bear of old was now given the moniker Teddy to bring in the crowds (see Chapter 7). Cooke's Circus Pantomime included on the bill a battalion of miniature Gordons – correctly costumed in busbies, red tunics and kilts – a suffragist incident, a fairy lullaby, a Japanese girls' ballet and a procession of lanterns. 'Mr Anderson' the clown entertained young and old alike in Dundee in the 1890s. When 'The Original and Only Sanger's Circus, Hippodrome and Menagerie' visited Edinburgh's Iona Street for four days in June 1911, an eclectic mix was on show. Described as 'A performance of Reputed Excellence and the talk of two Hemispheres' the show contained Sanger's Famous sea lions, Pimpo and his Teddy Bear, The Aeroplanes ('the Sensation of Sensations'), football dogs and the elephant dentist, amongst other delights. The show then moved to Bathgate, Falkirk, Stirling, Perth, Forfar and Brechin before finishing off in Aberdeen.

The Scots' passion for acts that brought the wider world magically before their eyes can best be seen in the example of American illusionist Lafayette (Sigmund Neuberger). Upon arriving in Edinburgh's Empire Theatre of Varieties on Nicolson Street in May 1911, having toured through Wales and England, Lafayette was greeted with enthusiasm. For his act he made himself up as an African and used that ethnic prism to reflect various celebrities. The new attraction was the seemingly mechanical teddy bear, popular for simulating a human child's mannerisms. Inside the costume was Alice Dale, who masqueraded as an ordinary bear displaying childish naiveté. But tragedy struck when fire, caused by an arc lamp or paper lantern, erupted during one of Lafayette's tricks, the draught taking the flames across the floodlights towards the stalls. The band played the National Anthem as the crowd carefully left the venue, but eight were found dead. Never to fulfil his planned appearance in Dundee, the Californian Lafayette died aged thirty-eight and was buried at Edinburgh's Piershill cemetery. His interment was made a rowdy occasion by the mass of Edinburgh's citizenry who turned up to pay their respects, requiring extra police to maintain order. Meanwhile Alice Dale, aged seventeen, and Joseph Coates, her fourteen-year-old understudy, both also killed in the fire, were buried in Sheffield with great emotion. In the spirit of 'the show must go on' in October of 1912, the King's Theatre advertised Lalla Selbini, 'The only successor to the GREAT LAFAYETTE', who was presenting his productions of the Lion's Bride. Lalla Selbini was the bride in that production, and it suggested that only she knew the secrets to his illusions. Selbini added Donald Ross, a Scottish comedian, Gilbert Girard, an animal impressionist, and various other turns to the evening's entertainment that sold well and achieved much applause.

It is difficult to dissect humour as a contributor to national identity if one examines *Punch*, for example, since almost all representations of Scots were either Highlanders knowing that the bright lights of London would never be home, or that whisky was always the punchline. The bagpiper and the fishwife were turned into a geographical representation of Scotland in Bartholomew's comic map advertising Philp's Hotels in 1882. Some jokes at this time poked fun at the discomfort with the new technology of the age. Thus the elderly lady up from the country looking in after the pageboy opened the door, replied, 'This room don't suit me at all. It's that small and stuffy.' In response 'Buttons, with bag in hand, continued to hold the door open, without making any remark. "I tell you," went on the old lady, "I won't have this room, and as for sleeping in one of them folding beds, I simply won't do it!" The boy could stand it no longer. "Get in, please, Madam," said he, with a weary expression on his face. "This ain't your room; it's the lift."' Or the old lady, hearing someone say the 'mails are very irregular', replied, 'It was just so in my young day – no trusting any of 'em.' Some, however, wanted to make the most of the new technology to spread Scottish culture. The Sunderland Burns Club was keen to campaign for the BBC to have more Scottish-themed radio programmes in 1913, a debate that continued to rumble throughout the twentieth century.

Scottish comics did take their fame at home to a wider British and international audience. W. F. [William Flint] Frame (c. 1847–1919) was a Glasgow-born comic billed as 'The Man U Know' and 'The Phunniest of Phunny Phellows' who made his name in the city's 'free-and-easy' theatres of the late nineteenth century. Touring Canada and the US in 1899, he played at Chickering Hall in New York, where he was joined by a soprano, a contralto, a violinist, a pianist, a piper and dancers to perform a range of 'humorous Scotch songs', the ladies singing 'Auld Lang Syne', 'Annie Laurie' and 'Ye Banks and Braes'. Frame's success came by playing up both lowland and highland stereotypes, an approach followed by the nation's greatest comedic export, the Portobello-born comic actor and performer Sir Harry Lauder (1870–1950). Living in Arbroath during his teenage years and then in Hamilton where he worked as a miner, Lauder built up his act and resisted the temptation to go full-time too soon (waiting until 1895) or to try his skill in front of London audiences before firmly established in Scotland. Once ready, he played down his dialect to make his mark in London and overseas, but played up the theme of the Highlander in dress and speech to gain international acclaim. He first appeared in New York in 1907 and also appeared at the inaugural Royal Variety Performance in 1912. Lauder became a strong supporter of the military, encouraging recruitment, entertaining the troops and launching the Harry Lauder Million Pound Fund in 1917. Lauder composed popular songs with Scottish themes and was always ready to entertain with his lowland patter, although rejecting Will Fyffe's (1885–1947) offer of the song 'I Belong to Glasgow' (1920) helped the latter Dundee-born entertainer top the bill in London and be invited himself to give royal performances.

We cannot laugh at ourselves, it would appear, without taking on board the objectification of others. We may claim irony, but London, American and royal success added credibility to 'our' performers Frame, Lauder and Fyffe. Credibility also came to composers Hamish MacCunn and William Wallace for success achieved outside of Scotland. Writers such as Carolina Oliphant and Jane Porter tailored their work to gain readership in a British and diasporic market, while German-born composer Mendelssohn provided a soundtrack to Ossian that was copied by Learmont Drysdale and others at home.

Did it help to believe in the performance because external others valued the art? We value it too, but now we enter the word of self-objectification. Did we appreciate the culture for ourselves, or because outside recognition heightened its worth? Did the culture follow a particular theme – broadly, romanticisation – because it fitted the world-view of ourselves or others? Or both? We, in return, objectified other ethnicities, including English, American, Arabic and African, as well as animals in order to be entertained. Ethnocentrism worked both ways. The never-ending circle of ourselves and others continues on its world tour. Next stop, something fundamentally Scottish: our religion.

9

Believing Ourselves

Scotland was a Calvinist nation, even if not all Scots were Calvinists. This meant that schism was well known to the people. The willingness of Scots to split doctrinal differences can make it challenging to find a period when church affairs have not been anything less than fundamental to life and society. With most at stake was the Church of Scotland, the national church, whose structures, discipline and 'style' have been seen to carry the nation's cultural and national ethos. Like the Anglican version of Protestantism to the south, the Church of Scotland was an Established religion – the state's church. But whereas Anglican bishops sat in the House of Lords and Anglicanism was the religion *of* state, the Presbyterian variant exchanged bishops for government through the presbytery and the annual General Assembly each May. The Church of Scotland was likened to the 'official' church of the people, with above 80 per cent adherence to it or, as the splits began, to Presbyterianism more generally.

The system of government in the Church of Scotland was based on the independence of the congregations to elect their elders and ministers. Together they formed the kirk session and oversaw religious discipline. Some elders from the kirk and all ministers made up the presbytery. The Westminster Confession of Faith (1647) defined the relationship of the church in Scotland to the Scottish state, and continued to bind that relationship after 1707. The national church played a central role in the provision of poor relief before 1845 (see Chapter 7) and education before 1872 (see Chapter 8), and in everyday life throughout the period. Religious beliefs were carried into the home, school and workplace, just as they were into the church – what historians call 'religiosity'. To understand ourselves as a religious people we must turn the focus upon church structures and how religiosity was sustained more widely.

URBAN ADHERENCE

The local clergyman had a vital social role in nineteenth-century society, and the church was central to community. Sir John Sinclair had used the clergy's local knowledge as well as their education when compiling his marvellous *Statistical Account of Scotland* in the 1790s. Returning the favour, the Committee for the Sons and Daughters of the Clergy raised the suggestion to the General Assembly of the Church of Scotland in 1832 that the parochial clergy should again provide a description of their parishes for the follow-up *'New' Statistical Account*, which appeared throughout the decade from 1834. The place of the minister as an authority figure would continue as the clergy publicly debated doctrinal issues, but also as they strove to maintain a moral influence in a world quite different from that revealed in the first returns to Sinclair: in matters of baptism, marriage, pastoral care and social discipline as well as the provision of religious instruction.

Rapid urbanisation posed particular problems for Scotland's churches. As well as rivals for employment, housing and relief, in-migrants brought different beliefs and forms of religious practice. Scotland had a population on the move with a consequent loss of the social control from neighbourhood and family: any notion of the face-to-face society was unstuck as long-held authorities were undermined. The cellular housing that resulted from the subdivision of older central housing stock created an element of facelessness and neighbourhood turnover. For the organised religions, ill-formed social hierarchies replaced the paternalistic society of the eighteenth century with 'disorder'. The gin palaces and backroom drinking dens brought danger to Scotland's morals. Where there was poverty or crime, then the abuse of alcohol was the first target of the reformers' zeal. The underlying fear of public inebriation, and the social ills that were readily attributed to excess imbibing, were projected as a consequence of the word of God no longer being heard by large sections of society.

The challenges facing organised religion were based on contrasts drawn. The dichotomies of the age were powerful pillars of interpretation: the contrast between pious rural society and secular urban society; the contrast between notions of respectability and the eligibility to poor relief. At first sight it was a crisis of faith, that secularisation was on the march in a society rationalised through industrial work and instrumental education. But there was a disconnection between religious attendance and belief, and recent scholarship has confirmed that religious belief was begotten and sustained as strongly as ever, as continuity in this time of change. And even if statistics are to be used, then rather than the great upheavals of the 1840s finding Scots shying away from their churches, attendance remained steady or in places grew, peaking in 1905. This suggests that the secularisation of Scottish society did not begin in earnest until the twentieth century, lagging behind modernity's arrival, yet still contemporaries feared a loss of godliness amongst the masses.

That Scotland's various church leaders shared concerns over the threat of urbanisation to the number of adherents was seen in their innovative and expansive action to reach out to Scottish society. Their first target was the apparent mismatch between where the new concentrations of people lived and where the churches were to be found. Thomas Chalmers became convener of the Church of Scotland's Committee on Church Extension in 1834. Three years later he estimated that 40,000 individuals in Edinburgh were without church facilities and that while nine churches had recently been built, there was as many as thirty churchless congregations in the capital. In Glasgow, by comparison, he estimated that 60,000 were churchless. The Evangelical wing of the church used each approximation as evidence that more congregations should be established close to where the industrial workers were now located.

To bring religion to the urban people, Chalmers had experimented with a 'Godly Commonwealth' of small cooperating
communities, first in the parish of St John's in Glasgow (1819)
and later in Edinburgh (1844) as part of an expansion of sixty
parishes in the city. Chalmers projected that this experiment
of elders taking a proactive role in the lives of their community would be the means through which the poor could reject
state aid or state patronage and be independent of all but faith.
Writing in *On Political Economy* (1832), Chalmers argued that
neither free trade nor social legislation could achieve lasting
social improvement. The permanent wellbeing of society was
to be secured by educating people in the communal values of
benevolence and cooperation through the parochial structures
of the national church. It was an influential rhetoric with worldwide appeal that spoke to the challenge of bringing religion to
the anonymity of the city. Having formed the Glasgow City
Mission in 1826, David Naismith took these ideas of personal
intervention abroad and was instrumental in the establishment
of city missions in England, Dublin and New York.

THE DISRUPTION

Tensions within the Church of Scotland over how aggressively
to build new churches in the towns and cities soon came up
against a structural disconnect between the present and the past.
Probably only the Scots would have split their church in two
for something that seemed from the outside to be so unspec-
tacular as the stale issue of patronage. The Evangelical ministers
within the Church of Scotland had grown frustrated in their
campaign to persuade the Parliamentarians at Westminster to
remove patronage, a right claimed back to John Knox and the
Reformation. The General Assembly of 1834 passed the Veto
Act to allow male heads of families in the parish to reject a
patron's choice of minister, to protect against the 'intrusion' of a
minister who did not have the support of the congregation. But
the government continued to side with the landowners and the
Court of Session found the Veto Act an infringement of the civil

rights of the patrons and the ministers they chose, a decision confirmed by the House of Lords in 1839.

Following on from the failure of Lord Aberdeen's attempt at reframing the Veto Act in a compromise motion in 1840, the church in 1842 issued its statement of ecclesiastical jurisdiction through its Claim of Right. The Claim asserted Christ as the head of the church and the church's independence in spiritual matters: 'a line of demarcation between things civil and things ecclesiastical [is] clearly established, and the exclusive jurisdiction of the Church Courts in ecclesiastical matters thoroughly secured'. Recalling the Glorious Revolution of 1688 as well as the 1707 Union, the Evangelicals in the Church of Scotland divided civil and ecclesiastical matters – or 'governments', as was the language used. Moreover, the church claimed complete control over spiritual and ecclesiastical matters; yet Lord John Russell countered that such matters could not avoid the reach of civil courts merely because they were ecclesiastical concerns. The consequence, he suggested, was that the Veto Act would set aside the Act of 1712 made by the British Parliament. Despite these ghosts being evoked, scholars have generally warned against regarding the Disruption as a nationalist event in political terms, yet it was culturally important for what it meant for the ethos of the Scots.

Unable to secure the Evangelicals' aims in the Assembly, the retiring Moderator Dr Welsh read out their protest statement. Chalmers led the walk from the Assembly to a temporary gathering at Tanfield Hall along with a crowd 300 strong: 38 per cent of the ministers and around 40 per cent of the church's congregations would eventually leave. The 474 ministers and probationers who signed the deed of demission left their manses, glebes (parish land) and stipends behind once Chalmers' 'Affectionate Representation' was adopted by the General Assembly and set out the basic structure of the Free Church. The ministers freshly loosed from their pulpits preached on hillsides, in barns and upon water, wherever they could find a space and a landowner who sympathised with the cause. The pull of the new church varied. In Glasgow the popularity of the

Free Church was a development out of the church extension
movement that Chalmers had campaigned so vigorously for.
In the towns it was the most active of the new-moneyed middle
classes, a younger generation of the bourgeoisie than those who
remained, who were its most potent proponents. In the Borders
support came from one-time Seceders who had rejoined the kirk
in the hope of its evangelisation. In the Highlands and Islands,
particularly in the west, the Free Church was another institution
of protest by people who had long suffered under the old institutional order and their social leaders. Figures show predominance
of secession in urban over rural areas. And there was little, if any,
Free Church presence in the predominantly Catholic islands of
Barra and South Uist.

One of the features of this spectacular event was the energy
put into it – a middle-class response from a group who had
forgone £100,000 a year. Nor was it a knee-jerk response.
Detailed planning allowed the new church to quickly build
churches and begin paying ministers their stipend. Most materi-
ally the establishment of the Sustentation Fund was planned in
advance and organised thereafter with efficiency and without
sympathy. At the first meeting of the Free Church Assembly,
687 congregational associations had been formed, with 239
already up and working, having contributed £17,000 to the
central fund. In addition to that, £105,000 had been contributed
to build churches: within five years 730 new churches and 400
manses had been or were under construction. A new teaching
college was established in Edinburgh and Sunday schools were
set up to cater for the young. Those with money or the ability to
raise loans dominated the kirk session.

Some remarkably energetic champions aided the Free
Church's inauguration. Dr Robert Candlish (1806–73), who
was influenced by Chalmers' preaching in St John's and was
Minister of St George's West in Edinburgh in 1834, had organised the 'Scotch Convocation' of ministers to discuss their
prospects and responsibilities back in 1841. Thomas Guthrie
(1803–73) was another great fundraiser whose sense of social
responsibility lay behind his *Plea for Ragged Schools*, advocat-

ing for non-sectarian schools. Guthrie's *The Gospel in Ezekiel* sold more than 50,000 copies. At the instigation of Candlish, Hugh Miller (1802–56) became editor and later proprietor of *The Witness*, the Free Church newspaper. The geologist from Cromarty had come to the attention of the non-intrusionist leaders following his letter to Lord Brougham opposing the state over the Auchterarder case. *The Witness* promoted the Free Church and passed social comment on matters of the day.

Later reflection suggests that the Disruption was no victory for the Church of Scotland or for the Free Church. After the reform of 1845, neither had the opportunity to administer poor relief or maintain the prominent quasi-governmental role present before the split. But the process of creating a new church did confirm to Scots the importance of Presbyterianism. These two churches, along with the newly merged United Secession Church and Relief Church (formed into the United Presbyterian Church in 1847), meant that in 1851 Presbyterianism could claim over four-fifths of Scotland's adherents.

THE CENSUS OF RELIGIOUS WORSHIP

Patronage remained one of the major points of division between the three main Presbyterian churches: it was the cause of sixty disputes between 1843 and 1869 before being abolished in 1874. These debates internal to the churches should be analysed in conjunction with the Census of Religious Worship taken in 1851. Together they were the pivotal points of crisis for the Church of Scotland.

The outcome of the 1851 census of religious worship is notoriously difficult to interpret with any confidence. The census was taken as Parliament debated whether state aid should be extended to keep pace with the extension movement. It is difficult to say what constitutes low or high attendance and what, if anything, appearance in church on any given day indicates about religious belief, or how religion might influence actions in everyday life. With communion only taking place once or twice a year in the Church of Scotland – occasions that would garner larger gatherings – it meant there was one less pressure to attend weekly, although other inducements applied.

There was no compulsion to complete the census form, meaning that underestimates are likely, but it does show trends in Scotland's worship. Those forms returned reveal that 32.2 per cent identified with the Church of Scotland, 31.7 per cent with the Free Church of Scotland, just under 19 per cent with the United Presbyterian Church and 2 per cent with the Reformed Presbyterian Church. It meant that all but 15 per cent were attending Presbyterian worship, a figure of sufficient magnitude to surprise many (some contemporaries thought it high, others who expected a figure nearer 100 per cent thought it low). The results also appeared to offer proof that non-attendance was highest among the industrial working classes in the towns and cities. This sustained those who argued against the extensionists that rather than there being insufficient churches, many were half-empty and secularisation was taking root.

CHURCH DISCIPLINE

After 1860 the Church of Scotland slowly regained its member-ship and the Free Church and United Presbyterian Church grew at a slower rate. The Episcopal Church, by contrast, remained small in these decades, but grew after the 1870s. The kirk session was one part of the Church of Scotland's administra-tive structure that connected godly discipline to social discipline and from that intervened in the lives of the parish. The evidence conflicts on whether kirk session discipline was biased against lifestyles with a strong emphasis on sexual immorality and the consequence of too much drink, and that it predominantly pun-ished those of lower social standing who lived in less respect-able areas of the community than others. One study of the Glasgow records shows a concentration on sexual offences, but no discrimination for class within a remit that covered unethi-cal business transactions and fighting, libel and profanity, and drunkenness. The kirk session, comprising the minister and a group of elders, were selected for their own piety and industriousness and looked to measure those standards against their adherents' conduct. It was a control that changed mid-century with a move away from communal interference if it was believed the matter was one of individual choice. Too much pressure and the individuals concerned would simply not show themselves again, or would change parish; by the 1870s, historian S. J. Brown notes, elders were reluctant to interfere in the lives of women who may, indeed, have been wronged and were not themselves culpable.

RELIGIOSITY

A re-analysis of the 1851 census by C. G. Brown, among others, has disputed the contemporary conclusions that the larger the town or city, the greater the secularisation was, or that the working classes were less likely to attend church than the middle classes. The statistical correlations do not bear out these conclusions and the figures themselves are too weak to show the great variety of churchgoing, where there was much local and regional difference. The kirk session may also have begun to take notice of the important role women played in promoting religion in the home. Children were continually exhorted to learn prayers, say grace before meals, recite the Shorter Catechism, learn proverbs and sing hymns. It was not uncommon for the family's father to read Scripture on Sundays and the mother to be involved in daily prayers and the encouragement of something approaching pious behaviour. Despite the inevitable rejection of such conduct, or its variable imposition, working-class biographies examined by religious historians show the strong influence of religion in the lives of the poor. They show that religious belief was important in an everyday sense, even if not formally indicated by church attendance. Interviews conducted on men and women born between 1872 and 1906 found that 50 per cent of working-class fathers would regularly attend church, a figure matched in Wales but higher than those relating to various counties of England.

Other types of sources used by historians to measure reli-

gious feeling include the diaries of missionary workers who
went round the doors. This again provides mixed evidence. The
belief that God spoke in dreams and visions, a belief sustained
by the Anabaptists and the Quakers, had a certain appeal to the
illiterate sections of the working classes. Most of the literature
stresses the apathy and the indifference of the nineteenth-century working class to religion. However in both the National
Religious Census in 1851 and various smaller religious censuses in a number of localities in 1881, there was again much
variation.

By the choice of the congregation, the sermon tended to be
unscripted, inspired by God although the tendency for waffle
led some ministers to move to the written sermon and, for the
most well-known clergymen, the published sermon. Church
interiors became more decorated in the later part of the nineteenth century and singing was begun mid-century within the
United Presbyterian Church, although two more decades passed
before hymns rather than sung psalms were heard in the Church
of Scotland, with organs having been permitted (after much
debate) in 1866. Adherents would shop around for the minister,
and sermon, of their choice. Millwright John Sturrock attended
three services one Sunday as he searched for his favoured place
of worship in 1860s Dundee.

A further division in the choice of religion was the social
distance maintained through the system of pew rents. This was
widely used throughout the nineteenth century, even by the
most working class of denominations. Pew rents were not in
themselves offensive, but problems arose when there were sharp
gradations in rent, with associated differences in the quality of
seating, or when no free seats were provided for those unable
to pay. Some churches went out of their way to attract the rich.
Other churches benefited from rich middle-class patronage in
return for personal salvation – all to the detriment of the poor's
attendance. New churches were built specifically for the middle
classes, with the poor priced out. There was, then, a gap in the
market for religion – which Dissent's Evangelical activists were
quick to grasp (see p. 217).

The Scottish Episcopal Church continued to survive through-out this century, shorn of much of its Jacobite heritage and the tag 'the English church in Scotland'. Its bishops had met with George IV during his visit to Edinburgh in 1822, and it has been estimated that there were around 10,000 Anglicans in Glasgow in 1839. Around a quarter of the Irish migrants into Scotland were Episcopalians from the north and, as S. J. Brown notes, they brought a strong vein of anti-Catholicism with them. It was a different version of Protestantism:

> To Mr. Ramsay's in the evening – a brilliant room of Episcopalians, quite a different atmosphere from Presbyterians. All full of this morning's meeting; Mr. Addison was perfectly happy with his speech, and gave me the purport of it – either very simple or very vain. Archdeacon Williams a good pursy body: – 'The Episcopal Church is a looxury they don't understand in Scotland.' He said to the ministers on quitting the Assembly: – 'Take care what you are about; you are making history.' The Government still draws 24,000*l.* of Church revenues from Scotland, waiting till the Scotch should become Episcopalian.

It did sound like a lively gathering and the healthy sales and numerous reprints of Ramsay's *Reminiscences of Scottish Life and Character* (1858) confirm that the Dean of Edinburgh had an ear for a good story. A Gaelic Episcopal Society was formed in 1832, but it struggled to retain its ministers with only limited funds as it preached in the Highlands rather than catering for Gaelic-speaking migrants in the cities.

This contrast was more widely felt. S. J. Brown confirms that the harsher aspects of Calvinism seemed increasingly unappeal-ing in the 1820s and 1830s. Predestination, limited atonement and eternal punishment were downplayed in favour of the love of God and forgiveness to sinners. By the end of the period the Westminster Confession of Faith no longer bound the minis-try of the Scottish Presbyterian churches, confirmed first by the United Presbyterian Church (1879), then the Free Church (1893) and finally the Church of Scotland (1914). In 1908 the Church of Scotland invited the United Presbyterian Church to again consider union. By 1911 it was thought best to take

a year of reflection and in 1913 the Church of Scotland sent
a memorandum upon which concrete negotiations could take
place.

ROMAN CATHOLICISM

Resulting from the Relief Act 1829, Roman Catholics in
Scotland no longer suffered from exclusion from public office
or from employment in the universities. Petitions were sent to
Parliament from various parishes in Scotland throughout the
1820s opposing the removal of these restrictions, but this had
died down by 1832 and in that decade the number of Irish
Catholics in Scotland grew as the need for a cheap and flexible
labour force was created by the rapidity of industrialisation.
Most Irish Catholics, however, came in the period of potato
famine from 1846, and over the next – remarkably quick – five
years, this rapid influx revived much of the earlier rhetoric of
hostility. The number of Irish and Scots Catholics found in
the religious census was necessarily low because there was so
little organisation or churches within which worship could be
contained. In 1858 Roman Catholic priests could join and minister in the armed forces. By 1878, when the Roman Catholic
hierarchy was restored, there were around 330,000 Catholics in
Scotland, rising to 365,000 in the 1890s and 513,000 in 1913.

Just as the Church of Scotland of the 1830s tried to
Christianise the town dweller, the Roman Catholic Church in
Scotland embarked on a vigorous church-building programme.
In the 1860s and 1870s, this generation of Catholic migrants
was noted for its devotional activity, including the display of
crucifixes and rosary beads along with the observance of holy
days. The priests attempted to recruit adherents through ultra-
montane devotions (proclaiming the infallibility of the Pope),
and the Catholic Poor Schools Committee was led by those principles and the imperative to convert. In this it was remarkably
successful as a church, increasing the numbers who attended on
a Sunday in particular. It was difficult to persuade other Scots
that there was no conflict between being a Roman Catholic and

being a Scot, simply because that religion marked out the Irish migrant. Yet in the 1870s the Irish saint Lawrence O' Toole was depicted by the Irish National Foresters Benevolent Association as it publicly emphasised its role alongside the Ancient Order of Hibernians in alleviating poverty amongst its brethren in Penicuik, and similar associations existed in other parts of small- and large-town Scotland.

Where Roman Catholicism was strongest in the communities, aggressive Protestantism was frequently to be found. The Irish Scots were less accepting of Presbyterian dominance compared to the Scots Catholics, adding to the national differences. The Ulster-Unionist support found in Glasgow was exploited by the Tories to take urban votes away from the Liberals, linking to the Orange Order to direct their message to individuals not otherwise found in a pew. Scholars have argued that even those who rarely attended mass and were likely to be considered by the parish priest as 'bad Catholics' would still be staunchly loyal to the church and opposed to marriage outside the faith or acceptance of charity from a Protestant organisation.

From small beginnings at the start of the 1840s, the Edinburgh Irish Mission and Protestant Institute developed over the following ten years into a vitriolic critic of what it termed 'Popery' in Scotland. A series of lectures against Roman Catholicism by William Leckie, later of the Scottish Reformation Society, eventually erupted into rioting in 1841. In 1851 one of the diversions of the Protestant youths in Greenock was to plaster the priest's door with filth, and the agitation of that year gave rise to two Protestant journals, *The Bulwark, or Reformation Journal* and *The Scottish Protestant*. They are examples that show the melange of popular opposition to Roman Catholicism within sections of Scottish society. A meeting of the Conference of Scottish Protestants in Edinburgh in 1854 attracted 760 church and lay representatives to castigate the effect of Catholicism 'on all that made Britain great'. Bible Protestantism demanded the cooperation of the Free Church with the Establishment in this matter, and were such a cooperation attained, the Secularists and Papists would, they insisted, soon be overwhelmed. The

Orange Order in Scotland had its membership strength in Protestant Irish migrants and their Scottish-born descendants, particularly in the west of Scotland but also in and around Edinburgh and Dundee. During the commemoration of the battle of the Boyne (1690) on 12 July and throughout the 'walking' (or 'marching') season each year, the Orangemen took possession of the streets to loudly display their Protestant faith and political Unionism.

REVIVALS

Revivalism had been ongoing in Scotland since the start of our period. Itinerant preachers were familiar visitors to various parts of rural Scotland, welcomed most where the presence of the Church of Scotland was weakest. Powerful and emotional, itinerants were usually at the heart of revivalism, and there were Catholic preachers also. At the Unish Revival of 1841–2, led by Tormod Saighdear, much clapping, shouting and swooning abounded as news of the spiritual excitement travelled by word of mouth. Revivalist preachers from America landed in Scotland to enhance and lead revivals in faith, first in Aberdeen in 1858 and then throughout Scotland in 1859 and later in 1873–4. Parish reports to the Free Church of Scotland's Assembly in 1861 found almost two-thirds indicating local interest in revivalism. It was the Free Church rather than the Church of Scotland who warmed most to the movement, hoping to rekindle the excitement of 1843, but still hesitancy remained. Long prayer sessions, sometimes over several days, would be conducted, at times led by those outside the church and done with fervour and excitement. The revivals of the 1870s involved the Americans Dwight L. Moody and Ira D. Sankey who attracted large crowds to hear their uplifting message and songs, claiming thousands into their midst. The revival movement increased church attendance generally and had some impact on lessening interdenominational rivalry, but it hardened opposition to Catholicism. To be 'awakened' was (nearly always) to be Protestant.

WOMEN AND WOMEN RELIGIOUS

Through the doctrinal battles of Scottish Presbyterianism, women were absent from the institutional decision making of the churches, despite making up the bulk of the congregation. Women could not be ordained as ministers or elders. They had, however, been increasingly influential since 1800 in the religiosity of the people, an important corrective from C. G. Brown. The woman in the home was charged with the purity of the family, and Evangelicals, reformers and governments alike understood the family structure as the moral bedrock of society. In the first half of the nineteenth century in the Gaelic parts of the Highlands, liturgy, prayers and scripture were repeated in the memories of the people rather than in the printed books of the church or the tracts of the evangelist. With no readily available Gaelic Bible until 1801, their availability in Skye after another twenty years was still the cause of much enthusiasm, in schools especially. Blasphemy, intemperance and crime were all aspects of male society that women could be seen to help alleviate, influencing their family and peers, building up defences against the morally weak. Women religious were on the frontline of educating children as the Roman Catholic Church re-established its chapels, schools and societies in the second half of the nineteenth century. The Sisters of the Immaculate Conception, the Sisters of Mercy and the Ursulines of Jesus serviced community Sunday schools, industrial schools, convent schools and poor parish schools. As Kehoe has shown, Scottish-born convent superiors were chosen over Irish, French or Italian superiors to inculcate Scottishness in those they taught, especially through their control of girls' schools.

To be pious Christians, then aspects of masculine behaviour had to be curbed; God expected His men not to fall into the ways of depravity and drunkenness. When the moral lives of women were written up in hagiographic form mid-century the favoured outcome of the sketch was a man's conversion and final devotion to God. In novels and in improving and secular press, the moral offensive was widespread. Men were addressed

Figure 9.1 *Scottish Catholic banner depicting St Margaret (on the reverse) and the Lion Rampant, 1908. © National Museums Scotland. Licensor www.scran.ac.uk*

in masculine ways, appealing to their sentiments as men, but in the hope that their world-view would be closer aligned with feminine piety. Muscular Christianity in the form of the rambling society or the Clarion cycling club was an outward response to this preaching. Contemporary autobiographies, too, would tend to chart the life from the irreligion of the self or the parents, to an epiphany leading to salvation.

An inevitable reaction came later in the century when evangelical women were seen to have too much influence, to be too judgemental, but it was a sign of how much piety in life was used to structure everyday behaviour from eating to washing, drinking and working.

DISSENT

Over the three decades since 1832, three events can be identified that led to a growth in the popularity of the Dissenting religions. The first is the Disruption in the Established Church in 1843 that broke the primacy of a single Established Church. The second was the Irish potato famine of 1845–6, which accelerated migration to Scotland and especially helped the Roman Catholic Church to grow into a significant force. The third was the union of the Secession and the Relief Churches in 1847 to create the United Presbyterian Church, a strong Dissenting group. Most of the remaining Seceders (the Auld Lichts) rejoined the Established Church in 1852, and the bulk of the covenanters in the Reformed Presbyterian Church joined the Free Church in 1876.

Dissent in Scotland was about the patronage of the state in the appointment of ministers. The belief that some of the divisions that had once loomed so large were now lessening pushed the disestablishment movement into full swing in the 1870s. The Church of Scotland had petitioned Gladstone to remove patronage in an attempt to bring the other Presbyterian churches into its fold. Gladstone refused, and the Free and United Presbyterian leaders responded by pushing forward proposals for disestablishment in 1872. When the new Disraeli government abolished

patronage in 1874 rather than reconciliation of the three main
Presbyterian churches, it led to the union of the Free Church
and the United Presbyterian Church and a pact to disestablish
the Church of Scotland. As S. J. Brown has argued, '[f]or many
Scots, disestablishment meant the liberation of their national
religion from control by the "British" state'. The Church
of Scotland survived as an establishment by mobilising its
own patriotic claims to being the national church, petitioning
Parliament in 1884 and arguing the church's place at the heart
of Christian Britain. The debate shows just how split this institutional basis of identity had become. Both were true reflections
of Godly Scotland, and both were right.

OUTSIDE THE WALL

'Well Johnnie, what saw you in church?'
'I saw a man bawling in a box, and no man would let him oot.'

Although it was thought in the *North British Review* that the
religious condition was better in Scotland than in England, still
the 'sunken classes' were 'the irreligious classes' who failed to
attend church. Yet churches were also sources of working-class
self-help, as well as various mixes of radical, conservative and
diffident interpretations of Christianity. Rather than Scots being
increasingly unchurched, the churches were foci for a web of
religious promotions. Bible and tract societies distributed literature to the masses, especially from the 1850s, with a combined
print run of eight million tracts produced by Peter Drummond
of Stirling over the mid-century decade. Whether in the form of
small-sized tracts for posting at home or overseas, larger tracts
for distribution at meetings or novels for longer reflection, a
whole gamut of advice was distributed to the people. Home missions were a response to the irreligion in the city, beginning in
the 1810s and most active from the 1850s, although there were
early fears that it would be an encouragement to unconstrained
Evangelicalism and personal faith to the detriment of the church
as an institution. The Salvation Army was established in its

present form in 1878 and already had 100,000 members by 1900. The particular strengths of William Booth's Army lay in the discipline imposed upon its its members and the opportunities for the working class to be involved in the Christian act of providing charity to the very poor. First formed in Glasgow in 1883, the Boys' Brigade was part of the Militia Movement and the Volunteer Movement – despite some protestations to the contrary – and involved the young in drill and outdoor pursuits. The Roman Catholic Church in Scotland sponsored its own Boys' Brigades, such as that in Motherwell, and the movement remained interdenominational. For the opposite sex, the Girl Guides was formed in 1910 after so many girls joined the scouting movement detailed by Baden-Powell in *Scouting for Boys* (1908).

Despite there being no legislation prohibiting Sunday opening, cultural entrenchment called for Sunday to be a day of rest with no outside work, travel, commerce or entertainment other than attendance at church. The Committee for Promoting the Better Observance of the Sabbath arrived to stem the tide of irreligion as it affected personal and family behaviour. Underpinning their campaign was the Commandment: 'Remember the Sabbath day, to keep it holy. Six days shalt thou labour and do all thy work, but the seventh is the Sabbath of the Lord thy God'. Seamen advocated for their day of rest, but steamboats were notorious as floating bars – and Sabbitarians fought many long battles against Sunday trippers. Others argued that control should be relaxed, especially for the labouring classes who had no other full day without work. In the 1860s debate raged on whether the New Testament did in fact preclude outdoor recreation.

OTHER BELIEFS AND NON-BELIEFS

Along with the three Presbyterian churches that prevailed over the institutional expression of their faith in Scotland, a number of other denominations came under the banner of Protestantism. When the Free Church papermaker Charles Cowan first stood in Edinburgh for election, to the 1847 Parliament, he was

Table 9.1   Religious adherences of voters for Charles Cowan, 1847

Free Church of Scotland	563
Presbyterian	493
Established Church of Scotland	157
Baptists	71
Congregationalists	69
Episcopalians	35
Secessionists	20
Wesleyan	9
Friends	8
Roman Catholic	7
Unitarians	6
Reformationists	2
Glassite	1

an unexpected success, defeating the renowned historian and politician Thomas Babington Macaulay. In preparation for his re-election in 1852, Cowan's supporters conducted a religious survey of all those who had previously given him their vote. He received just over 2,000 votes, with 1,441 of the voters declaring their religious adherence.

The dominance of the Free Church and the (United) Presbyterian Church support for this Liberal, who was fighting on a ticket of opposition to state support for the Roman Catholic seminary school at Maynooth in Ireland, shows the political motivation of those who were outside the Established Church of Scotland. The long tail of religious faith gives some indication of the range of denominations represented amongst Edinburgh's voting public.

Regarding such activity as pagan in origin or simply influences of the Roman Catholic Church, the Presbyterian churches did not celebrate Christmas and Easter. Paganism did have its adherents but it was difficult for them, as it was for agnostics and non-believers, to make their views public. The secularist movement gained some support throughout Britain following the radical thinker Charles Bradlaugh's formation and presidency of the National Secular Society (1855–90), and through Bradlaugh's partnership with Annie Besant in the 1870s, peaking in their notorious trial for publishing information on birth control in 1877. Within the labouring classes a mix of the secular and temporal ideas sustained the Chartist churches and the search for a workers' 'jubilee' (emancipation). This was not the realisation of a socialist utopia, but a better balance between the needs of the employer and the conditions experienced by the workers, with the goal of using religion as a means of achieving inter-class cooperation. Socialist Sunday schools were another manifestation of this interplay of the modern industrial world and strands of an increasingly influential social gospel.

Notwithstanding firm adherence to organised religion in Scotland, for some churchgoers there was no conflict between their faith and their belief in the existence of the fairy folk, superstition more widely and the power of magic. Hugh Miller, the geologist and editor of the Free Church's *The Witness*, recalled without judgement that when voyaging down Loch Maree in 1823 a visitor was told by the boatman, in Gaelic, that 'Yon other island [Eilean Suthainn] is famous as the place where the good people [fairies] meet every year to make submission to their Queen.' Such stories were easy to believe. Those said to have second sight, able to see both the spiritual world alongside the world around them, were heeded but thought cursed as they envisioned the state of dead friends and relatives. The research of historian Elizabeth Ritchie has shown that 'healing wells' were found throughout highland Scotland, where the healing power of the water was readily conflated with the touch of the saint. Because Roman Catholic theology was more accepting of the use of physical objects to meld mind, body and soul, the well did not straightforwardly carry the overtones of magic it did within the Presbyterian community. Incantations using objects or rituals were persisted with, as was walking around the well three times and leaving a token of appreciation. Highland Scots had a ready supply of narratives of the otherworld of fairies and kelpies, of healing rituals, of prophecy and of the insight of 'keen-eyed men' and 'peering-eyed women'. The Fairy Bridge on Skye was the place chosen for Unish Revival meetings from 1841 as well as for preaching and communion. Elsewhere, such as in Shetland in the 1890s, folk belief remained forceful within aspects of women's culture: folk cures for humans and animals alike and beliefs associated with fishing and farming were part of contemporary life as it structured women's retelling of their shared heritage.

Spiritualism and animism also worried theologians. James Bailie Fraser wrote to Sir George Mackenzie in 1843 to discuss 'animal magnetism' and clairvoyance, or 'ultra vision'. Fraser set up an experiment to establish if a young woman 'who shows the highest class of Phenomena', upon entering into a trance, could describe the contents of his Inverness drawing room while she was in Edinburgh. The Victorian obsession with the accoutrements of mourning manifested itself in a fascination with the afterlife. Arthur Conan Doyle had been so convinced he had felt his brother's death in South Africa, while he himself was in England, that it confirmed his conversion to spiritualism. Doyle toured tirelessly giving lectures on the topic in his final years, often meeting with ridicule. He was also to support the authenticity of the Cottingley Fairies photographed by the children Elsie Wright and Frances Griffiths in 1917. Animistic religions similarly raised eyebrows in Scotland. Explaining the issue in 1910, Professor W. P. Paterson said that animism – ascribing a soul to natural and inanimate objects – was the natural philosophy of uncivilised man. He likened the way a child looked upon his or her dolls or teddy bears to the way 'the savage looks upon his idols'. This produced laughter, but 'in the case of the Animistic heathen, who took it very seriously, [it was] a crushing and destroying nightmare weighing upon his soul'. These beliefs were deemed both a 'terror and immoral superstition' to society that should be resisted within the 'civilised world'.

This increasingly complex interplay of scientific and religious belief was a feature of the later Victorian years. Charles Darwin famously delayed publication of *The Origin of Species* until 1859 as he wrestled with his religious convictions. A later cause célèbre with Scottish origins was the discovery and authentication by Sir Arthur Keith of the Piltdown Man as a previously unknown early human. Keith was born in Old Machar,

Aberdeenshire in 1866, and upon graduating from Aberdeen University in 1888 he went to the goldfields of Thailand as a physician before returning to work in London, being Conservator at the Royal College of Surgeons (1908) at the time of the Piltdown discovery. That there was such doubt regarding the veracity of this extant evidence of early man (and it was indeed a hoax) is perhaps suggestive of how interspersed science and faith had become in Edwardian Scotland. Spiritualism, the Cottingley Fairies and healing wells all seemed to offer, for some at least, new scientific ways to link present-day life with that of our ancestors and what was to come in the afterlife. This was a far cry from the spiritual and social bind of the kirk session, or reciting the Shorter Catechisms in school. Yet Scots had learned new ways of conducting and controlling themselves, and this forms the theme of the next chapter.

10

Controlling Ourselves and Others

The pull of the earth's gravity has been undeniably consistent in keeping the Scots on the ground, but what stopped them from acting like a bunch of mavericks with no responsibility for their actions? What rubbed Scots up the wrong way, and what did they try to do about it? How did the Scots protest? We have seen the importance of religious activities in the everyday, but how else did the Scots deliver social order to their lives? These are the questions covered by this chapter. Part of being 'a people' is acting in socially acceptable ways, valuing certain action over others and condemning unacceptable behaviours. Societal stability develops from a mixture of structure and action, of rules and regulations, which construct the social norms that control 'individual and group' behaviour. Nothing is as enveloping as gravity, of course, but still a remarkably powerful set of negotiated constraints culturally formed can be delineated to explain how the Scots controlled and governed their nation, stewarded their land and policed their public behaviour and that of others.

CONSTITUTION AND POLITICS

The Scots have a long and continuing history of interaction with their southern neighbour. After more than two centuries of monarchical union and a century of political union, the experience of British government was well known in 1832. From the remnants of the Dundas family's political dynasty, the Scottish politicians knew how to work the system. The year

1807 brought little to mark the centenary of Union, but still
the clauses of that legislation were invoked as Parliamentarians
came to negotiate the first major expansion of the electoral
franchise in 1832.

Some Scots could not see the benefit of extending the franchise. Sir John Peter Grant, from the line of Rothiemurchus,
summed up a Parliamentary debate on changing the representation of Edinburgh by making a wider point: while there might
only be thirty-three individuals enfranchised with the vote in
Scotland's capital, they held a public trust, and so he believed
it counter to the articles of Union to debate their position.
Otherwise, he speculated, Scotland would be governed like a
province or colony, a situation against the best interests of the
'general welfare of the united kingdom'. Others, such as Sir
George Clarke, wondered why Edinburgh was being singled
out for this alteration to the ancient privileges of the city, when
such rights, or 'delinquencies' as yet unproved, were no different from those granted to the boroughs and cities of England.
Clarke mused that the great advances Scotland had made under
the present system in the arts and sciences and in the moral
condition of the people meant there was no need for franchise
reform.

It suggests, for these Scots at least, some confidence in the
ability to exert control within the pre-reform structure, that
those who identified with the nation could govern Scotland
effectively. Yet at times it was difficult for the Parliamentarians
to maintain the moral high ground when they were so distant
from their kingdom. As the various elements of franchise
reforms and democratisation were debated, comment was made
that much of this was going on in London, not Edinburgh. Sir
Thomas Dick Lauder was one such politician resented for being
embedded in the politics of London rather than those of home:

> He swears that he was check'd in Fife,
> That he's lo'ed Scotland a' his life,
> That o' her cause in every strife
> He will be the promoter.
> An' aff he's set frae Lunnon town

Wi' English law an' English gown,
An' to Auld Reekie he is boun'
To catch a Scottish voter.

Nor did poet and contributor to *Blackwood's Magazine* William Edmonstoune Aytoun escape the satire, acquiring the moniker 'Union Laddie' for questioning the value of the 1832 reform and for his views on what the Union settlement was thought to be. Pro-reform rallies were held as the legislation was being discussed first for England, and post-reform celebrations celebrated the success of that legislation and the Scottish equivalent. Glasgow and Edinburgh hosted gatherings of tens of thousands of people and these were mirrored in other parts of the country. Scottish and British symbolism that mixed Wallace with the Magna Carta was on display at the Edinburgh rally; the tradesmen were warned, and successfully it would seem, to moderate their behaviour and show the world that they, too, were equivalent 'men of property and intelligence' worthy of the nation's trust. What further confirmed the Scots' approval for these changes was the reward their voters bestowed at the urban ballot boxes to those candidates who identified with the Whig party, meaning those who had pushed hardest for the £10 franchise. Voters had the benefit of casting two votes. They could cast those for two candidates of the same political party ('straights') or for candidates of different parties ('splitting'); alternatively, they could decide to use only one of their votes so not to benefit another candidate ('plumping').

While working men continued to make the case for their Parliamentary representation, the Scottish Chartists forged a platform that mixed electoral reform with worker interest. The Chartists were among the earliest to campaign against the Corn Laws and the landlords' interest, and leaned more towards 'moral force' rather than the physical alternative to make their claims. The movement was not separate from its more rumbustious southern equivalent, and aggressive posturing was part of their armoury, but the Scottish Chartists preferred to fight for social justice by invoking the Old Testament and the language of religion. Later better known for his detective work in the US, Allan Pinkerton shows this social morality both as a Glasgow Chartist and as a teetotaller in 1839. And rather than mobilise the worker through examples of the violent disturbance and the rhetoric of Feargus O'Connor, periodicals, cheap printed circulars, newspapers and preaching at Chartist churches were all part of the campaign. Generally it was peaceful, but riots did on occasion break out, such as the one in Glasgow in 1848 that led to five deaths.

The second reform of the Representation of the People Act, in 1868, kept the £10 property qualification but added household suffrage, including occupiers and owners (of 12 months' duration) and £10 lodgers. From this change, around 100,000 adult men were added to the burgh franchise with a further 38,000 added in the period up to 1880, making Scotland's burgh electorate that year 198,669, with a further 95,000 enfranchised in the counties. Although the skilled workers were now included, this was, in the phrase of political historian Michael Dyer, a lopsided reform. It changed the basis of the burgh electorate to household suffrage, but redistributed seats in a way inconsistent with regional growth in the population, and the legislation did not give those in the counties the same privileges as those in the towns. More importantly, the legislation did not enfranchise women.

All male householders, renters and landowners, again at the £10 value, gained the right to vote in the third Reform Act of 1884, the main intention being to provide country votes with the privileges already in place for the urban electorate. In addition to each returning two Members of Parliament, Edinburgh and Glasgow also elected an additional MP voted for by the students and staff of the respective universities, a privilege that also applied to St Andrews and Aberdeen universities. One perhaps underrated reform of this period was the Ballot Act 1872 that brought in private voting. No longer were poll books to be published showing name, address and vote. It meant a potential run of rich historical sources was at an end but the Scots were protected in expressing themselves through the ballot box without fear of reprisal. They would continue to develop a strong coalescence of political and religious welfarist interventions with the formation in the 1870s in Glasgow of the Christian Socialist movement, led by John Glasse, a Church of Scotland minister. There was also a strong Christian message to socialism as it developed in the 1880s and 1890s. Socialist Sunday schools and Labour churches were interlinked with Clarion clubs held fast by the Christian Socialism of key leaders, Keir Hardie especially.

POLITICS OF THE NATION

The Reform legislation brought Scottish politics out of its late-eighteenth-century phase of management into a history of party formation, influence and discipline. Not exactly the same electoral structure as England, but close enough, and when Scottish national identity formed around the working of the Union bargain it did so within this structure.

When the nation within Union was debated, it was because 'we' were losing something of ourselves to an unresponsive Other – the British state (rather than Catholic Ireland). It was never a dominant fear, if membership of nationalist groups is the measurement, but still it structured Scots' lives through the objectification of their national past. That the Scots' concerns were real and practical and not simply posturing is evidenced by town council representation on – and support for – the two nationalist organisations of the Victorian era: the National Association for the Vindication of Scottish Rights (NAVSR) in the 1850s and the Scottish Home Rule Association (SHRA) from 1886.

The need for an association to guard the religious and political privileges of the Scots under Union was first argued in a letter to *The Scotsman* on the eve of the 1852 general election which warned of increasingly centralised government at Westminster. In a follow-up contribution to the same newspaper the next week, the plan was introduced for the formation of a society to protect the independence of local decision making. The first gatherings of the NAVSR were held in Edinburgh and Glasgow the next year, with the movement gaining support from all manner of local and national politicians. As an organisation it was effectively run out of the home office of return migrants and brothers James and John Grant, ably supported by their half-pay soldier father James and the politicians Charles Cowan and Archibald Montgomerie, the Earl of Eglinton and Winton. The town councils in Scotland had sent representatives to subscribe their support and it was they who organised and collated a series of petitions to Parliament. Criticised for its many aims and objectives, the Association's campaigning targets united around heraldic slights and imbalances in public spending and taxation that appeared to show Scotland paying more and receiving less than its fair share. The reason, they claimed, was that Westminster had shifted its focus away from domestic matters under the strain of running the Empire – governing others, not ourselves. The domestic nation was also neglected by the bureaucratic tendency to centralise functions in and around Whitehall. Edwin Chadwick extolled the benefits of centralised knowledge for the implementation of sanitary reforms. But what these nationalists knew as 'local national' affairs were poorly served from decisions made by faceless 'functionaries' who did not know the local situation and were always likely to push costs onto municipal rates. The Association's Unionist-Nationalism supported the bargain of 1707 by reforming the eighteenth-century political arrangement to better govern in the local national age.

Both James Grant in 1853 and the later home rulers sent petitions to Queen Victoria. Petitions and addresses to the Queen were exempt from postage and petitions sent to Parliamentarians and the Lords were also free of postage charges if under 2lb in weight. The Australian Scottish nationalist Theodore Napier claimed over 100,000 signatures in 1898 for the largest of these pleas to Her Majesty, securing support from Scots in Canada, Australia and New Zealand, South Africa, the Transvaal, India and the US among them. Napier insisted that both England and Scotland had ceased to exist in 1707 and that the proper way for the English to consider the matter was to wonder at being called

Irish, because they were proud of being English, 'not because the Irish are to be considered an inferior race'. But some newspaper correspondents thought perhaps the best colloquial name for the United Kingdom and its empire was 'Wiscie' (Wales, Ireland, Scotland, Colonies, India and England), such was the levity they ascribed to Scotland's complaints.

William Gladstone's 'zealous support' for a home rule scheme that would reduce the burden on the Imperial Parliament developed from analyses rooted in the nationalist arguments of the 1850s. His proposal for devolution was premised on local government as the constitutional solution: 'If you ask me what I think of Home Rule, I must tell you that I will only answer when you tell me how Home Rule is related to local government.' He summed up the spectre of government overcentralisation in London, the very basis of the NAVSR's analysis of Scotland's ills. But Gladstone's reluctance to jeopardise his priority of home rule for Ireland led him to cool his support for the Scots.

Gladstone's reluctance in this matter persuaded disaffected Liberals to form the Scottish Home Rule Association in 1886. In the previous year an impressive array of Scotland's nobility, MPs from both Conservative and Liberal parties, plus representatives of the parochial boards, town councils and public bodies, had packed the Free Assembly Hall in Edinburgh under the banner of a 'National Meeting'. Edinburgh's Lord Provost, Sir George Harrison, argued that there ought to be more than one national life in the British nation, that it was difficult to pass a Scottish Bill without £10,000 being spent on it and that the Scots were proud of their separate institutions from England (adding to the amusement of the audience that the English were welcome to their own institutions, those that suited them better). Future Prime Minister A. J. Balfour, in supporting the first resolution of the meeting that more satisfactory arrangements were needed for the better administration of Scotland, answered the charge that by emphasising the differences between England and Scotland then the inevitable ending would be something akin to home rule, declaring that 'all in this room, like him, were at one in thinking that no legislative act had been so fruitful of good consequences to the countries concerned, as the act of Union between Scotland and England'. Balfour would act as President of the Local Government Board between June 1885 and January 1886, Secretary of State for Scotland in 1886 and Chief Secretary for Ireland between 1887 and 1891 when the landlord issue and home rule were particularly acute. The gathering were merely 'asking for the carrying out of a thing which was stipulated in the Act of Union', suggested the Marquess of Bute (John Patrick Crichton-Stuart). The nationalists argued that the eighteenth-century Union was now too inflexible to manage the complex affairs of Scotland and England and their Empire: the tightening of the bonds between Britain and America and between Belgium and Holland were examples cited of unintended separations when there was no willingness to decentralise power. The pressure paid off and a Scottish Secretary and Scottish Office (or Scotch Office, as it was first styled) were established in 1885, although proposals for a home rule Parliament, or the federal concept of Home Rule All Round (devolved legislatures for England, Wales and Scotland, along with Ireland), lacked sufficient support.

The idea of a 'union of the Empire' brought Irish speakers to address the first congress of the SHRA in 1886. Those who supported Scottish home rule believed that too often the Irish nationalist voice was raised with nothing heard to balance it. To this end, speakers T. W. Russell and the Rev. Dr Hanna of Belfast argued that the changes proposed by Charles Parnell would be dangerous: 'He would not allow a rat or a mouse in all Ireland to move except under the cognizance of the police (hissing and interruption).' The visitors argued that Ireland would be pacified by disestablishment of the church, and if achieved the

> three kingdoms will be joined by this act in stronger bonds of union, and the people of England, of Scotland, and of Ireland would vie with each other in the exhibitions of loyalty to the person and to the Throne of Her Majesty.

Charles Waddie, honorary secretary of the Scottish Home Rule Association, attempted to rouse support in Ireland for Scotland's cause in 1896, but was rebuffed. 'Englishmen don't like Irishmen, whereas the average Englishman has the greatest respect for a Scotsman,' he concluded. Writing to *The Times* on the 'Grand Committee Dodge', Waddie wondered how it would operate if all seventy-two Scottish MPs plus a smaller number of English, Irish and Welsh members were taken out to debate Scottish issues. Would it happen in some back room, or after business in the chamber had finished at midnight or 2 a.m.? And would Parliament continue with British legislation if debates were concurrent, a crazy situation when the English Solicitor-General, the Home Secretary and the Duchy of Lancaster, plus former Prime Minister Gladstone, were all Scottish MPs? Waddie regarded the development of the Grand Committee as a sop to Scottish demands as Parliament moved on Irish Home Rule, still avoiding the case for Home Rule All Round: 'Home Rule for Ireland alone or first is too preposterous to need further argument against it. It stinks in the nostrils of every thinking man,' he railed against the realities he faced.

As the Victorian age began to fade, the Young Scots Society was formed in 1900 and became part of the 'New Liberalism' at the 1906 general election. And it was during the 1910 general election that the Society became extraordinarily active, distributing thousands of pamphlets and holding hundreds of meetings on behalf of liberalism rather than sketching out the practicalities of establishing a Scottish Parliament.

SUFFRAGE

While nationalists argued for Scotland's rights, they made little if any mention of women. This is not to assume, however, that women were excluded from the electoral franchise unthinkingly. The framers of the 1832 electoral reform stated that those entitled to vote would be 'men of property and intelligence'. Women as with the non-property-owning majority were barred, lacking the stake in society that property ownership entailed.

Both groups were absent from 'public life', at least as it was understood at Westminster or the office of the Lord Advocate. But while men might change their material well-being and thus gain what became the £10 franchise, women of all social standings were excluded from voting in a Parliamentary election or for standing for election to Parliament.

Yet there remains strong evidence of women's political involvement. In the early 1830s abolition of slavery and workers' welfare were popular causes, with sixteen emancipation or freedmen's aid societies established by women prior to 1868 and twenty-three Chartist associations in the 1840s. Women, as has been discussed earlier, were at the forefront of religious education both in the schools and in the home, and undertook formal involvement in local government after 1872. Parliamentary ridicule and defeat for John Stuart Mill's attempts to include women's suffrage as part of the electoral reform bill for England and Wales in 1867 prompted the forming of a wave of women's suffrage societies up and down the country. Edinburgh's National Society for Women's Suffrage was formed at the end of that year and before the Reform legislation for Scotland had wound its way through Parliament. By the time the women's vote was again denied at the 1884 reform there were twenty-four women's suffrage societies in Scotland, a campaign that continued to gain support from the earlier abolitionist and Chartist activities as well as from the active role of women in home and foreign missionary and welfare societies. The fight for the women's vote continued in auxiliary branches of the main political parties throughout the 1880s and through trade unions in the 1890s, with strong support from Keir Hardie and Tom Johnston. An article on women's suffrage read before the Dundee and District Women's Liberal Association in December 1899, for example, confirmed that suffrage was not about giving all women the vote ('so unreasonable') but for them to have the same rights as men. Canvassing and 'tea-partying' was no longer of value, as the Women's Liberal Association pushed for a serious political and philosophical analysis of women's exclusion.

Figure 10.1 '*On the Warpath*'. *After a hammer was thrown into a Dundee post office window, the local suffragettes were likened to North American Indians by cartoonist Tom Ross in 1912.* © *Dundee Central Library. Licensor www.scran.ac.uk*

Depictions are found in songs and postcards of the early twentieth century ridiculing the disorderly home of the suffragist, their timorous husbands and neglected children. This was a reaction to the increasing visibility of the campaign. The Glasgow and West of Scotland Association for Women's Suffrage was formed in 1902, and ten years later the Scottish Churches League for Woman Suffrage formed on the basis that sexual equality meant political equality. In between, the Scottish Federation of the National Union of Women's Suffrage Societies was created in 1909 to coordinate campaigning, and had some sixty-five suffrage societies affiliated by 1916. Suffrage women opposed the intrusion of the state's decennial census into their lives in 1911. The Scottish universities and male societies offered support for a campaign that became more aggressive and violent in the Edwardian period. Scots-born Marion Wallace-Dunlop went on hunger strike while in prison as a means of highlighting the suffrage cause, and it became a well-used tactic, with the first occurrence in a Scottish prison by Ethel Moorhead in 1914. In 1912 Moorhead had broken the glass at the Wallace Monument and in 1914 was implicated in an attempt to burn down Burns' cottage in Alloway. At this point most suffrage campaigners shifted their attention to the war wounded and the development of political alliances with the Labour party. In the Representation of the People Act 1918, female householders and wives of householders aged over thirty were given the vote; after a further expansion in 1921 an equal franchise was achieved in 1928. At this point, in a nation of more women than men, the larger population had a stake in society. To paraphrase Virginia Woolf: 'How could Scotland belong to a woman, how could she be a part of it, if she did not have the vote?'

POLICING

Within the constitutional and electoral structure that governed their nation, Scots did not lose sight of the need to control their everyday society. To be 'who we are' was about regulating (socially constructed) behaviours as much as it was about the positive rhetoric of the nation. Contemporaries perceived moral depravation as the major failing of modern urban society, and transmission of immorality into crime and disturbance was feared to undermine civil society. While the idea of 'being Scotland' was a carefully constructed identity, it remained susceptible to challenge by 'deviant' behaviour. Policing the nation, and controlling ourselves, was about self-governing too.

Modern policing in Britain dates back to the 1829–56 period. Low-quality recruits and a concomitant instability in numbers bedevilled mid-Victorian policing. The force was primarily concerned with maintaining social order and protecting property, being generally poorly equipped to detect crime. It was not until he had emigrated to North America mid-century that Allan Pinkerton formed the detective agency that took his name. Occasionally there would be a sensation, such as the trial of Madeleine Smith, accused of administering arsenic to her French partner Émile L'Angelier in March 1857. The trial focused attention on the quality of the evidence gathered as much as the offending poisoned cocoa, leading to her acquittal. But most crime was blunt and simplistic, generally the consequence of too much alcohol.

Contemporary reports were quick to use the term 'riot' to describe many social disturbances that were little more than family fights brought out into the streets or some youths looking for entertainment by throwing stones. In law, a disturbance became a riot when the magistrate or delegate reads the Riot Act to the crowd, instructing them to disperse or face arrest. Scots gathered together to protest, make noise or make mischief for all manner of reasons. Like the pre-industrial past, riots were often fundamentally conservative, the claim protested being nothing more than a demand to return to a previous state of affairs or a means for the people to assert their social values when there appeared no other recourse. In Durness in Sutherland, a group of around 400 men and women 'armed with bludgeons and other weapons' gathered in 1841 to attack the local Sheriff-Substitute and Procurator Fiscal. The protest was a reaction to Lord Reay's plans to end fishing and introduce sheep farming, a plan that sought the removal of a number of crofters who had fallen behind with their rents. The two men were threatened with their lives if they stayed the night in the parish; some proposed to destroy their horses and gig, others to strip them naked and turn them out on the rocks. The *Inverness Courier* called for sufficient military force to be sent 'to teach the misguided people that the laws of the country must and will be vindicated, and those to whom the execution of them is entrusted protected'. But it was a sign of the tensions that existed between customary practices, obligations, property and the rule of law.

Rural and urban food riots and smaller disturbances were not unknown in Victorian Scotland, and again they tended to be conservative, looking to restore prices and agreements previously held. A riotous crowd formed in Paisley in 1855 when it was found that the local wholesalers had colluded to increase the price of potatoes by 1s to 5s per stone. After a public meeting at which protests were voiced – but before further peaceful protests could be carried out – an effigy of the chairman of the associated potato dealers was burned and his premises stoned over a two-hour period. The events prompted a similar disturbance at Johnstone the same week against the grocer who acted as the marker for potato prices in the town.

As well as a day of celebration, the monarch's birthday was a popular day for voicing grievances in Scotland, as it was more widely in Britain and within the Empire. On board one emigrant ship to New Brunswick in 1840 the passengers cleaned up their appearances and were served pudding by way of festivity for the day, but at home the monarch's birthday celebrations could easily get out of hand, showing evidence of flammability simmering in the streets. When a great number of trades lads and schoolboys gathered in Perth 'mischievously inclined, as wont is' in 1843, they happened to 'hoot and buffet' a couple of soldiers from the 68th depot stationed in the town. The two soldiers were rescued by a group of comrades who reacted by taking over the main streets of the town, assailing all who came near, with many 'cruelly beaten by this band of lawless and infuriated soldiery'. The soldiers swept the street left and right, carrying sticks scooped out at the head and filled with lead. Finally quelled by a sufficient gathering of police and special constables, sixteen were jailed and the regiment was quickly marched off to Stirling.

While the majority of urban disturbances were relatively minor, the authorities' response would often (even to contemporary eyes) appear heavy-handed. A snowball riot by a group of Edinburgh University students in 1838 caused problems for the local police force stretched by a concurrent cotton spinners' trial. The local press complained about the military being called

238

out for such an incident and were impressed that the Procurator Fiscal was able to bring context to the charges:

> He would be most happy if none of them were found guilty – (Cheers) – That there could be no doubt that some of them had been apprehended innocently – (Cheers) –but the Police – (Hisses) – had no alternative in a row but to law hold of any they could get – (Loud Hisses).

In a similar example, a group of Glasgow University students rioted in 1846 over the seemingly innocuous blocking of a lane previously used for upwards of forty years as a short cut. The students were armed with sticks and stobs, with around 200 in the mob. The arrival of the police led to an altercation, with eleven students taken down to the police station, but not before a number of street lamps were broken. Fined two guineas each, the students then retired to College Green where funds were raised to reimburse the guilty parties, and removing the offending gate once again they ensured older customs won out over the rule of law.

Working-class crime and disturbance was feared most by the local authorities, so when in Glasgow a meeting on the Green of the destitute unemployed was hijacked by a 'band of blackguards intent on plunder' in 1848, the police responded in force. The gatherings had been going on for a while as those without work sought to get hired, with 4,000–5,000 in attendance. The sparks came from speeches that became more insistent '[t]o do a deed worthy of the name of France!' and the march to the town hall. After a long night of disturbance over 100 were lodged in the police station. It was the prompt for some 'ill disposed boys bent on mischief alone' to go on a copycat rampage around the High Street and Princes Street Gardens in Edinburgh, breaking the windows of the Royal Institution and the surrounding streetlamps, but not, as in Glasgow, breaking into the shops. The crowd travelled up to George Square and back north to the New Town. At various points the cry of *Vive la République* was heard, but otherwise it would appear there was no political motive.

OUTSIDERS

'Outsiders' in a community have long been targeted by sections of the host society. The arrival of immigrants from Ireland from the 1830s and at an increased rate from 1846 led to a number of tensions, from both the competition they brought to employment and accommodation, and the growth in Roman Catholic adherence to a level not seen in Scotland since before the Reformation. Scare stories began to permeate the pages of the secular press. In 1847 the *Glasgow Herald* reported on hundreds of navvies having taken possession of the streets of Hamilton, brandishing clubs and sticks, who had 'assaulted every Scotch person they could meet with'. Similarly, a simple case of troublesome drunks being arrested in Edinburgh's Cowgate took on an ethnic dimension and one of authority challenged when the intoxicated Irishmen in the care of the police were released by passing soldiers. With Irish labourers looking on and others supporting the soldiers in the ensuing melee, the disturbance escalated and the police fled.

The Scots were also fed regular stories of ethnic violence involving Irishmen in other parts of the world. The *Dundee Courier* in June 1844 reported news carried in the steamship *Hibernia*, recently docked in Liverpool, of the 'dreadful and disgraceful' riot between Protestant Americans and Irish Catholics, likening it to the Gordon riots of the 1780s. The following year the same paper condemned a group of visiting Irish navvies who attacked the home of 'a decent worthy Protestant Englishman' in Canada. It was reported further that the locals looked forward to the completion of the canal work that would precipitate the navvies' return to America. Regularly the *Caledonian Mercury* and *Glasgow Herald* carried similar stories from throughout England, including in 1852 an 'Orange Riot' at Liverpool and a 'Romanist Riot' at Stockport.

This rumbling tension continued over the next quarter of a century and intensified during the lead-up to the restoration of the Roman Catholic hierarchy. When a number of Protestant firebrands organised a gathering on Glasgow Green in April

1878 to burn the Pope's image and a copy of his allocution-
ary letter confirming the restoration, they were met by many
thousands of Orange Order and Roman Catholic witnesses.
Following warnings of likely trouble, the disturbance that
then developed was met by a large police presence, with the
magistrates standing ready to read the Riot Act if needed.
Restabilising the Roman Catholic Church was evidence that
that religion could no longer be labelled simply the preserve of
Irish migrants, but was again a Scottish church, would however
take time to be accepted. With the debate still raw for some, the
next year the local police learned that a riot was threatened for
the Kinnaird Hall in Dundee if a seemingly innocuous lecture
by the Rev. F. G. Widdows entitled 'The Mass as taught in the
Church of Rome' went ahead.

It was against this backdrop that the Scottish Roman Catholic
Church encouraged the pursuit of separate communal activities amongst its adherents, in ways divorced from the Scottish
working class but still loyal to the British state. 'Their own'
church halls, clubs and associations were the cultural means of
achieving what theorists term the pillarisation of civil society:
keeping traditions distinct, but not so to create a completely
separate public sphere. Still, sometimes maintaining these pillars
of difference appeared to lead to isolation rather than communal strength. In January 1862 'Hibernicus' complained that the
creation of Catholic reading rooms had gone too far and was
now a point of sectarianism:

> No sooner has the initiative been fairly taken, than the Catholic
> clergymen – those from whom above all others, we expected sympa-
> thy and support – launch forth the thunders of the pulpit against us
> . . . And why do they condemn our reading rooms? Simply because
> they are not under their immediate control – because the promoters
> did not ask their liberty – because the books, newspapers, etc., are
> not under their immediate censorship – and because they are of a
> secular and educational tendency.

More nationally, the creation of Hibernian Football Club
in Edinburgh (1875) and Roman Catholic teams in Dundee

(Dundee Harp in 1879) and Glasgow (Celtic in 1888) would continue this pillarisation, but not separation, from Scottish civil society. By these means Roman Catholic adherence was losing its Otherness in wider Scottish society, a trend further evidenced from estimates that suggest around 16 per cent of Scottish Roman Catholics enlisted into the British army in 1914, rising to one-quarter in some parts of Glasgow. Contemporaries, though, were often blind to such trends, and discord orchestrated by the Church of Scotland's leadership as well as Protestant jingoists against the believed foreigners of the Church reached further peaks during the 1920s and 1930s.

AWAY GOALS

Alongside political and doctrinal sectarianism in Scotland during the second half of the nineteenth century, and despite attempts within the world of football to bridge cultural solitudes, sporting occasions were the backdrop to criminal activities that were readily ascribed to ethnic discord. What was believed to be a premeditated disturbance by a group of Irish railway workers caused consternation at Ayrshire's Eglinton Park racing track, for example, in May 1842. Numbering around 200 people, the disturbance began at the end of the day's events. Armed with bludgeons, the navvies attacked 'all and sundry' with age or sex no protection, resulting in 'some helpless females being knocked about and cruelly used'. Described as 'brutal savages', the navvies cleared the racecourse before threatening to march into Irvine to 'sweep the town to destruction, and to beat every Orange – in the country!' At Paisley racecourse in 1857 when a policemen decided to arrest an 'ill-looking Irishman' he was promptly attacked by one of the miscreant's companions; there were various stand-up fist fights amongst the navvies and a more serious disturbance broke out later in the evening. Later reports suggest, however, that this was no fight between Orangemen and Ribbonmen, but the result of a group of Glasgow 'blackguards' using the races as cover to cause mischief.

WORKER UNREST

For the ordinary Scot, as for the Irish navvy, the police formed
the cutting edge of wider attempts to impose new standards
of urban discipline. Laws to regulate public behaviour, from
throwing snowballs to public drinking, increasingly filled the
books of police by-laws in the town. These came about because
the police were under pressure from the magistrates and groups
of ratepayers concerned with the protection of property. The
result was to make the policeman an unpopular figure to many
Scots.

The police in Kirkcaldy 'roughly handled' striking masons
in 1878, with the ringleaders of the strike sentenced to four
months, sixty days and forty days respectively. When in the
same year workers from Dundee were brought to Wick to
replace those in the herring trade who went on strike after poor
trade had reduced their wages, a disturbance led to broken
windows and a number of assaults, the investigation of which
was not aided by the community. A similar lack of support was
forthcoming during a strike by colliers in Beith who had lost
work and rejected the offer of reduced wages (5s to 4s per day),
with new hands hired in their place. A crowd stopped the sale
of the poinded effects of five fishermen in Beck near Stornoway.
And as late as 1888 a riot occurred at the Emigrants' Home,
Maxwelltown Place on the south side of Glasgow when two
newly arrived Irishmen got into a fight that soon involved 200
of the men who had been in Scotland for only a week. Two
policemen carried the Home's proprietor senseless from the
building, and while reinforcements were being waited on those
police locked inside endured a 'warm time' from the 'cowardly
ruffians'. Those who had lost their jobs to the Irish then gathered ready to join in the fight, but the early control taken by the
police avoided further conflict. Fifty-two of the labourers were
sentenced to thirty days' imprisonment without the option of a
fine.

Never an everyday occurrence, riot, disturbance and street
crime neverthless served to feed contemporary Othering of

groups and ethnicities in Scottish society. That process of imagining outsiders within the nation both strengthened and weakened the homogeneity of the people. 'Othering' within Scotland was as persuasive to identity formation as the headline-grabbing Unionist-Nationalism of the nationalists. In neither case were 'them' and 'us' clearly defined, a complexity that can also be applied to the analysis of late-century agitation over land ownership.

LAND AGITATION

The ownership of land was a preoccupation of the Victorian Liberals just as 'the land' was central to 'being Scotland' (Chapter 1). Most acutely in Ireland's case where it was tied up with the issue of home rule, in Scotland land agitation came to the fore around the issue of absentee landlords and the continuation of the crofters' way of life. The two sides were contrasted in the Land Commission evidence of 1883:

> The fish that was yesterday miles away from the land was claimed by the landlord the moment it reached the shore. And so also were the birds of the air as soon as they flew over his land. The law made it so, because landlords were themselves the lawmakers, and it was a wonder that the poor man was allowed to breathe the air of heaven and drink from the mountain stream without having the factors and the whole of the county police force pursuing him as a thief.

The crofters and their radical allies in the burghs established the Highland Land Law Reform Association to politicise demands for land redistribution and fair rents. Newspapers like *The Scotsman* were hostile to their case, preferring to support the landowner and the rule of law. Disturbances were sporadic and localised, but of sufficient intent that the exaggerations of the lowland and English newspaper editors caused much alarm.

Napier's report from the Land Commission was published in 1884. The legislation it spawned two years later increased security of tenure in the crofting counties together with the trend towards 'land raids', initiated in Lewis, through which crofting families reclaimed land that had already been cleared. These events seemed to set the highland and crofting counties apart with their own culture, politics and legislation but in other ways they showed how deeply the Highlands were integrated into a greater Scotland. When the Napier Commission took evidence in Morvern, an area that had suffered clearances and loss of population after the potato famine, an association of Morvern people resident in Glasgow financed their barrister. Crofting – a very precarious way of life at best – was now legally enshrined, and done so to protect an important part of 'being Scotland'.

AT THE END OF THE LEASH

Land agitation was a conflict over how land was stewarded to maintain a way of life. While economically less dominant (with the decline in the numbers employed in its associated sectors), but still important, the land retained its ideological centrality to ourselves as Scots. As a people, the Scots also sought control over and care for animals on the land and in their towns. The great and the good made up the Perthshire Society for the Prevention of Cruelty to Animals in 1872, its patrons including Lord Kinnaird, the Earl of Kinnoull, Sir William Stirling-Maxwell, Arthur Kinnaird, MP for the town of Perth, William Smythe, the Country Convenor, and Lieutenant-Colonel William McDonald, with Lord Provost John Pullar as the Society's President. Yet the courts found it difficult to impose sanction on those charged with mistreatment of animals, especially if it was part of working life. A hunting dog working on the Dyce estate of Sir William Forbes in 1874 was witnessed receiving twenty lashes from the riding whip of gamekeeper Andrew Dickson, but weak legislation meant the charge was not proven. Similarly, the charge in 1883 against an Aberdeen engineer that he seized a cat by its hind legs and threw it against the ground before stamping on it was not proven. In contrast a ten-year-old Dundee boy was sent to an industrial school in 1896 after being found guilty of forcing a cat into the boiler-room fire in a washing house and burning the animal to death.

Social control, authority and the treatment of animals clashed uncompromisingly over the practice of cock fighting. Here birds were decorated with sharp spurs with the contest resolved through defeat by death. Gambling was the chief attraction of the challenge. The *Caledonian Mercury* asked in 1839, 'Does such a thing exist in lovely Fife,/ 'Mong men called Christian – men of education;/Or in some distant heathen land, where strife/ And ignorance prevail at every station?' The answer was yes it did occur in Fife, and despite the Cruelty to Animals (Scotland) Act 1850, which subjected transgressors to a penalty at a daily rate not exceeding £5, cock fighting continued on the farms and back alleys of rural Scotland. The *Dumfries Courier* reported news of a cock fight on board a steamer in Dublin Bay in 1884, the contest pitched between the North of Ireland and Liverpool for a purse of £200. The onboard participants seemed to get away with it, and only occasionally was the local constable able to break up a contest, such as in the case of the twenty-two men, mainly miners, convicted of cock fighting at Rambleton Plantation between Kirkcaldy and Kinglassie as late as 1891. That this was no isolated example was seen when later arrests in 1892 led to the legislation being challenged and deemed by the Court of Judiciary not to explicitly include cock fighting. With the police now lacking the power to intervene, the practice came into the open with large crowds of around 500 people not uncommon in the western Lowlands. There is also evidence of extensive cock fighting in Renfrewshire, with betting ranging from 2s to £1. Less organised, but still open, a 'motley crew drawn from various parts of Fife' participated in an afternoon cock fight near Markinch in May 1895.

MAKING NICE

Land agitation is one of the strongest examples of how a society based on obligation and conviction would react when that trust was broken; cock fighting drew ire for its encouragement of gambling as well as for the cruelty inflicted. This evidence of discord leads to one further question for the national sense of self: how nice were Scots to one another? It is all too easy to get caught up in elegant or verbose contemporary speechmaking where linguistic restraint was a fashion. Even polemic was nothing if not polite. The reformer's description of wanton behaviour was just as measured, and the response recorded, but perhaps not received, tended to employ more than four letters in the chosen words. For all the middle-class refinement that so dominated the historical record, Scottish everyday life in Scotland was a coarse affair. Grocers selling whisky and giving drams to women was objected to, but it was not uncommon, and there was an exchange of correspondence between the police committee and Burgh of Campbeltown over 'the number of drunken women that prowled the streets at night' in the 1840s. The Sheriff of Oban described Constable John MacFarlane as 'a worthless tippling person' who had been 'drilling ragged ruffians as soldiers'. Constable Neil Rankine was cautioned over his 'irregular behaviour', particularly in having tasted the tinkers' whisky. Finally, there is the story of how Dr Blair reacted when a rude fellow chose to insult him by not giving the customary right of way to someone coming in the opposite direction: 'I never give the wall to a scoundrel, Sir.' 'I always do,' said the doctor, sidestepping away. Not always nicely, then, but the Scots were controlling themselves and others.

11

Emigration and Diaspora

The view from Canada Hill on the Isle of Bute offered one final glimpse of loved ones sailing off for a life abroad. Some would return – perhaps as many as a third – but most would not. For those on board, the fading sight of faces long known would magnify the reality of departure. With the physical connection to their nation at an end, Scots migrants relied on letters, relatives, neighbours, groups and an expectation of reunion in the afterlife to maintain their bond with home. Why did so many Scots make this journey to the unknown? Why did so many, less obvious in the historical record, also make the journey to Ireland and England?

Comparatively, Scotland was coming out of its greatest period of philosophical analysis into an industrialising economy: more jobs than ever before were created as the nineteenth century advanced and the standard of living, however unevenly, rose. Inevitably perhaps, economic realignment brought social dislocation. The trauma of highland eviction and clearance before 1860 was increased by the forces of the free market which inexorably, to contemporaries, pressed Scots to leave their homes for a livelihood elsewhere. The uneven and cyclical influence of capitalism broke into relationships that had seemed invariant, forming processes that weakened ties to place, shaping the rationale to move on. The first decade of the twentieth century experienced yet further economic realignment and impetus to migrate overseas. As was argued in Chapter 6, both the dependence on the overseas market and the level of Scottish capital

investment overseas were indicative of weakness in the home
economy.

OUR EXTENDED SELVES

The Scots who did not live in Scotland have a different history
from those residing in the nation. They may have been born
in Scotland, or be second or later generation Scots, or affinity
Scots, identifying with Scotland through marriage or cultural
osmosis. They count as Scotland's extended self. It is remarkable, indeed, that Scotland should remain comparatively so ethnically and religiously coherent when its people were so disposed
to migrate: the people left, but the Scots at home remained
comparatively unchanged. For those who did leave never to
return, and for affinity Scots, then 'being Scottish' involves their
objectifying their personal history through cultural symbols of
the nation. Denying the agency of the Scottish experience in this
way did not mark the development of false consciousness, as is
often assumed, but rather the ideological means of perpetuating
the national self when away as much as back home.

A MIGRATORY PEOPLE

Despite Scotland's long history of overseas and internal migration, a continuous run of emigration statistics is only available
from 1825, based on ship muster rolls. Prior to 1863 the figures
obtained through the Passenger Acts include only steerage and
not cabin passengers, and the Scots who left from English and
Irish posts before 1853 are not traced (and it is most likely
emigrants to Australia and New Zealand who were under-
reported here). There are some disembarkation statistics for the
United States (1820) and Canada (1829), but the evidence is
not comprehensive. From what demographers have been able
to gather from the official record, an estimated 2.33 million
Scots made their way overseas between 1825 and 1938, a figure
that is certainly an underestimation. Every region of Scotland
experienced net outward emigration in every decade between

1861 and 1914. In the decade 1921–30 Scotland lost 110.5 per cent of its 'natural increase' (the difference between the crude birth rate and the crude death rate) to emigration. In the period under scrutiny here, it lost half its natural increase. To add some scale, this figure was 1.5 times higher than the equivalent figure for England. Only the greatest European exporter of people, Ireland, was above this level, and if Scots who moved to England are included, then Scotland was the winner of this unwanted competition. While it is therefore difficult to discern the exact number who left for a life elsewhere, estimates suggest that one in every two Scots had some life experience – direct or otherwise – outside of Caledonia.

The numbers of Scots leaving the nation can be split pre- and post- the potato blight of the 1840s, giving 1860 as the tipping point. The economic conditions in sending and receiving countries had changed, information was better and steamships made quicker and more regular passages, including one's return. In the period 1861–1911, male migrants outnumbered female migrants for every decade, and this tended to be the pattern for earlier decades too.

There are distinctive features that structure Scotland's migration story and the creation of the nation's diaspora: the Scots were leaving an industrial economy that was expanding; they were leaving an urbanised and urbanising nation; it tended to be individuals, not families, who migrated; and, after 1860, most of these people came from the towns. Underpinning this migration was a rising population that could no longer be sustained in the countryside. As Devine notes, there was a substantial group of non-inheriting children of farmers who, along with farm servants and country tradesmen, could not sustain a living that was possible for their grandparents. With the banning of the subdivision of holdings, fewer people had access to the relatively small amounts of land that would keep a family from hunger.

Under-population was a problem that created a demand for migrants in the 'white colonies', especially if those workers had some experience of industrial work, and this suited the Scots. A number of spinners who saw their wages and then their jobs

Table 11.1 Net out-migration from Scotland, 1861–1930

Decade	Net out-migration	Net out-migration as % of natural increase
1861–70	116,872	27.7
1871–80	92,808	19.8
1881–90	218,274	41.0
1891–1900	51,728	10.4
1901–10	253,894	46.8
1911–20	226,768	53.6
1921–30	415,768	110.5

Source: Flinn et al., *Scottish Population History*, p. 441.

disappear in the 1830s were attracted to the opportunities overseas. And Highlanders, most of whom had some familiarity with seasonal work with the manufacturers of lowland Scotland, made up the bulk of Scottish migrants before the 1840s, then to be replaced by Lowlanders who had endured the cyclical employment of modern industry. The Scots' desire to migrate to what in most cases was a less developed urban infrastructure came from their attraction to the nascent urbanism (with access to an amount of land) their parents would have known, and they were able to progress its development at a speed unthinkable in their homeland.

NOT SO FAR

The 'forgotten diaspora' is perhaps the best way to describe the Scots who left for near neighbours England, Wales and Ireland: some emigrants, the others migrants. While it was the case that in every decade from 1861 to 1911 more Scots migrated overseas than to a destination elsewhere in Britain, the numbers involved are not insignificant. Some 670,808 Scots are estimated to have left Scotland for other parts of the UK between 1841 and 1921, a figure that peaked in the second half of the century. And while more men than women went overseas, male and female migrants were more or less evenly split in their choice of leaving Scotland for elsewhere in Britain.

Table 11.2   Scots' migration to England, 1841–1921

Decade	Number
1841–51	74,314
1851–61	81,738
1861–71	96,274
1871–81	98,315
1881–91	90,711
1891–1901	98,210
1901–11	68,177
1911–21	63,069

These internal migrations within Britain created distinct groupings and clusters. One of those communities, the Ulster Scots, has been sustained longest in Scotland's migration story. With Belfast geographically closer than London, and sea travel typically more favourable than journeying south by land, the Scottish and Irish people have shared society, culture and trade. By mid-century, as the Irish and Ulster economies suffered under post-famine population loss, only around 10 per cent of migrant Scots made the journey over the Irish Sea, a smaller proportion than, say, in the seventeenth century, and these later generations were probably the children of Irish migrants into Scotland. Yet Belfast was the first city outside Scotland to publish an edition of Robert Burns' poems, a cross-channel connection confirmed in 1844 when the poet's son and namesake visited the city to enjoy a supper in honour of his family. Enthusiasm for Burns peaked with the 1859 centenary of the poet's birth when 300 gathered to celebrate his memory, but thereafter membership of Scottish-themed clubs and societies went into abeyance, leaving the Belfast Benevolent St Andrew's Society, formed in 1867, to carry the associational identity of the Scots in the city.

The short sailing across the Irish Sea and the fractious religious interplay that closeness engendered was reflected in Scots' political actions in the north and south of Ireland, as it was for those of the Irish in Scotland. There was no simple Othering between these communities, but instead a complex mix of isolations and commonalities that were shared. In the 1880s and 1890s, when the Belfast Scottish Unionist Club campaigned to protect the 1801 Union between Britain and Ireland, support for Irish Home Rule was being canvassed back in Caledonia. And when the Scottish Home Rule Association's Charles Waddie toured Ireland looking to muster support he heard few friendly voices, whereas the Highland Land League found common ground when the target was landlord absenteeism.

Returning from the near diaspora, Scots brought culture, experiences and capital to their homeland. England, most of all, offered Scottish migrants higher wages, a wider pool of marriage partners and substantial trade and credit networks. London, Liverpool and Manchester were where most Scots were to be found. Of all, London was the greatest attraction. The English capital gave the opportunity for the kind of prestige not available anywhere else. The historic pull of that metropolis that overcame normal levels of distance decay to surge in population from the early modern period has impacted population move- ment within Britain to an extent greater than any other city. One count suggests there were more Scottish associations in London than in any other city.

Confirming the preference for internal migration that was close to home, a Scottish presence had led to St Andrew's societies being formed in Manchester (1876), Barrow (1878), Bradford (1886), Liverpool (1890) and York (1894). Historian John Burnett has found evidence of the Scottish communities in England holding galas, dinners and balls in order to raise funds to help with the relief of Highland Scots and rural Irish devastated by the potato blight of the 1840s. In the second half of the nineteenth century the Scots outnumbered the Irish in the north-east of England, a pattern contributed to by the industrial similarities with Scotland's west coast. Highland and east-coast Scots were also to be found within the shipyards of north-east England, to the extent that Hebburn, the residential area in Tyneside, became known as 'Little Aberdeen'. Presbyterian churches, Orange Lodges, Boys' Brigade groups and pipe bands were part of the network of this 'Scottish colony'. 'Hail Brither

Scots O' Coaly Tyne, We meet again for Auld Lang Syne' was the telegram sent by the Sunderland Burns Club to their Newcastle counterparts at their inaugural Annual Dinner of 25 January 1897. A number of Burns clubs were in the region and affiliated to the Federation of Burns Clubs based in Kilmarnock. Significantly, the Sunderland Burns Club hosted the first meeting of the Federation outside Scotland in 1907.

The philanthropic imperative for those Scots and their families in need of help was the objective of the Scots' Society of St Andrew formed in Hull in 1910, and to 'strengthen the ties which bind Scotsmen resident in or near Hull with their native land and to promote social intercourse amongst them'. It was a small community, with Scots-born making up 1 per cent of the town's population in 1891 and when 2,700 Scots were enumerated in 1921 it was nearly double the figure of Irish-born residents. Their help extended to those Scots passing through. As the Society's first President explained: 'They were in another country and they wanted to see each other as much as possible, and to help their poorer brethren.' Groups such as the Darlington Burns Association (formed in 1906) started out with a desire for ethnic exclusivity but became more open to all nationalities as the decades progressed. This, from the near diaspora, is a first look at how the socio-economic experience of Scots migrants was homogenised through culture: to strengthen ties with home and to foster ethnic association when away.

THE EMIGRATION EXPERIENCE

Popular perceptions of Scottish emigration often reflect the extremes of how emigrants fared in their new homes. On the one hand are accounts of exiled Highlanders and horrendous voyages followed by tales of settlement woe, while on the other is the image of the canny Scots, who came to dominate in business, education and politics. Emigration historian Malcolm Prentis finds that while contemporary diarists recorded anguish at their leaving, these farewells became less effusive as the century wore on. But there was an insistence on getting the last look of the native land and solace from prayers that the journey would lead to a better life. Having a minister on board, with a Gaelic speaker when needed, would lead to much reflection and singing of psalms.

The Passengers Acts were tightened in 1832 following sufficient evidence of onboard conditions deteriorating dangerously after deregulation three years earlier. The prevalence and danger to health of overcrowding, the owners' installation of temporary decks when people rather than timber were the cargo and the deprivation of light or ventilation beneath deck were all turning the emigrant ship into a coffin ship. The spread of tuberculosis, typhus and then cholera were feared not just by the passengers but also by the receiving ports. Along with an attempt to tax the ship owners 15s per passenger coming into New Brunswick to help pay for their medical treatment, an emigrant bond of £10 and the insistence that no passenger would become a cost to the local authorities for one year was imposed in Nova Scotia. The quarantine costs at Grosse Isle were payable by the boat owner and were doubled for those who left without sanction of the government office in London.

When the Good family left Glasgow in 1841 bound for Canada they were immediately disappointed with the onboard conditions they encountered. The tobacco they had paid for in advance was not forthcoming and the water was described as the colour of porter. When storms came, they couldn't cook and sea water flowed through the hatches. Their journey involved an enforced three-week delay circumnavigating the coast of Newfoundland, and the poor weather delayed the passage so much that the captain put everyone on reduced supplies: half a pound of biscuits per adult per day and eight gills of water. During the wait, a woman who gave birth died for want of medicine. In all it took nine weeks and two days to reach land and despite Good believing otherwise this was not overlong, falling within the range of the forty to ninety days needed to cross the Atlantic in that year, and quicker than the average summer passage of seventy days.

The longer journey to Australia gave more opportunity for Scots to compare their cultural preferences with those of their fellow passengers (and crew) from other nations, especially those from England and Ireland. Around 850 diaries remain extant from these passengers, of whom women and those in steerage class are under-represented. The accounts illuminate the onboard tension between boredom and the need to maintain social order, where the captain of the vessel, the ultimate authority, kept some distance from the passengers. Observance of the Sabbath and some reading of scripture was recorded as behaviour marking the Scots out from those they travelled with, divisions confirmed by the captain's practice of separating the ethnic groups into different eating, and therefore socialising, areas. This tendency to stick with their own kind was part of the Scots' emigration experience that sustained associational, philanthropic and business activity upon arrival and which took a number of generations of settlement to unravel.

AGENTS

Notwithstanding the individual and family decision making that underpinned emigration, outside agents and influences helped facilitate the process. In the 1830s the Colonial Office began to advertise Australia as a destination for common labourers and artisans, offering £12 to the shipmasters for every migrant they delivered. Returning home to Greenock from New South Wales in 1837, the Presbyterian minister John Dunsmore Lang was honoured with a public breakfast at which he took the opportunity to promote a new home for destitute Scots. It was highland society he was referring to, but with an eye on Britain more generally he extolled how wonderful it would be to have an ally with British culture, spirit and religion elsewhere in the world. His aim was to 'take the Highlanders before they withered, and plant them in fertile Australian soil'. In total he persuaded 4,000 Scots to make the journey.

Otherwise it was the highland laird who for many was the de facto agent, and while emigration was once an unwelcome drain of labour, from the 1830s it had become a rational response to destitution. In this decade it was out of step to maintain as *Fraser's Magazine* did in 1838 that 'we do not like emigration; it is to the social what bleeding is to the physical'. The agent countered by pointing out that by going en masse, Highlanders were able to resurrect their culture in a new land, to transplant their community, and thus 'emigration was both the death *and* the resurrection' of their society.

The work of agents kept emigration, and all that it offered, as a valid strategy to escape from poverty. After 1851 the Highland and Island Emigration Society sent 5,000 destitute Highlanders to Australia. By 1886 there were as many as sixty private societies helping Scots to migrate. The National Association for Promoting State-Directed Emigration and Colonisation itself had nine affiliated societies. They offered financial and other practical advice, explaining the nature of the land and climate soon to be encountered. At various times in these decades the argument was raised for the state to pay the cost of the emigrant's journey, and to provide land for those newly arrived, but most were there on the back of savings, a loan or indentured service.

Information on the transplanted community overseas was varied: in 1910 Lord Brassey reported back on the attractions of the Dominion of Canada, and its 'illimitable resources', to the annual conference of the Association of Chambers of Commerce. A century earlier there were around twenty accounts published on Upper Canada that continued to circulate mid-century. Scots expected to find the overseas territories 'empty' other than of those Scots and Europeans who had migrated before them, thinking little that there might be substantial numbers of indigenous peoples. The majority wouldn't know quite what to expect, hence the importance of guides that were bought, recirculated and passed on, with extracts published in the newspaper and periodical press. Robert MacDougall's *Ceann-iùil an fhir-imrich do dh'America mu-thuath; or, The emigrant's guide to North America* (1841) was published simultaneously in Glasgow, Oban, Keith and Inverness. MacDougall emigrated with his father and brother from Perthshire in 1836 and returned to Scotland in 1839 before leaving for Australia two years later. Otherwise information on the practicalities of food and material costs, on the weather, the soil and access to water was also sent home in personal letters that often exhorted the relatives to join in the new life. Writing home, James Good recounted that he hadn't seen many Paisley folk; that his neighbours were all Pennsylvanian Dutch; that animals were plentiful; that his wages were good, but still he needed replacement parts sent out from Paisley for the family's loom.

For this migrant 'home' was maintained in the communications and movements of family and friends rather than his immediate settlement, and confirmed the importance of the postal system and later the telegram and steamship to maintain connections between Scotland and its diaspora. At the time Good was writing, the cost of a transatlantic letter to Scotland was $1.12, but only 41c if sent via New York. There were no transatlantic postage stamps in Canada prior to 1851 and letters were folded with a seal; postage was paid in advance, but sometimes also upon receipt. In the 1830s and 1840s it took around seventy days for post to reach its destination, and travellers were often entrusted with mail for relatives.

When Karl Marx pointed out in 1853 that 80 per cent of migrants in the previous six years were Celts, it was not a racial but an economic analysis. A logical extension to the argument that emigration was a solution to the social and financial drain of adult underemployed was that it could be applied equally successfully to orphans. Dr Thomas Barnardo argued that colonies should not be populated simply with the morally undesirable, an argument that built on John Galt's cry for the Scottish middle class to head to the emigrant nations for the eventual good of Scotland. Barnardo had sent 28,689 children over to Canada by 1914 and 2,343 to Australia by 1920. The Barnardo Boys went on a fundraising tour of Scotland in 1875, with rooms crowded to excess by those interested in hearing of this work, and Scottish boys could be picked up by the Society when in England. William Quarrier, who started out his working life as a boot and shoemaker, provided the Scottish equivalent. His passion for helping orphans blossomed after he met Annie McPherson and with financial help from Thomas Corbett established his first Orphans and Destitute Children's Emigration Home in Glasgow (1871). Within two years Quarrier was looking after 136 children in the city, with 2,137 allowed to stay overnight during a twelve-month period. Quarrier's first children taken to Canada sailed in 1872; numbering thirty-one, their families contributed £10 to the cost of passage. At later dates Marjory Harper counts 400, then 700 going out; and in 1898 Quarrier established a distribution centre for these orphans at Brockville, Ontario.

TO THE WORLD

Adult Scots were to be found in many more parts of the world than the nation's orphans. They had long migrated east to Scandinavia, the Low Countries and Continental Europe. The Scots, with vision, attempted to establish their own colony separate from England's trading possession on the Isthmus of Panama, the ill-fated Darien scheme that not only sustained loss of life but also proved such a drain on Scottish capital at the end of the seventeenth century. Still, the Scots looked for opportunity and a life outside the nation, and Argentina and Paraguay were part of their South American exploits. In the nineteenth and twentieth centuries, Scottish economic and permanent migrants headed for India and South East Asia, North America, the Antipodes and Africa. It is to evidence from these case studies that we turn to explore how diasporic groups objectified the nation's historical past in order to support migrant settlement.

Of all overseas migrants leaving Scottish ports, around one-quarter left for the US in the period 1830–44, rising to 55 per cent during 1845–53 and peaking at 76 per cent in 1890–4. In the 1830s and until 1844 Canada was the preferred destination for these migrants, although we cannot discount those who then moved on to the US. Canada took anything between 10 per cent and 25 per cent of the total, which spiked in 1910–14 at nearly

60 per cent. Australia temporarily took a majority of Scotland's migrants after 1853 with the discovery of gold. South Africa only attracted reasonable numbers at the end of the century, reaching 20 per cent of Scots migrants as the century turned, but return migrants from the Cape were almost equal in number to those arriving, indicating that conditions were not as favourable as was hoped. In 1913–14, 47 per cent of Scottish migrants (compared to 36 per cent from England and Wales) described themselves as skilled and over 50 per cent did so in the 1920s. Of those for whom we have occupational information in this year, the skilled tended to head for the US and South Africa and the unskilled for Canada.

INDIA AND SOUTH EAST ASIA

Despite losing its monopoly in 1834, the East India Company continued to have an influence into the nineteenth century, with Scots maintaining a significant presence in the financial sector. In Hong Kong the headline-making Scots Sir William Jardine and Sir James Matheson – a memorial to Matheson was built in Lews Castle, Stornoway – are leading examples that help show that this was less a story of settlement as one of sojourning. India and Hong Kong were worker outposts where Burns suppers never attracted the same community involvement as they did in North America, instead tending to be smaller and more private affairs for the cultivation of business and personal links.

Scottish involvement in this region was closely tied to British imperialism, which itself was at its most bombastic. A visit by the Duke of Edinburgh to Ceylon on 30 March 1870 was commemorated in an expensively illustrated memoir of the occasion. It was a red-letter day: 'never was Orient sky more cloudless' – and after the 'Oriental silence of respect', there came 'cheers, such as British lungs know how to give'. But it was India that remained symbolically so important to Britain's imperial power, Queen Victoria gaining the title Empress of India in 1876. India was the location for Scottish women's missionary interventions; the spread of Presbyterianism abroad was an extension of vibrant religiosity at home. The Edinburgh Ladies' Association for the Advancement of Female Education in India (founded in 1837) was part of a significant conjunction of women's public activity and religious endeavour. The 'few friends', for example, who contributed £20 to the Scottish Ladies' Association for the Advancement of Education in India during February 1846 represented one of many small involvements that had a cumulative presence. Others included Agnes, daughter of David Livingstone, and her husband A. L. Bruce, who were founding members of the Royal Scottish Geographical Society (1884), with research indicating a high female presence in the thirst for geographical knowledge.

While it was the case, as religious historian Andrew R. Ross has pointed out, that Scotland's three greatest missionaries – John Philip, Robert Moffat and David Livingstone – were not of the Church of Scotland, but of the chapel movement, it is estimated that between 1829 and 1900 the Church of Scotland supported 252 missionaries and the Free Church of Scotland 335 missionaries overseas. The churches supported the 'civilising mission', with Scottish branches of British imperial organisations such as the Imperial Federation League to the fore. Scotland welcomed the World Missionary Conference in June 1910, hosted in the Assembly Hall of the United Free Church of Scotland. Over 1,200 representatives from missionary societies around the world were in attendance.

CANADA

Rather than sending the missionary from home, the Scots' philanthropic engagement with the people of Canada was to organise associations and societies to provide pecuniary relief and only then to structure fraternity and class relationships through a prescribed reading of Scotland's history. Scots first arrived in any numbers from the 1770s. Settlement in the Maritimes and Lord Selkirk's colonisation of Rupert's Land's Red River Valley from 1812 were first, before movement into Upper Canada in the 1820s and 1830s. Some of the very first signs of these settlers forming a group identity came through St Andrew's societies. Named after Scotland's patron saint, these were philanthropic organisations generally led by the middle classes and the economically better off with the aim of helping indigent Scots. The criterion set to qualify for aid was Scottish birth or lineage to great-grandfather or grandfather, although this was opened up over time. The St Andrew's Society of Montreal, formed in early 1835, aimed in part to promote British values and institutions as distinguished from the Francophone majority. In a history of the organisation compiled in 1844, founding member Hugh Allan makes plain that even if the goals of the Society 'are strictly limited to charity and acts of philanthropy, [its formation] was partly caused by political circumstances'. As a group they supported the Loyalists, as philanthropists they cared enough to raise a subscription for a group of migrants from Lewis stranded for the winter in 1841. The same year the St Andrew's Society of Quebec formed to provide help for recently arrived Scottish emigrants, with others formed to serve the Scottish communities in Hamilton (1835), Toronto (1836), Kingston (1840) and Ottawa (1846), all established settlements along the St Lawrence and Lake Ontario. The societies each required two physicians to give advice and to recommend to the Board of Managers who was worthy of their help. They also had two chaplains to visit the sick and distressed persons nominated by the Board. Meetings were advertised in the press, and subcommittees were established to frame the constitution and the subscription rate. In contrast, Caledonian societies offered more sporting activities for immigrant Scots, mainly curling, but also racing and strength games. Sons of Scotland societies, meanwhile, were a means for the labouring classes to insure themselves against loss of employment and death, their local branches or camps given names redolent of home.

Immigrant cultural societies were legion in the diaspora and thus attract scholarly attention for what they indicate about mixing national identity in a new land. Burns societies and celebrations littered North America. The Burns Literary Club of Toronto, for example, was founded in 1896 after a public

meeting commemorating the poet's death. The Club's membership was restricted to fifty people and the city gained its Burns
monument in 1902. References to Burns and Scott were abun-
dant throughout the Scottish-Canadian papers of the period.
There is hardly an issue that does not refer in some way to
either the works of these two writers or the men themselves:
a 'Burnsania' column was a frequent feature in the *Scottish
Canadian*.

USA

Key to Scottish associational life was its interconnectedness
within the diasporic location it was based, spreading and deepening involvement in the construction of self when away from
home. The American example provides strong evidence of this,
notably the numerous Burns celebrations held mid-century
in New York. The Grand Celebration at Tammany Hall on
Tuesday 25 January 1856 was described in the *New York Times*
as a day to warm the heart of any Scotsman because 'It was dear
to every warm heart of the world.' The company consisted of
some 300 'sons of Scotia' who heard from the speechmakers
that their fellow Scots were '[t]he Worshipers and Workers out
of Liberty in all Climes and Countries . . . They are the leaders
of humanity, by the light of whose intellect a happy future is
developed . . . in the brotherhood of mankind'. Two years later,
the Burns Club of New York celebrated the ninety-ninth anniversary of the poet's birth at the Metropolitan Hotel at which
they were entertained by piper William Clellan dressed in the
'Gaelic costume'. The flags on display blended Scottish, English
and American sensibilities: the St Andrew's Cross, the Flag of St
George and the Stars and Stripes. The toasts were to the 'birth
day of Nature's own poet', 'the genius of Burns' and 'Scotland,
the land of our fathers', followed by 'America, the land we live
in'. In 1858 the poet was paired with John Knox as the 'two
kings of Scotland' since the times of Bruce. The next year, the
hundredth anniversary, kindred associations throughout the
world telegraphed simultaneously at 10 p.m. New York time.

Figure 11.1 *The unveiling in New York's Central Park of the first statue to Burns in the diaspora, 1880. Designed by Sir John Robert Steell, it was placed alongside an earlier statue of Walter Scott. Casts of the likeness were later used for statues in Dundee, London and Dunedin. © Dumfries and Galloway Museums Service. Licensor www. scran.ac.uk*

At the Astor House event in New York, the Burns Society's anniversary report noted with pride that

> The Pulpit, the Press, and the Bar furnished some of their ablest representatives; and men eminent in every honourable position presented an assembly distinguished for intellectual excellence and high character, probably never surpassed in the city of New York on any similar occasion.

The published report of the New York event ran to 136 pages and was produced for the local libraries. When the New York Scots Society chose Scottish-American industrialist and philanthropist Andrew Carnegie to deliver a eulogy to the poet in 1888 they were able to not only fill the hall to excess, but to fill it with an audience 'who could not hear enough of the poet's praises or his songs. There were encores galore . . .'

NEW ZEALAND

The associational activity of the Scots in Canada and America was crammed with philanthropic endeavour and cultural reflection, mostly centred on the poetry of Burns, with some mention of the literature of Scott and Hogg, the songs of Lady Nairne and the romances of Jane Porter. Curling was the mainstay of the Caledonian clubs, but the growth of Highland Games was not seen until later in the twentieth century. The Burns celebrations were remarkably similar in form and function, confirming Scottish history as an egalitarian benefit to the world when viewed through a Burnsian lens. It would appear that Scottish history was packaged similarly but still differently in the Antipodes. In New Zealand and Australia, the associational activity of the Scots was centred much more firmly around musical and sporting cultures, with some evidence too of a distinct identity within the colonial military.

The census of 1858 recorded slightly fewer than 8,000 Scots in New Zealand and around 4,500 Irish; by the 1870s it was the Irish who were coming on assisted and nominated migration schemes in much bigger numbers. In 1848 the Free Church of Scotland along with the New Zealand Company led the Scottish Settlement Scheme in Otago. From the 1860s Scottish associations began to form in that region and throughout the islands. These were primarily Caledonian societies and Thistle clubs, but also St Andrew's and Burns clubs, and regionally specific associations such as Orkney and Shetland associations. It is estimated that in 1871–81, 4,640 Shetlanders migrated to New Zealand out of a population of 31,000. The Caithness and Sutherland Association (founded 1873) expanded the next year to include Orkney and Shetland in its remit, offering aid to migrants as well as sending relief funds back to Scotland. Research by Angela McCarthy on emigrant diaries shows that Scottish migrants favoured mentioning their specific origins, be they Skye, Paisley or Dundee, rather than simply their nation. One survey indicates there were around 100 Caledonian societies and another twenty Burns, Gaelic and Thistle associations formed in the second half of the nineteenth century. In the view of a contemporary in 1890: 'recent negotiations between the Auckland Caledonian Society and Burns Clubs elicited the fact that the Caledonians are numerically four times stronger than the others'.

AUSTRALIA

After European migration based mainly on the forced settlement of convicts, the free movement of people to Australia begin in the 1830s. In the period 1831 to 1900 just under 1.5 million, excluding convicts, migrated there from the UK. Half were assisted by fare subsidies that depending on government policy ranged from 33 per cent to 79 per cent of the cost. Australia's Scottish associational culture dates from 1840 with the formation of a St Andrew's Society in Victoria (then Port Philip). As the network of societies became more entrenched in the first decade of the twentieth century, the Victorian Scottish Union was formed to better coordinate the many games, social events and musical gatherings that were taking place. It was a challenge since numerous rural Caledonian societies continued to run their separate annual gatherings despite the Union's attempts to regulate the competitive aspects of their games. The Union was involved with the 'British not English' campaign of 1906, the work of the Scots Patriotic Association in Glasgow and, notably, the campaign in 1911 to preserve the Australian army's kilted regiment in face of government moves to abolish it.

Despite the monarchical loyalties of Australian Scots, Burns was not forgotten. Perth looked to form a Burns club in 1896 because 'there were very many Scotchmen who had little opportunity of meeting unless some such club was formed'. Many of those present spoke in favour of the club, despite fear of overlap with the local Thistle club, and promises were made of book donations to form the nucleus of a Burns library. Concurrently in Brisbane, there was willingness to cooperate with plans for a joint Caledonian Society and Burns Club. Planning their forthcoming musical event, with a musical subcommittee formed, they had received a gift from the Greenock Burns Club of a bound programme for their event on the previous 25 January.

AFRICA

While the sporting and musical impulse was strongest in Antipodean Scottish cultural formation, the Scots migratory inclination towards Africa developed not for settlement but for missionary success, projecting Christianity to the 'dark Continent'. David Livingstone (1813–73) became the most famous of all Victorian missionary explorers for his exploits in Zambia. Before him, Mungo Park (1771–1806) made his name through his search for the source of the Niger and later the Rev. Dr Robert Laws (1851–1934) took over Livingstone's work in Malawi. In associational terms, then it was the London Missionary Society, energised by its Scottish missionary foot soldiers Robert Moffat and John Brownlee, that led the way. But others joined in. When the American Colonization Society held a public meeting in Aberdeen's East Church in 1833, its aim in coming to Scotland was to garner support for its efforts in Liberia to develop an independent African settlement, the Christianising of Africa and the abolition of the slave trade. The Glasgow Ladies' Association for promoting Female Education in Kaffraria [South Africa] was formed in 1839. For both these societies, the cause was one of 'liberty, humanity and religion' in order to bring an end to slavery in the British colonies.

Otherwise it was a sojourning experience for Scots in Africa, foremost in the Southern Cape. The gold and diamond rushes of the 1880s in the Rand brought Scots over. Scots also experienced farming life and military life. The vast majority of railway engineers in the dominion came from Scotland and England. Without enough experienced engineers in the Cape it was more than just national prejudice that led Sir David Hunter to prioritise his own kind for building the network.

The exported engineers also created jobs at home as British railway companies benefited from 'home preference'. And Scottish engineering companies made use of this culture of imperial trade to move from one market to the next. When in the 1860s Scotland's west coast industries no longer found sufficient demand for their machinery from the West Indies, they quickly shifted focus to the markets of the Far East and South Africa to rebuild their businesses.

Because Scotland's migrants to this part of the world were predominantly missionaries and (temporary) economic sojourners rather than settlers, it meant the use of Scotland's historical past was less well developed within their associational activity. Only after the gold rush and the development of industrial infrastructure were Scots present in sufficient numbers to sustain any range of cultural, philosophical and scientific institutions and associations. John Mackenzie dates this to 1914, by which time the periodicals and newspapers in circulation (such as the *South African Scot* from 1905) had created a civil society to sustain the Cape's ruling autocracy within which the Scots were prominent. Importantly, MacKenzie argues, the romantic nostalgia these societies presented was a reaction to the harsh conditions faced by Scots trying to make a living there.

In each example – wherever the Lion Rampant, the Saltire

and the Union Flag flew – the Scots used the communicative power of objectification to bring themselves together associationally. Through culture, history and business, emigrant Scots offered up a framework for other Scots – participant or not, but cognisant – to imagine a transplanted home. And if we accept that around one-third of these Scots returned, and that trade, letters, telegrams, newspapers, philanthropic and missionary aid, associational affiliations and popular literature criss-crossed the oceans, then diasporic Scotland was not lost to homeland Scotland.

ENCOUNTERS WITH INDIGENOUS PEOPLES

Scots' encounters with indigenous peoples – through the process of 'Othering' – similarly had the power to link Scots abroad with those at home. Over 300 years of Scottish involvement in the Arctic fur trade meant both races had gone beyond 'them and us'; this was the case for the powerful such as Lord Strathcona, Governor of the Hudson Bay Company (HBC), as it was for the Orcadian workers engaged by the HBC when its boats took on supplies at Stromness harbour en route for Canada. Indigenous encounters shaped understanding of self. When, for instance, the Rev. William Bell warned his fellow Scots in *Hints to Emigrants* (1824) of a 'moral as well as a natural wilderness' in Upper Canada, he was referring as much, if not more, to the highland Scot and Irish labourers he was familiar with, as to the Algonquin and the Mississauga Indians he had come across. These were discoveries, reflections and negotiations around race embedded in familiar cultural constructions. If in the eighteenth century heathens in the colonies were likened to the heathens at home, each rejecting religion, in the next century race was tied to class, and to the peripherality of Scotland.

Scholars have emphasised what was common between Scottish Highlanders and Native Americans. The preponderance of an oral culture, the use of myth and the common experience of being colonised was an affinity recognised by contemporaries. For instance John Ross, seven-eighths Scots and leader of the

Cherokee removal to Oklahoma, raised $190 from his people on hearing of the plight of the highland poor from Philadelphia fundraisers in 1847. Ross's own home was described as something akin to a Scottish manor house. Further, so many Orkney men returned home with Native wives that a school was erected in South Ronaldsay especially for the education of mixed-race children. Historian Ferenc Morton Szasz suggests the most articulate of these was Alexander Kennedy Isbister. His father worked for the HBC and his mother was a Cree. Isbister moved from Red River in Canada to King's College Aberdeen (graduating in 1842). Later taking the position of dean in a teacher-training college, he petitioned the government over the treatment of mixed-race children. Szasz finds many examples of Scoto-Indian children who through education or hard work in business were successful within America and Canada. Contemporaries, for sure, were full of stories indicating the similarity of Scottish highland and Red Indian dancing, although this is an ethnographical comparison still in need of further nuance.

Race relations between Maori and highland Scots have been analysed as neither benign nor reflective of cultural domination, and contrasted through a range of encounters. Contemporary reflections on race were sometimes poorly analysed. The *Dundee Courier* explored in 1846 'The Capacities of the Negro Race', showing their military, political, commercial and artistic successes, while an article on the 'Permanence of the Negro' in the *Caledonian Mercury* (1862) claimed a law that all savage races are doomed in the face of civilisation, except the Central African Negro: 'their barbarism, or semi barbarism, seems fully capable to live side by side with our civilisation'. The Mohicans and the Maoris were intellectually and morally more advanced than the Negroes, it continued, but still the latter were the strongest.

A DIASPORIC HALL OF MIRRORS

Emigrant encounters with indigenous peoples, and the stories they read in their guidebooks, did little to suggest to the Scot that he or she was ever at an advantage over the Native. Most of the guidebooks lauded the steadfast confidence of the Native Americans as a people, bemoaning the negative rather than beneficial effects of western 'civilisation' on Native behaviour – especially in teaching them profanity – and the greater hardships migrant Scots faced without indigenous knowledge of everyday life in the backwoods. Failure was frequently economic, too. Many only planned to 'make their fortune', or at least some boost to their income until trade at home picked up, but this didn't always work out. Some soon had no money to live on, or found the competition for jobs as intense as it was at home; they longed for familiar familial support. The philanthropic societies helped with the cost of passage home, and were willing to dole out funds when the husband or father died. Criminal activity and simple homesickness were causes of return, as was mental illness. The letters home, diaries and emigrant guides make regular mention of homesickness.

Along with St Andrew's and Caledonian and Thistle societies to inculcate community formation by the self-objectification of national history, the Scots also transplanted mechanics' institutes, circulation libraries, insurance and assurance societies, and numerous other friendly associations besides. Less overtly 'Scottish', but with a clear Scottish influence on their aims, operations and conduct, each could have been transferred seamlessly back to any Scottish town or city of the period. This makes it not only part of everyday Scottishness transplanted abroad, but further confirmation of the connection maintained between the Scots' home and wider self.

This use of associational culture outside the nation reflects a continued attachment to how life was lived at home. The ways in which 'being ourselves' formed in the mirror of ourselves and others carries the final chapter to its conclusion.

12

Being Ourselves

Being ourselves in the mirror of the nation reflects others within its boundaries. The century from 1832 records a steady unravelling of the Scottish people who by various indicators have been seen to be remarkably homogeneous. With around 80 per cent of the population Presbyterian by mid-century, and a population that was home to few born outside the nation, the appearance of Irish migrants in such numbers could hardly go unnoticed – rising to some half million by time hostilities engulfed Europe in 1914. But Scotland's borders had long been open to immigrants, sojourners and visitors. The Scots were sufficiently welcoming that donations were raised for Benevolent and Strangers' Friend societies in the larger port towns to support outsiders. These charities provided relief to 'honest folk in distress who belonged to distant places', doling out funds irrespective of nationality or religion. Although in one case, in 1832, an Italian national tricked the Society in Edinburgh after seeking the cost of passage from Leith to London for himself and a companion, only to remain and give the tickets to others. Such aid was part of wider information and commercial assistance available for locals and outsiders alike. Along with its Watt institution, reading room and literary institute mid-century, Dundee's Cowgate housed a Baltic coffee house (trading exchange) to help coordinate the city port's increasingly internationalised trade. The numbers coming into Scotland were always dominated by the flow exiting Ireland, but there was an increase in immigration from Eastern Europe at the end of the nineteenth century, figures inflated by the census recording place of birth rather than nationality. In response, the 1901 census authorities attempted to obtain the nationality of all in Scotland who were foreign born, but the criterion was applied unevenly by the enumerators and those with British-sounding names were classified as British.

The proportion of English-born people living in Scotland increased steadily each decade beginning in 1841, from 1.5 per cent to 4 per cent of the nation's population in 1921. Never great in number, most were found in the Borders and the central belt. These communities, however, were not without an associational presence. The St George's Benevolent Society of Glasgow had relieved twenty-one English people in 1882, while another seventeen had been sent back across the border. Meeting on St George's Day, its year end, the Society had just over £24 in the bank. As became a feature of the twentieth century, English-born affinity Scots could be seen to enact a strong cultural influence. Addressing a large soiree in Glasgow city hall to celebrate recent Crimean victories in November 1855, Professor Nichol described himself as an Englishman, a resident of Glasgow, a cosmopolitan and a European. He argued with no little pomposity that with his background – as an outsider – he was ideally placed to compare Glasgow's response to that of other places, commending the support amongst the local working class for the war. The urban areas were increasingly important to Scotland's contribution of men to the British army; there was a decline in its military recruitment from the countryside between 1841 and 1891. Highland regiments not only contained a good number of lowland Scots but were also augmented by English- and Irish-born soldiers: in this period 60 per cent of the Cameron Highlanders were known as the 'Whitechapel Scots', neatly mixing generational and affinity Scots in each nation's near diaspora.

The kind of institutional help for the English was less forthcoming for Scotland's gipsy population, and here numbers and nationality are much harder to determine. The death of Scotland's 'King of Gipsies' made front-page news in 1882, however, when John Mills died aged sixty at Gartaberrie in Old

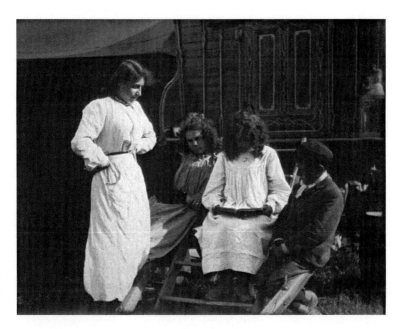

Figure 12.1   *English gipsy children encamped near Newton Stewart,*
c. 1906 – looking their best in vibrant white pinafores for Andrew
McCormick, provost of the town, local lawyer and sympathiser to their
culture. © *Whithorn Photographic Group. Licensor www.scran.ac.uk*

Monkland. Held in high esteem 'by this nomadic race of people'
in the district to which he belonged, 'his word was law'. Mills
had thirteen of a family with his 'Amazonian wife', but only two
lived to maturity. This, it was assumed by the *Dundee Courier*,
was because of the hardship of his unsettled life. It was a widely
held assessment, and the school boards and local magistrates
tried hard to 'save' gipsy children by discouraging itinerancy.

By 1891 foreign-born residents of Scotland had increased 50
per cent over the previous decade. Predominantly Europeans,
there were 17,651 'foreigners' in Scotland in 1901 and 24,739
by 1911, mainly living in Glasgow and the western Lowlands.
The breakdown of the 1901 figures shows 11,908 males
and 5,684 females designated as foreigners: of those 7,609

were Russian (working mainly in mining and tailoring); 3,105 Italians (predominantly bakers); and 2,570 Germans (employed in a variety of trades).

Edinburgh's modern Jewish community dates from 1816 and Glasgow's Hebrew Congregation was formed in 1823; however, only thirty-one were returned in the 1831 census as Jewish, and around 200 a decade later (of whom around half came from England, the rest being European immigrants). In the 1870s more Jews arrived in Scotland from London to work as tailors, such as those who migrated to take up employment with Arthur & Co. of Glasgow. The Garnethill Synagogue opened in 1879 and by 1891 half of Glasgow's Jews were living in and around the Gorbals, with much of the remainder having succeeded sufficiently to move to the city's southern suburbs. Part of Glasgow's necropolis was given over to Jewish burials and by 1914 the city had the largest Jewish community in Scotland, numbering around 10,000; there were a further 1,500 located in Edinburgh and smaller numbers elsewhere.

Historian Kenneth Collins has argued that the Scots were either benevolent towards Jews that were escaping Russia with their lives, or were keen to proselytise their conversion to Protestantism. They were much more readily accepted into the Calvinist world of work than the Catholic Irish. As early as 1838, and despite the small numbers we have seen locally, the presbytery of Edinburgh heard from the capital's Jews' Society the importance of converting Jews by reference to 'their past history, their present state, and their future prospects'. The General Assembly struck a committee the next month to follow this intention; focused mainly abroad, it was authorised to take money from any who would give it. The London Society supplied the committee with Bibles and other materials for conversion: 'It was a happy era,' the Assembly heard, 'that gospel should be preached to the Jew as to the gentile.' By the century's end, the decision of a Jewish family to convert to Presbyterianism caused a stir in the local Jewish community, with letters sent to the *Edinburgh Evening News*, including one from the city's rabbi, the Rev. J. Furst, who wrote that the man was an illiterate labourer who did not understand the vows he had taken. He had come destitute from Newcastle and only the help of a Jewish woman had allowed his family to join him.

Certainly Jewish practices and faith raised some confusion in parts of Scotland. A Jewish watchmaker from Edinburgh, R. J. Davison, caused amusement before Sheriff-Substitute Henderson at Cupar in 1895 when he claimed the sale of a watch to Andrew Bell was conducted through the man's wife, in the belief she was 'master of the house'. More sinister, however, was the murder of elderly spinster Marion Gilchrist in 1908 and the subsequent trial and conviction of Oscar Slater, an unsound conviction overturned in 1928 with concerns raised about anti-Jewish prejudice colouring the witnesses, the investigation and the trial.

HEARING THE VOICE OF OTHERS

The familiarity and integration of English, Irish and European migrants into Scotland, along with regular visits from gipsies, tinkers and travellers, weakened both the insularity of 'being ourselves' and the foreignness or singularity of Scotland's Other. Conflict existed, as Chapter 10 has shown, but the waters of difference were sometimes less than clear. The extent of the internal movement of Scots (see Chapter 5) and of emigration to other parts of the world, and the continuing relationship with that diaspora (see Chapter 11), likewise undermined the rigidity and exclusiveness of the 'national' category in the dichotomy of them and us. Othering *within* Scotland had just as much cultural power. And here scholars have emphasised the attractiveness of the Celtic sublime as a metaphor for the whole of Scotland, with Highlanders, kilts and tartan to the fore despite these being a people who in urban Scotland roused feelings that ranged from romance and sympathy to fear and contempt. If the objectification of the Highlands had any influence on the Scots, then it came from voices heard above the din of modernity. Can we read anything into the fact that what is believed to be the earliest recording of Queen Victoria's voice was made at Balmoral?

It took the comfort of 'home' for this notoriously reticent and self-conscious of monarchs to allow Sydney Morse to make the recording on a Graphophone in 1888.

Cultured in the writings of Walter Scott, the visitors who came to even lowland Scotland sought 'exotic ordinariness' in the scenes and scenery the nation had to offer, and were shocked when confronted with something other than expected. Lady Eastlake's impressions of Scotland's capital in 1845 focused on Arthur's Seat, the Braid Hills, the city's environs of high hedges and villas that reminded her of England: 'then come château-like erections and farmless fields, and you are in la Belle France'. But as she entered the city her eyes fixed upon 'dingy walls, and dark stairs, and lolling heads at windows, and dirty children at doors, with trolloping girls and daredevil boys, and men home from work – snobs passing from the counter, and milliner-girls flopping, flounced from the workroom'. It was not what she had anticipated; it did not fit the sublime trope. Frances Kemble was another who wrote of her travels in Scotland not meeting expectations. Travelling by train and then open carriage between Glasgow and the Highlands in the 1860s, heading out to Loch Katrine and a tour of the Trossachs, it was on her return leg that she was compelled to reimagine Scotland's most populous city: 'the second night was much better than the first; but as those [impressions] were small, this is not saying much'. She clearly struggled to consume the reality of life before her eyes as 'being Scotland'.

While urban Scotland was not what visitors looked for, Scott's home at Abbotsford most certainly was, and it became the nation's first international heritage attraction, led by the enthusiasm of Thomas Cook's tourists. Visitors travelled to the banks of the River Tweed from all over Europe to see the inspirational domestic world of the Wizard of the North and peruse his collection of historical artefacts from the nation's romantic past – a special visitors' walkway and entrance was built mid-century to shield the family from the hordes. The sites and associations of Burns, before long, had become attractions for 'trade tourists', amongst others. The English Chartist leader Robert Gammage visited the industrial west in the 1880s, touring Ayr and Cummnock to give lectures on the rights of the worker. Gammage had been introduced to a Scottish readership in 1865 when the *Glasgow Herald* reproduced his writings in the *Newcastle Chronicle*. He took time out from his work to visit what he really 'wanted' to see: the area he called the 'land of Burns'. After staying with a 'hearty Chartist and his wife', Gammage recounts his experience:

> They did all in their power to make me feel myself at home, and to do so was not difficult. On the following morning, I arose almost with the dawn, and made my way to the monument erected to the memory of Burns on the banks of Doon. By payment of four pence I soon obtained admittance, and examined all I wanted to see. Looking through the window all the inside, there was full to the view the testament which the poet is said to have presented to Mary the last time they ever met on earth. Close to the spot there stood the 'Twa Brigs,' old and new, which all readers of Burns have read of. Returning, I passed Alloway Kirk, the scene of the witches' capers, described in 'Tam O' Shanter'. I soon arrived at the celebrated cottage in which the poet was born, and which was then licensed for the sale of drink. I called for a glass of whisky, and soon got into an agreeable chat with the hostess, a middle aged woman, and one of the most fluent talkers I had ever met. I stayed about half an hour. She showed me everything connected with the name of Burns, even the bed on which he was born. The bedstead was a curiosity, not that it was of itself very different from others, but because of the way in which it had been hacked about by numerous visitors.

Unlike Eastlake and Kemble, Gammage got what he was after, in his case a sense of revelry and scene-setting that fitted a pre-conceived visualisation of the poet's life. He may have been seduced by the somewhat romantic engravings D. O. Hill produced for *The Land of Burns*, published in Glasgow in 1840, yet it was not scenery but life that attracted this union leader.

What links these three voices with Victoria's is their search for the 'domesticated picturesque' – an older, more natural lifestyle that was otherwise lost in the tumult of modernity.

They insisted Scotland's singularity lay not in the technology of modernity, but in the survival and triumph of community and landscape.

Yet technological modernism did define the age, and it did commodify and reproduce – like never before – Scotland in the objectified form. The growing band of tourists to Scotland, like the Scots themselves, had access to all sorts of information to help them find this version of ourselves. George Bradshaw published a shareholder's guide that reported the length and year of completion of Scotland's railway lines, how the finance was raised, who the directors were, what the rules and agreements for the lines were, their relative accident rates and receipts per mile for each classification of ticket, with comparable information for England and Wales and more limited intelligence on the colonial railways. These dull statistics laid bare the infrastructural investment through which Scotland was consumed at 'railway speed'. More than that, the publisher also provided charming accounts in *Bradshaw's Railway Guide to Paris*, which included times of Church of Scotland services in the French capital, and guides describing the historical context to journeying through Scotland on the British and European railway network. More picturesque still, *The Caledonian Railway's Guide to Tours in Scotland* quotes Byron and Scott to set the prospect for its travellers, providing a pull-out sheet of pink pages with 'Hints to American Tourists visiting Scotland'. Whether landing in Liverpool, Southampton, London or Glasgow, Americans were told the most satisfactory routes north and the means of calling a cab, with a full table of junctions and minor routes also provided. Sepia and coloured photographs, poetry, and brief historical and cultural descriptions illuminated the journey through the Borders and Gretna Green towards Aberdeen, with brief accounts of the towns along the way, highlighting any appearance of Robert Bruce, William Wallace, Red Comyn and, most frequently, Walter Scott. Occasionally the more prosaic would appear: thus the traveller to Glasgow was invited to marvel at its water supply from Loch Katrine, bringing in 42 million gallons daily to the city, but also, too, at the Valhalla of Glasgow

(George Square). Paisley, on the other hand, was historicised not through its textiles but through its eminent poets Alexander Wilson, Robert Tannahill and Christopher North. The guides, when they could, drew attention to their most regal traveller, Queen Victoria, who used the steam railway to travel to and from Balmoral in Aberdeenshire. It was Victoria, after all, who had discovered what 'being Scotland' was all about and her voice, most powerfully, shaped how Scots heard of their own place within Empire.

THE QUEEN'S VIEW

When Victoria used the telegraph to contact 'every part of her vast Empire' from Buckingham Place in her diamond jubilee year of 1897, replies were received within fifteen minutes: the first came from Ottawa, quickly followed by the Cape, Hong Kong, the Gold Coast and Australia. Other responses came from Simla, Singapore, Adelaide, Lagos, Newfoundland, Colombo, Antigua, Bombay, Madras, Barbados and elsewhere besides. Here she was at the heart of her Empire. But when Victoria took herself off to Balmoral, her government, backed by *The Times*, wondered how she could be so absent. Scotland, here, was the 'otherworld'.

Yet this 'otherworld' was in its own way central to the British Empire and it would be wrong to downplay the impact of the simple decision made by the reigning monarch and her husband to purchase a relatively modest hunting lodge in Deeside near Aberdeen. Looking at the lasting influence of this choice, sociologists Tom Nairn and David McCrone have analysed the cultural influence of the domestic life of the most powerful woman in the world conducted in the backwaters of the northern part of Britain. They see this decision as creating ideological power, warranting an 'ism' to be appended to the name of that lodge to signify its importance. There are five elements that were to sustain the penetration of Balmoralism within the Scots' identity. The first of these was Victoria and Albert's choice of Scotland and the rejection of options in Wales and England, marking 'Royal Deeside' as the most essential of Celtic escapes. Then there are Victoria's highland journals (1868 and 1884), which enchanted their readers with tales of highland living and her domestic life of exotic ordinariness; third, the popularity of hunting for sport which marked a new phase in highland land management as well as the cultural consumption of the Highlands as pleasure grounds; fourth, the physical connection, by road, rail and telegraph, that was created between an Imperial monarch, her Empire and the Celtic periphery, a direct line of communication *The Scotsman* highlighted in reply to the sniping editor of *The Times*; and fifth, the cult of Celtic imagery, of tartan, Paisley shawls, watercolours of her highland menservants and the Highland Games she patronised.

Importantly, Balmoral was no shielded retreat. The noted Aberdonian photographer George Washington Wilson was invited there to photograph the house in 1854. In 1868 Victoria published the first extracts from her highland diaries to immense success, a later edition including Wilson's photographs. The previous year she had ordered forty views of the area around Balmoral and Loch Lubnaig from the Dundee photographers Valentine and Co., further fixing 'her view' as 'the national view'; Loch Tummel, 'The Queen's View', despite the name pre-dating Victoria, was the most celebrated example. Victoria made Balmoral known to the wider world, fixing it as 'authentically Scottish' to the international gaze. While partly based on the birthplace of Prince Albert, the Schloss Rosenau in Saxe-Coburg, but also inspired by Abbotsford, Balmoral was a fantasy country house which in turn stimulated the 'Scottish style' in art, decor and buildings. On evenings the royal couple would sit side by side on the tartan sofa at the grey stone hearth, with a huge Gaelic dictionary spread out on their knees. They read by candles nestled in holders of silver thistles, sprouting from a central shaft of stag horn, set on a base of silver stag heads interspersed with cairngorms. Through her Balmoral life, through Balmoralism, Victoria had constructed for Scotland the everyday signifier, the banal semaphore, of the nation.

EXHIBITING OURSELVES

Paying visitors were not able to tour Balmoral and see its romantic ornamentation during Victoria's lifetime, but they readily consumed the tittle-tattle of her life, as reported in the Aberdeen-based *Balmoral Correspondent* with the news then picked up by the broadsheets. International exhibitions and museums were further examples of how Scotland's material culture was internationalised and objectified for consumption at home. The attraction of the library was common amongst a number of naturalist, mechanics' and philosophical societies, but so too was the small permanent collection of artefacts or sometimes the more extensive ad hoc exhibition. Aberdeen Mechanics' Institution designed an 'Exhibition of Fine Arts, Natural History, Philosophy, Machinery, Manufactures, Antiquities and Curiosities' in 1840 in the hope of raising sufficient funds for a permanent home for these objects. Displays ranged from working locomotive engines, a diving-bell, a letter press and glass blowing, to paper in various stages of manufacture, a cheetah or hunting leopard, a vampire bat, Borland's Patent Water-Meter, a lunar circle and sun dial; portraits of Alexander Bannerman, Cleopatra, Stirling Castle, John Knox 'Preaching before the Lords of the Congregation' and a French image of Ossian; plus a glass case of famous staffs: one previously owned by Charles Edward Stuart and another by Napoleon Bonaparte as well as the stick presented by Robert Burns to Mr Thomson of Edinburgh in 1793.

Visitors to Aberdeen's local and Scotland's national exhibitions experienced the transmission of objectified culture in non-verbal and non-written ways. Edinburgh's International Exhibition of 1886 was more European in focus, but it did contain Imperial exhibits alongside stalls promoting Bartholomew the mapmakers and Morison, the Glasgow-based globe makers. The Glasgow International Exhibition of 1888 was sufficiently profitable to fund significant decorations to mark Victoria's visit to the site. Included amongst the banners and mottoes was a welcome arch at Buchanan Street displaying a decorative crown with the words 'God Save the Queen' and 'Long to Reign over Us'. This exhibition was more completely a celebration of Empire, featuring exhibits from the colonies alongside examples of Scotland's industrial output. The royal connection with Glasgow was maintained in 1901 when the Duchess of Fife and her husband opened the first international exhibition of the new century. Their tour began in the Grand Hall, then moved to the industrial exhibition and then the new Art Galleries, which cost £250,000, of which £50,000 was the surplus from three years earlier. Displayed throughout the 73 acres of Kelvingrove Park, the exhibits attracted 11.5 million people and carried a greater sense of Scotland's literary and cultural distinctiveness.

In these international exhibitions Scots chose to represent 'ourselves' to the outsider by prioritising industry and manufacturing in Empire (see Chapter 6). At the World's Fair at Chicago in 1893 Scotland's industrial ingenuity was again featured. Firms from the Clyde were represented in the sea and railway transportation sections – the pneumatic tyre for the bicycle and tricycle was shown and described as 'a great revolution' – along with fishing, small manufacturing successes and whisky. All the while, the exhibitors hoped their American audience would discover more of Scotland beyond their ample knowledge of the amber bead.

PICTURE YOURSELF

Feeling and touching Scotland was a big appeal of these modern museums and exhibitions, but 'picturing ourselves' was repackaged further in the developing age of mechanical reproduction. The photograph was not simply a means to document and preserve the nation 'frozen in time', but offered a new medium to consume an objectification of Scotland and the Scots at a geographic and temporal distance, in almost any quantity. The first people to appear in a photograph were a Parisian shoeshiner and his customer in 1838. The exposure time of Louis Daguerre's 'Boulevard du Temple' was ten minutes, so when we begin to see Scots photographed in the 1840s and 1850s formal portraits dominate the early experiments. Standard artistic metaphors were retained. David Octavius Hill and Robert Adamson chose to imagine Ossian in their portrait of the blind Irish harpist Patrick Bayne in 1845. And the photograph was first placed in comparison with the oil painting rather than perceived as an alternative form of art. Perhaps the most ambitious series of early photographs were the calotypes taken of the Disruption ministers in 1843 ready for the much longer process of committing the images to canvas. Ossian and Presbyterian division, the choices were well made.

The Scots, however, were not to neglect more 'authentic' images. Elizabeth Eastlake was one of the first to realise, in 1857, how the photograph could capture the human condition, perhaps influenced by her awakening to urban Glasgow. In the analysis of Tom Normand, this approach made the visual documentary the Scottish norm, to be later taken up by those working with the moving image. Thomas Annan's pictures of the newly opened Loch Katrine water system and of Edinburgh's streets in the 1860s similarly had their greatest impact when the signs of industrial activity were foregrounded, with people incidental, lurking in the background.

Professional and amateurs alike experimented with the technology. It became possible to offer Scots a window on emigrant life before they finalised their decision. Alexander Henderson left Scotland for Canada in 1855 and became known for his images of the St Lawrence River of the 1890s experiencing its annual flood near Montreal. His photography was admired for its art and dreamlike qualities in exhibitions shown abroad. It was, for sure, a contrast to the scenery and life poses recorded by Ishbel Gordon, Lady Aberdeen, who travelled through Canada with her Kodak camera in 1890, capturing life for potential female migrants.

By the mid-1860s George Washington Wilson was producing over 50,000 prints each year, setting the standards for others to follow. In the 1870s and 1880s Valentine and Co. were making their money from selling scenic views; their popularity was enhanced further by the ability to 'print' copies in the

1890s and then by the production of postcards at the turn of the century. For a flat rate of 1d, an image of Scotland could be sent to any country within Britain's possessions and protectorates in 1902. Clearly pushing the boundaries of this postal union, one of the first photographic postcards to be sent from the South Pole shows Gilbert Kerr, having travelled with William Bruce's Scottish National Antarctic Expedition (1902–4), playing the bagpipes to an emperor penguin, placing ourselves with others at the edge of the world.

The number of photographers and photographic shops increased. In the 1890s Motherwell's photographic artist James G. Sinclair offered high-class work at moderate prices and Sharp's Photographers had branches in Hamilton, Coatbridge and Strathaven. The chances were that rural rather than urban depictions would dominate the commissions. R. J. Morris has noted that there were very few kilts in the pictures of Valentine and Co., whereas fisher folk figure disproportionately, satisfying prevailing notions of the picturesque self in ways that perhaps more representative urban trades could not. By contrast, the images that recorded the work of the increasingly popular naturalist societies did see a preponderance of kilted gentlemen going about their work of discovery and classification. As an interloper, the camera operator captured both the outsider's sense of Scotland, and, dictated by sales, the Scottish insider's perception of self.

CELEBRATING OURSELVES

It is suggestive also that perhaps the most active nationalist proponent of marking Scotland's historical past through associational activity came from a foreigner: the Melbourne-born Theodore Napier, whom we have already met petitioning Queen Victoria in 1898 for precision in the use of 'Scotland not Britain' during public debate. Influenced by his Scottish parentage, Napier was an outsider with a cogent vision of Scotland as a Jacobite nation. He was most active in the 1890s but was rarely silent at any time from his first journey 'home' to Edinburgh in 1859 until his final return home to Melbourne in 1913. Napier was a member of the St Andrew's Society of Melbourne, a fellow of the Society of Antiquaries of Scotland, a Companion of the Order of St Germain, honorary Secretary for Scotland of the Legitimist Jacobite League of Great Britain and Ireland, and member of the Royal Oak Club of Edinburgh. He joined the Scottish Home Rule Association in Scotland and a range of literary societies. Each year he commemorated Bannockburn, Culloden, the execution of Mary Stuart and the Glencoe massacre, campaigning for Bruce's victory to be marked by a public holiday. He was active in the Scottish Anniversary and Historical Society and commemorated the life of Wallace by decorating the patriot's statue in Aberdeen, continuing even when people stopped coming to see him.

No wonder another outsider, the *Belfast Newsletter*, accused Napier of going on an endless round of anniversary celebrations in 1900. Not everyone agreed with this Australian-Scot, especially with his Jacobite sympathies. He was socially marginalised and thought too eccentric and volatile. *The Scotsman, The Aberdeen Journal, The Times, The Pall Mall Gazette, The Argus* (Melbourne) and the *Sydney Morning Herald* all at one time or another presented him in an ignominious light, but were at other times sympathetic. He had a public falling-out with home ruler Charles Waddie, yet Napier's energy contributed to creating the modern framework whereby national history could transform into heritage. With the consumption of our historical selves enhanced by an outsider using the rational, rule-based association as his medium, it gave suitable lineage and tradition to our identity.

NEVER AWAY

Indeed, there has been no shortage of leaders and people of influence within the national movement who, like Napier, were not born or raised in Scotland. One-time leader of the Scottish National Party and anti-war campaigner Douglas Young (1913–73) was born in Tayport in Fife but was a child of the diaspora as his father worked for twenty-six years in India. His mother made the trip home for his birth, one of twenty-six crossings that she made between the two countries. Young grew up in Jagatdal near Calcutta; for his education he was sent to Edinburgh's Merchiston Castle School aged nine. His academic career as a classicist was equally peripatetic, taking him to Aberdeen (Scotland), Hamilton (Canada) and Chapel Hill (United States). Nationalist firebrand Wendy Wood (1892–1981) was another child of the diaspora: she was born in Kent, but her parents removed her to South Africa when she was only a toddler. She, too, returned home for her education, but home was Kent and then London before she moved to Scotland as an adult to write and broadcast. And perhaps two of the most known nationalist supporters of all, author Compton Mackenzie (1883–1978) and poet Christopher Murray Grieve (1892–1978) were returnees. Edward Montague Anthony Compton Mackenzie was born outside Scotland, in his case on the 'wrong' side of the border in Country Durham; Grieve was born on the 'right' side of the border, in Langholm. Grieve grew up in Scotland, headed to south Wales to begin a writing career he would later continue under the name Hugh MacDiarmid and returned to Scotland in 1919 after spells in England, Greece and France following enlistment in the Royal Army Medical Corps. Both, like Wendy Wood, adapted their birth names to adopt new personae (outside their born selves) in their cultural campaigning for the nation.

Each of these outsiders worked his or her way into mainstream Scotland through literary talents that translated into political voices 'of the nation'. As outsiders to the land, none could claim that 'being Scotland' was homogeneous or insular, yet each spoke to 'being ourselves' through his or her cultural inclusivity. Any number of examples could be found to show how emigrants also reflected upon their ancestral roots to explain their life course. These echoes may be artifice; these memories may be distortions; these claims may be misplaced, but they were forged within the interplay of ourselves and others. Two examples will suffice. The first is that of Tommy

Douglas: voted the 'greatest Canadian' in 2004 for his introduction of universal health care (Medicare), he was born in Falkirk in 1904 and was motivated to go abroad by challenging circumstances at home. His grandfather was an iron-moulder and a painter, amateur orator, local politician and Burns speaker. He was the chairman at the meeting in the town hall when Gladstone opened his famous Midlothian campaign in 1880. Douglas's mother's parents came from Auchterarder and Crieff, migrating to Glasgow in their early twenties. They were Gaelic speakers. His father fought in the Anglo-Boer war, leaving first for Canada in 1911. Tommy and his two sisters, his mother and his father's brother followed in 1912. His mother was a Baptist, his father a Presbyterian. There was 'a good religious atmosphere in the home'; they sat around 'singing hymns and some of the old songs of Bobbie Burns'.

Tommy Douglas's inspiration for a religious then political life championing Medicare mixed the social consciousness of his upbringing with his successful treatment for osteomyelitis – by the charitable actions of a Winnipeg orthopaedic surgeon – that had been first identified, but poorly treated, when he was still living in Falkirk. What couldn't be achieved at home, but which he believed should have been, drove his work with others.

Another whose rekindled memories of youth came to shape his consciousness of self outside the nation was John Muir (1838–1914). The Victorian land debate in Scotland had international repercussions for how it framed land ownership but also had much to say about land stewardship (see Chapters 1 and 10). As naturalist and voice behind America's first national parks, Muir was one of Scotland's more influential exports. In 1964 his home in Martinez, California was designated a National Historic Site; in 1976 he was voted the 'greatest Californian'. That state celebrates John Muir Day each 21 April, the naturalist's image is reproduced on the California quarter coin and the official California state tartan is based on the Muir tartan.

Muir was born in Dunbar; indeed, six of his seven siblings were born in East Lothian where his father worked as a merchant. He had been aware of American wildlife from his Scottish schooldays, when tales of the ornithologist Alexander Wilson were to be found in the schoolbooks he used before emigrating in 1849. Muir's intellectual influence on ourselves as Scots was not established in his lifetime, however. In the obituary submitted to *The Scotsman*, his birthplace and Scottish roots were all that were indicated of his local associations. Otherwise he was remembered for his honorary degrees from the universities of Harvard (1896), Wisconsin (1897), Yale (1911) and California (1913), although no comment was made on the fact that no Scottish university thought to do likewise. He was celebrated across the Atlantic for the discovery of the Muir glacier in Alaska, for his work in forest preservation, as well as for the creation of national parks in America. When in mid-January 1915 *The Scotsman* reprinted (uncorrected) reminiscences of Muir's life from the *Boston Globe*, his Scottish Presbyterian father and his birthplace, vaguely stated as near the Firth of Forth, were his only Scottish antecedents to be highlighted. Muir instead was described as 'naturalist, philosopher and patriot', as the newspaper lamented America losing one of the last of her pioneers. He was called a friend of presidents, railroad leaders and farmers, yet still he wanted to preserve the wilderness rather than tame it for farming or prospecting. So much of this could have been reflected back on Scotland; that it wasn't suggests a disconnect from ourselves as Scots that would not begin to be changed in the popular mind until John Muir Country Park was established in Dunbar in 1976.

Nonetheless Muir had recreated a personal bond to Scotland that he formulated in letters to his family, written during his only return 'home' to Dunbar. Not solely of his birth, the adult John Muir's Scottish identity became a mix of ourselves formed first in comparison with what he had studied, in standard contemporary objectification of the nation's history and landscape, and through a spiritual association of friends and family sealed with suitable ethnic language.

As he approached Oban on the steamship *Chevalier* in June 1893 Muir described everything as 'all beautiful . . . like the coast of Alaska' and that 'the heather is a good deal like Cassiope'. Reaching Dunbar in July he enjoyed a night of merriment with the publisher David Douglas. The next day Douglas toured him around Edinburgh and the sites celebrated in Scott's novels, the castle, churches 'full of associations' and to Queen Mary's Palace Museum. After another evening of merriment with Douglas, Muir reflected 'from feeling lonely and a stranger in my own native land, he brought me back into quick and living contact with it, and now I am a Scotchman and at home again'. In Haddington he visited Jane Welsh Carlyle's grave, sending two daisies from the site to his wife Louie Strentzel. He concludes his final letter by enclosing sprigs of bell heather for his cousins Wanda and Helen, writing:

> Dear Cousins,
> I am now fairly aff and awa' from the old home to the new, from friends to friends, and soon the braid sea will again roar between us, but be assured, however far I go in sunny California or icy Alaska, I shall never cease to love and admire you, and I hope that now and then you will think of your lonely kinsman, whether in my bright home of the Golden State or plodding after God's glorious glaziers in the storm beaten mountains of the North.

As he remembered the friends and family he had met, attempting a few words of Scots before settling his endearments in English, Muir said goodbye by quoting Burns: 'From scenes like these old Scotia's grandeur springs,/that makes her loved at home, revered abroad'. Overly sentimental, certainly, yet in composing this final dispatch to end an outsider's return to the land of his birth, Muir had taken the journey from being Scotland to being ourselves.

Further Reading

With the 1832–1914 period being awash with the printed text, throughout this book the reader will find evidence gleaned from government papers, institutional reports, newspapers, trade and post office directories, regional and national guides, maps, meteorological records, contemporary folklore and statistical investigations, as well as illumination from private letters, diaries, manuscripts and the wealth of detail contained in the *Oxford Dictionary of National Biography*. Much use has been made of the research conducted by Scotland's and others' remarkably industrious historians, with the following readings being of particular use, offering added depth to the issues examined.

INTRODUCTION

L. Abrams, E. Gordon, D. Simonton and E. Janes Yeo (eds), *Gender in Scottish History since 1700* (Edinburgh: Edinburgh University Press, 2006).

L. Davis, I. Duncan and J. Sorensen (eds), *Scotland and the Borders of Romanticism* (Cambridge: Cambridge University Press, 2004).

W. H. Fraser, *Scottish Popular Politics: From Radicalism to Labour* (Edinburgh: Polygon, 2000).

1: BEING SCOTLAND

C. G. Calloway, *White People, Indians, and Highlanders: Tribal Peoples and Colonial Encounters in Scotland and America* (Oxford: Oxford University Press, 2008).

T. M. Devine, 'Social stability and agrarian change in the Eastern Lowlands of Scotland, 1810–1840', in T. M. Devine, *Exploring the Scottish Past: Themes in the History of Scottish Society* (East Linton: Tuckwell Press, 1995).

K. Fenyő, *Contempt, Sympathy and Romance: Lowland Perceptions of the Highlands and the Clearances During the Famine Years, 1845–1855* (East Linton: Tuckwell Press, 2000).

I. G. C. Hutchison, 'Anglo-Scottish political relations in the nineteenth century, c.1815–1914', in T. C. Smout (ed.), *Anglo-Scottish Relations from 1603-1900* (London: The British Academy, 2005).

M. G. H. Pittock, *Celtic Identity and the British Image* (Manchester: Manchester University Press, 1999).

E. Richards, *A History of the Highland Clearances, Vol. 2. Emigration, Protest, Reasons* (London: Croom Helm, 1985).

M. Stewart and F. Watson, 'Land, the landscape and people in the nineteenth century', in T. Griffiths and G. Morton (eds), *A History of Everyday Life in Scotland, 1800 to 1900* (Edinburgh: Edinburgh University Press, 2010).

C. W. J. Withers, *Urban Highlanders: Highland-Lowland Culture and Urban Gaelic Culture, 1700–1900* (East Linton: Tuckwell Press, 1998).

2: WEATHER SCOTLAND WILL

K. Anderson, *Predicting the Weather: Victorians and the Science of Meteorology* (Chicago, IL: University of Chicago Press, 2005).

A Rural D.D. [David Esdaile], *Contributions to Natural History: Chiefly in Relation to the Food of the People* (Edinburgh: William Blackwood and Sons, 1865).

R. FitzRoy, *The Weather Book. A Manual of Practical Meteorology* (London: Longman, Green, Longman, Roberts and Green, 1863).

M. Hulme and E. Barrow (eds), *Climates of the British Isles: Present, Past and Future* (London: Routledge, 1997).

A. Mitchell, 'Popular weather prognostics of Scotland', *Edinburgh New Philosophical Journal* (October 1863).

F. Tooke and N. H. Battey, 'Temperate flowering phenology', *Journal of Experimental Botany*, 61, 11 (2010).

3: WE LIVE, WE DIE

M. Anderson, 'Fertility decline in Scotland, England and Wales, and Ireland: comparisons from the 1911 census of fertility', *Population Studies*, 52, 1 (March 1998).

M. Anderson and D. J. Morse, 'The people', in W. H. Fraser and

R. J. Morris (eds), *People and Society in Scotland, Vol. II, 1830–1914* (Edinburgh: John Donald, 1990).

A. Blaikie, 'Rituals, transformations and life courses in an era of social transformation', in T. Griffiths and G. Morton (eds), *A History of Everyday Life in Scotland, 1800 to 1900* (Edinburgh: Edinburgh University Press, 2010).

S. Browne and J. Tomlinson, 'A women's town? Dundee women on the public stage', in J. Tomlinson and C. A. Whatley (eds), *Jute No More: Transforming Dundee* (Dundee: Dundee University Press, 2011).

W. Ernst and B. Harris (eds), *Race, Science and Medicine, 1700–1960* (London: Routledge, 1999).

W. H. Fraser, 'Necessities in the nineteenth century', in T. Griffiths and G. Morton (eds), *A History of Everyday Life in Scotland, 1800 to 1900* (Edinburgh: Edinburgh University Press, 2010).

C. H. Lee, 'Scotland, 1860–1939', in R. Floud and R. Johnson (eds), *The Economic History of Britain, Vol. II Economic Maturity, 1860–1939* (Cambridge: Cambridge University Press, 2004).

A. McGrath, 'White brides: images of marriage across colonizing boundaries', *Frontiers: A Journal of Women Studies*, 23, 3 (2002).

W. P. Ward, *Birth Weight and Economic Growth: Women's Living Standards in the Industrializing West* (Chicago, IL: University of Chicago Press, 1993).

N. J. Williams, 'Housing', in W. H. Fraser and C. H. Lee (eds), *Aberdeen 1800–2000. A New History* (East Linton: Tuckwell Press, 2000).

4: URBAN SCOTS

D. G. Barrie, *Police in the Age of Improvement: Police Development and the Civic Tradition in Scotland, 1775–1865* (Cullompton: Willan Publishing, 2008).

T. M. Devine, 'Scotland', in P. Clark (ed.), *The Cambridge Social History of Britain, vol. II 1540–1840* (Cambridge: Cambridge University Press, 2000).

W. H. Fraser and I. Maver (eds), *Glasgow, Vol. II 1830–1912* (Manchester: Manchester University Press, 1996).

C. McKean, '"Beautifying and improving the city": the pursuit of monumental Dundee during the twentieth century', in J. Tomlinson and C. A. Whatley (eds), *Jute No More: Transforming Dundee* (Dundee: Dundee University Press, 2011).

H. Meller, 'Gender, citizenship and the making of the modern environment', in E. Darling and L. Whitworth (eds), *Women and the Making of Built Space in England, 1870–1950* (Aldershot: Ashgate, 2007).

R. J. Morris, 'Urbanisation and Scotland', in W. H. Fraser and R. J. Morris (eds), *People and Society in Scotland, Vol. II, 1830–1914* (Edinburgh: John Donald, 1990).

R. J. Morris, 'In search of twentieth-century Edinburgh', *Book of the Old Edinburgh Club*, new series, vol. 8 (2010).

G. Morton, B. de Vries and R. J. Morris (eds), *Civil Society, Associations and Urban Places: Class, Nation and Culture in Nineteenth-Century Europe* (Stroud: Ashgate, 2006).

R. Rodger, *The Transformation of Edinburgh: Land, Property and Trust in the Nineteenth Century* (Cambridge: Cambridge University Press, 2001).

V. M. Welter, *Biopolis: Patrick Geddes and the City of Life* (Cambridge, MA: Massachusetts Institute of Technology, 2002).

5: GETTING AROUND

A. J. Durie, *Scotland for the Holidays: Tourism in Scotland, c.1780–1939* (East Linton: Tuckwell Press, 2003).

A. J. Durie, 'Movement, transport and tourism', in T. Griffiths and G. Morton (eds), *A History of Everyday Life in Scotland, 1800 to 1900* (Edinburgh: Edinburgh University Press, 2010).

R. J. Morris, 'New spaces for Scotland, 1800 to 1900', in T. Griffiths and G. Morton (eds), *A History of Everyday Life in Scotland, 1800 to 1900* (Edinburgh: Edinburgh University Press, 2010).

P. J. G. Ranson, *Iron Road. The Railway in Scotland* (Edinburgh: Birlinn, 2010).

K. Veitch (ed.), *Transport and Communications. Scottish Life and Society. A Compendium of Scottish Ethnology*, vol. 8 (East Linton: Tuckwell Press, 2009).

6: WORKING SCOTS

T. M. Devine, C. H. Lee and G. C. Peden (eds), *The Transformation of Scotland. The Economy since 1700* (Edinburgh: Edinburgh University Press, 2005).

E. Gordon and E. Breitenbach (eds), *The World is Ill Divided:*

Women's Work in Scotland in the Nineteenth and Early Twentieth Centuries (Edinburgh: Edinburgh University Press, 1990).

E. Gordon and G. Nair, *Public Lives: Women, Family, and Society in Victorian Britain* (New Haven, CT: Yale University Press, 2003).

T. Griffiths, 'Work, leisure and time in the nineteenth century', in T. Griffiths and G. Morton (eds), *A History of Everyday Life in Scotland, 1800 to 1900* (Edinburgh: Edinburgh University Press, 2010).

R. Johnston, *Clydeside Capital, 1870–1920: A Social History of Employers* (East Linton: Tuckwell Press, 2000).

G. Morton and R. J. Morris, 'Civil society, governance and nation', in R. A. Houston and W. W. Knox (eds), *The New Penguin History of Scotland* (London: Allen Lane, 2001).

S. Nenadic, 'The social shaping of business behaviour in the nineteenth-century women's garment trades', *Journal of Social History*, 31, 3 (spring 1998).

C. Schmitz, 'The nature and dimensions of Scottish foreign investment, 1860–1914', *Business History*, 39 (1997).

J. Tomlinson and C. A. Whatley (eds), *Jute No More: Transforming Dundee* (Dundee: Dundee University Press, 2011).

C. Young, 'Financing the micro-scale enterprise: rural craft producers in Scotland, 1840–1914', *Business History Review*, 69, 3 (autumn 1995).

7: POVERTY, SPENDING AND SPORT

C. G. Brown, 'Popular culture', in T. M. Devine and R. J Finlay (eds), *Scotland in the Twentieth Century* (Edinburgh: Edinburgh University Press, 1996).

T. Collins, J. Martin and W. Vamplew, *Encyclopedia of Traditional British Rural Sports* (London: Routledge, 2005).

A. Crowther, 'Poverty, health and welfare', in W. H. Fraser and R. J. Morris (eds), *People and Society in Scotland, Vol. II, 1830–1914* (Edinburgh: John Donald, 1990).

M. Huggins, *The Victorians and Sport* (London: Hambledon Continuum, 2007).

G. D. Pollock, 'Aspects of thrift in east end Glasgow: new accounts at the Bridgeton Cross branch of the Savings Bank of Glasgow, 1881', *International Review of Scottish Studies*, 32 (2007).

N. Tranter, *Sport, Economy and Society in Britain* (Cambridge: Cambridge University Press, 1998).

D. Varga, 'Teddy's bear and the sociocultural transfiguration of savage beasts into innocent children, 1890–1920', *Journal of American Culture*, 32, 2 (June 2009).

C. Zutshi, '"Designed for eternity": Kashmiri shawls, Empire, and cultures of production and consumption in mid-Victorian Britain', *Journal of British Studies*, 48, 2 (April 2009).

8: READING, WRITING, TALKING AND SINGING

R. D. Anderson, *Education and Opportunity in Victorian Scotland* (Oxford: Clarendon Press, 1983).

R. D. Anderson, *Education and the Scottish People, 1750–1918* (Oxford: Clarendon Press, 1995).

W. Donaldson, *Popular Literature in Victorian Scotland* (Aberdeen: Aberdeen University Press, 1986).

W. A. Everett, 'National themes in Scottish art music, ca. 1880–1990', *International Review of the Aesthetics and Sociology of Music*, 30, 2 (December 1999).

D. M. Mason, 'School attendance in nineteenth-century Scotland', *Economic History Review*, new series, 38, 2 (May 1985).

J. McDermid, *The Schooling of Working-Class Girls in Victorian Scotland: Gender, Education and Identity* (London: Routledge, 2005).

S. Manning et al. (eds), *The Edinburgh History of Scottish Literature, Vol. 2 Enlightenment, Britain and Empire (1707–1918)* (Edinburgh: Edinburgh University Press, 2007).

G. Morton, 'Scotland's feminine nationalism: some distant views of Jane Porter', *Journal of Irish and Scottish Studies*, 4, 1 (autumn 2010).

G. Morton, 'The Scottish nation of Jane Porter in her international setting', in J. A. Campbell, E. Ewan and H. Parker (eds), *The Shaping of Scottish Identities: Family, Nation, and the Worlds Beyond* (Guelph: Centre for Scottish Studies, 2011).

B. Munro, 'The bothy ballads: the social context and meaning of the farm servants' songs of north-eastern Scotland', *History Workshop*, no. 3 (spring 1977).

9: BELIEVING OURSELVES

C. G. Brown, *The Social History of Religion in Scotland since 1730* (London and New York: Methuen, 1987).

C. G. Brown, *The Death of Christian Britain: Understanding Secularisation, 1800–2000* (London: Routledge, 2001).

S. J. Brown, *Providence and Empire: Religion, Politics and Society in the United Kingdom, 1815–1914* (London: Pearson, 2008).

S. J. Brown, 'Beliefs and religions', in T. Griffiths and G. Morton (eds), *A History of Everyday Life in Scotland, 1800 to 1900* (Edinburgh: Edinburgh University Press, 2010).

S. K. Kehoe, *Creating a Scottish Church: Catholicism, Gender and Ethnicity in Nineteenth-century Scotland* (Manchester: Manchester University Press, 2010).

H. McLeod, *Religion and the Working Class in Nineteenth-Century Britain* (London and Basingstoke: Macmillan, 1984).

E. Ritchie, '"A palmful of water for your years": babies, religion and gender among crofting families in Scotland, 1800–1850', in J. A. Campbell, E. Ewan and H. Parker (eds), *The Shaping of Scottish Identities: Family, Nation, and the Worlds Beyond* (Guelph: Centre for Scottish Studies, 2011).

J. Sawday, '"New men, strange faces, other minds": Arthur Keith, race and the Piltdown affair', in W. Ernst and B. Harris (eds), *Race, Science and Medicine, 1700–1960* (London: Routledge, 1999).

10: CONTROLLING OURSELVES AND OTHERS

M. Dyer, *Men of Property and Intelligence: The Scottish Electoral System Prior to 1884* (Aberdeen: Scottish Cultural Press, 1996).

S. Innes and J. Rendall, 'Women, gender and politics', in L. Abrams, E. Gordon, D. Simonton and E. Janes Yeo (eds), *Gender in Scottish History since 1700* (Edinburgh: Edinburgh University Press, 2006).

W. W. J. Knox and A. McKinlay, 'Crime, protest and policing in nineteenth-century Scotland', in T. Griffiths and G. Morton (eds), *A History of Everyday Life in Scotland, 1800 to 1900* (Edinburgh: Edinburgh University Press, 2010).

G. Morton, 'Scotland is Britain: the Union and Unionist-Nationalism, 1807–1907', *Journal of Irish and Scottish Studies*, 1, 2 (spring 2008).

G. Morton, 'Identity within the Union state, 1800–1900', in T. M. Devine and J. Wormald (eds), *The Oxford Handbook of Scottish History* (Oxford: Oxford University Press, 2012).

11: EMIGRATION AND DIASPORA

E. Breitenbach, *Empire and Scottish Society: the Impact of Foreign Missions at Home, c.1790–c.1914* (Edinburgh: Edinburgh University Press, 2009).

T. Bueltmann, *Scottish Ethnicity and the Making of New Zealand Society, 1850 to 1930* (Edinburgh: Edinburgh University Press, 2011).

T. Bueltmann, A. Hinson and G. Morton (eds), *Ties of Bluid, Kin and Countrie: Scottish Associational Culture in the Diaspora* (Guelph: Centre for Scottish Studies, 2009).

T. M. Devine, *To the Ends of the Earth: Scotland's Global Diaspora, 1750–2010* (London: Allen Lane, 2011).

M. Flinn et al., *Scottish Population History* (Cambridge: Cambridge University Press, 1977).

M. Harper, *Adventurers and Exiles: the Great Scottish Exodus* (London: Profile Books, 2003).

M. Harper and S. Constantine, *Migration and Empire* (Oxford: Oxford University Press, 2010).

A. McCarthy, *Scottishness and Irishness in New Zealand since 1840* (Manchester: Manchester University Press, 2011).

G. Morton, 'Identity out of place', in T. Griffiths and G. Morton (eds), *A History of Everyday Life in Scotland, 1800 to 1900* (Edinburgh: Edinburgh University Press, 2010).

M. Prentis, *The Scots in Australia* (Sydney: University of New South Wales Press, 2004).

12: BEING OURSELVES

W. F. Badè, *Life and Letters of John Muir*, 2 vols (Boston, MA: Houghton Mifflin, 1924).

B. Braber, 'The trial of Oscar Slater (1909) and anti-Jewish prejudice in Edwardian Glasgow', *History*, 88 (April 2003).

R. J. Morris, *Scotland 1907: The Many Scotlands of Valentine and Sons, Photographers* (Edinburgh: Birlinn, 2007).

G. Morton, 'Returning Nationalists, Returning Scotland: James Grant and Theodore Napier', in M. Varricchio (ed.), *Back to Caledonia: Scottish Homecomings from the 17th Century to the Present* (Edinburgh: Birlinn, 2012).

T. Normand, *Scottish Photography: A History* (Edinburgh: Luath Press, 2007).

L. H. Thomas (ed.), *The Making of a Socialist: The Recollections of T. C. Douglas* (Edmonton: University of Alberta Press, 1984).

Index